Jacques Pépin's
Simple and
Healthy Cooking

Written and Illustrated by Jacques Pépin

Rodale Press
Emmaus, Pennsylvania

Printed in the United States of America on acid-free ∞, recycled paper ♺

Cover and Interior Designer: Faith Hague
Cover and Interior Photographer: Angelo Caggiano

Library of Congress Cataloging-in-Publication Data

Pépin, Jacques
  (Simple and healthy cooking)
    Jacques Pépin's simple and healthy cooking / written and illustrated by
Jacques Pépin.
        p.   cm.
    Includes index.
    ISBN 0–87596–234–3   hardcover
    1. Cookery.   2. Low-fat diet recipes.   3. Nutrition.   I. Title.
  II. Title: Simple and healthy cooking.
  TX714.P458 1994
  641.5'638—dc20   94–29177

      ISBN 0–87596–362–5   paperback

Distributed to the book trade by St. Martin's Press

      6 8 10 9 7 5   hardcover
2 4 6 8 10 9 7 5 3 1   paperback

Visit us on the Web at www.rodalebooks.com, or call us toll-free at (800) 848-4735.

───── OUR PURPOSE ─────

*We inspire and enable people to improve
their lives and the world around them.*

Contents

Main Courses   98

Acknowledgments

The production of this book required the hard work of many very capable people. It is not possible for me to thank everyone individually for their help, but I would like to mention the names of a few people whose enthusiasm, dedication and support for this project bring their names immediately to my mind.

Debora Tkac, the executive editor, who brought me the idea for this book and then, after a great conference-style lunch at the Park Avenue Cafe in New York, convinced us all that we were on the right track; Jane Knutila, the art director; Faith Hague, the designer of the book, with whom I worked closely and whose wonderful artistic sense enabled her to show my artwork at its best; Jean Rogers, able, discerning editor; Kathy Diehl, copy editor; and Melinda Rizzo, production coordinator. I am especially grateful to Angelo Caggiano, photographer, for his terrific—and painless—photo for the jacket, as well as his absolutely stunning pictures of the food. Thanks, too, to Mariann Sauvion and William Smith for their simple but elegant food styling and to Barbara Fritz for her prop styling.

For graciously welcoming me into their home, I want to thank Pat and Sandy Corpora, whose vision and belief in our project was an inspiration. This list would not be complete, of course, without the mention of Susie Heller, my collaborator, with whom I've worked for many years on numerous books and countless projects; and finally, Norma Galehouse, my assistant, who pulled together all the various facets of the book to make my life easier and more rewarding.

Introduction

to all cooks
who believe, as i do,
that good cooking and good health,
are inseparable

i have spent most of the last 45 years in the kitchen. Even before my formal apprenticeship began at the precocious age of 13, I was in the kitchen of our family restaurant helping my mother, who was the chef. Then, and through all my professional years of cooking—whether in the French countryside, in Paris or, later, in New York and other parts of the United States—my primary concern as a chef has always been taste. It still is.

Nowadays, however, I have also become interested in defining healthy eating habits. With that goal in mind, I have begun to scale down my use of certain foods, such as butter and other fats, meats and desserts—in general, foods that are either fattening or high in saturated fat or cholesterol. This is a concern that should and must be addressed by chefs. With their knowledge of ingredients and flavors and how they interact, chefs are the best equipped to create well-balanced menus composed of savory dishes containing a minimum of fat.

It is not that I have eliminated butter, beef or sugar entirely; in fact, I have not eliminated anything at all. The difference is that I use smaller proportions of these foods and larger amounts of other more healthful ingredients in my recipes. And I take a greater interest now in trying to balance a diet and give it proper diversity, while still trying to make use of the best seasonal ingredients.

Cutting back on fatty foods is a handicap, but not an insurmountable task. A chef with the proper training, dedication and understanding of ingredients and how they work together in recipes can put that knowledge to work to create the kind of healthier, more balanced diet that so many people want today. Throughout this book, I tell how I made favorite dishes lighter in fat or calories. I used many different techniques, including skimming fat from homemade stocks, using vegetable cooking spray to sauté foods or grease cookie sheets, removing the skin from chicken, trimming all visible fat from meat before cooking and flavoring vegetables with garlic, herbs, vinegars and other ingredients that have a lot of flavor but little or no fat.

E veryone has his or her own opinion about what constitutes eating well. Most doctors, when asked about creating a healthier diet, recommend cutting back on fat. There is, however, a great deal of confusion about what reducing fat intake really means.

One gram of fat contains nine calories, which is more than twice as much as a gram of carbohydrate or protein has. So by reducing our consumption of fat in general, we can also cut back on our calorie intake. Some people think they need only be concerned with butter and other types of animal fat. They know these fats are not only saturated but also high in cholesterol. Yet they forget that some types of vegetable fat, such as coconut, palm and palm-kernel oils, are also highly saturated, even though these oils contain no cholesterol.

Many people also know that monounsaturated fats, such as olive oil, and polyunsaturated fats, such as corn oil, are much more desirable. But that does not give us license to consume large quantities of those healthier oils. Doctors still recommend that no more than 30 percent of the calories in our entire diet come from fat—with approximately equal amounts being monounsaturated, polyunsaturated and saturated.

Trying to calculate the percentage of fat in the diet is tricky and often leads to confusion. People think that every single food they eat must get less than 30 percent of its calories from fat. That's not realistic. Good nutritious foods like vegetables and salad greens, for example, are practically calorie-free. So adding even a minute amount of oil in the cooking of those vegetables or in the dressing of the salad increases the fat to more than 30 percent.

A similar situation sometimes occurs with certain meats, fish and poultry. Even very lean cuts of these foods can exceed the 30 percent level when they're served all by themselves. It's important to realize, however, that these foods aren't eaten alone. Combining them with bread, rice, pasta or other low-fat carbohydrates within the context of a menu lowers the total percentage.

Furthermore, instead of looking at one menu, doctors now suggest you look at an even larger picture, checking a week's intake to know whether you are within the recommended guidelines. One day you may splurge and consume more fat than is advocated, but the next day you may be below the suggested levels. The important thing is that the total picture is balanced.

nother issue I would like to address is the use of alcohol in recipes. I realize that some people do not consume wine and other spirits. Some of my dishes do call for wine, and I consider it an indispensable part of many of those recipes. In the case of stews and other long-cooking recipes, most of the alcohol evaporates during the cooking process, with just the flavor of the wine remaining. If you really prefer not to use the wine, substitute stock.

When liqueurs and other spirits are added to a sauce that requires no further cooking—often the case with dessert sauces—I've made them optional or given a nonalcoholic substitute, such as a fruit juice that's compatible with the dish. If your objection to alcohol is cost-related, and you feel you can't justify the expense of buying a bottle of Grand Marnier or cognac, for example, just to use a tablespoon or two in a recipe, feel free to substitute another liqueur.

What I have tried to provide in this book are healthful recipes that also taste good. This is not a "diet book," with all the negative feelings that epithet evokes. This is simple and healthy cooking that everyone can enjoy. I hope you prepare these dishes and share them with your family and friends in the good spirit that they were created to elicit.

menus

Mushroom and barley Soup

Fricadelles of Veal in tomate Sauce

Onion Papillote

Orange delice

*T*he creation of a menu involves putting dishes together in a coherent way. There are several factors that must be taken into account in this process.

First among these are seasonal considerations. I always try to use food in season. Abundant and mature, it is at its peak in terms of taste and nutritional value and is usually at its least expensive.

Economic factors also are important. I must determine whether particular ingredients are too expensive for the occasion. Although I might decide that I can't justify the cost of certain foods for a family dinner, I might buy them for a special party.

Another consideration affecting menu creation is time. I must decide whether I have time to do all that a certain menu demands. I would probably be more likely to prepare a menu that requires more time on a weekend, for example, than during the week, when my available time is limited and my main concern is to get a meal on the table quickly.

Individual taste preferences also play a role in the choice of what dishes to combine for a meal. Like most people, I tend to like certain foods together and rely on familiar combinations.

A final consideration in all menu planning—but especially so in this book, where I focus on the nutritional value of ingredients—is balance. Even when all the other considerations have been factored in, it is essential to have a balanced menu. This is always possible; it is merely a question of common sense.

One way I balance my meals is to include grain, bread, pasta and rice dishes in them as well as a great many vegetables and fruits. When using beef, pork and lamb, I specify lean cuts to keep the amount of fat down.

Even though salads are not always listed as a part of the menus that follow, they are omnipresent at my table, and I recommend that they be consumed daily. Extremely versatile, salads can be composed of almost anything, even leftovers from the previous day.

I have not listed bread in these menus, although in the European tradition— certainly the French—a meal cannot exist without bread. Bread has an added value: It reduces the total percentage of calories from fat at any given meal. So I suggest a slice or two of bread per person with the following menus. A glass of wine is also part of my daily fare, and I recommend it as a menu accompaniment here if it is within your means and doesn't conflict with your style of life.

You may notice that most of the desserts in this book are made with fruit or have a fruit base and contain very little fat. Ordinarily, I serve desserts at home only when we have guests; we usually end family dinners with fresh fruit.

Combining recipes into menus is important because some dishes by their very nature will always contain more than the recommended 30 percent of calories from fat. Green salads are a good example of this, since almost all the calories in them come from the oil that is in the dressing. When a salad is incorporated into a menu, however, the other foods help balance out the fat content.

In accordance with the recommendations of the surgeon general and other doctors, the following menus get no more than 30 percent of their calories from fat. Sometimes the percentage is considerably lower. The menus presented here are arbitrary, of course. I hope you will use them as guides to create menus that you, your family and your friends will enjoy. Bon appétit!

SPINACH-DUMPLING SOUP
TURKEY FRICASSÉE WITH BROWN RICE AND CUMIN
CAROTTES VICHY
STRAWBERRIES IN CREAMY ORANGE SAUCE

681 CALORIES
20% CALORIES FROM FAT

PICKLED VEGETABLES
APPETIZER WONTON CRISPS
VEAL STEW NIÇOISE
BASIC RICE
FRUIT SORBETS
SNOWBALL COOKIES

667 CALORIES
16% CALORIES FROM FAT

ONION SOUP GRATINÉE
PEPPERED PORK STEAKS WITH APPLE-VINEGAR SAUCE
HONEYED SWEET POTATOES
STEWED PRUNES IN RED WINE

862 CALORIES
20% CALORIES FROM FAT

VEGETARIAN BORSCHT WITH CREAMY HORSERADISH
PROVENCE PIZZA
MIXED GREENS
CUCUMBER-SCALLION DRESSING
OATMEAL AND CURRANT COOKIES

749 CALORIES
28% CALORIES FROM FAT

CHUNKY LENTIL SOUP

CHICKEN SAUCE PIQUANT

SPINACH AND CROUTON MÉLANGE

CRÊPES WITH CARAMELIZED APPLES AND PECANS

739 CALORIES
24% CALORIES FROM FAT

ARTICHOKES WITH ORIENTAL SAUCE

CHICKEN IN MUSTARD SAUCE

ORECCHIETTE PASTA WITH RED ONION

SWEET APPLE FLAKE CONFECTIONS

795 CALORIES
20% CALORIES FROM FAT

CORNMEAL AND VEGETABLE SOUP

LAMB STEAKS IN SWEET PIQUANT SAUCE

GARDEN-STYLE POTATO SALAD

SAUTÉED APPLE RINGS IN HONEY
AND MAPLE SAUCE

652 CALORIES
29% CALORIES FROM FAT

CARROT-WALNUT SALAD

SCALLOP WONTONS WITH TOMATO SAUCE

GREEN BEANS AND RED ONIONS

RASPBERRY SOUFFLÉS IN RASPBERRY SAUCE

692 CALORIES
22% CALORIES FROM FAT

SPINACH AND CHICKEN SOUP

SAUTÉED VEAL CHOPS WITH VEGETABLES

WHITE BEAN FRICASSÉE WITH CURRY

ANGEL CAKE

APRICOT SAUCE WITH DRIED FRUITS

1,106 CALORIES
16% CALORIES FROM FAT

VEGETABLE, LEEK AND OATMEAL SOUP

CHICKEN BREASTS IN CREAMY DILL SAUCE

ROASTED BEETS

CREAMY RICE PUDDING WITH DRIED FRUIT

807 CALORIES
11% CALORIES FROM FAT

APPLE AND MUSHROOM SALAD
BROILED PORK LOIN CHOPS WITH SAGE
GARLIC BROCCOLI
CITRUS-RAISIN COMPOTE   *759 CALORIES*
OAT BRAN AND BUTTER WAFERS   *21% CALORIES FROM FAT*

MUSHROOM-BARLEY SOUP
FRICADELLES OF VEAL IN TOMATO SAUCE
ONION PAPILLOTE   *639 CALORIES*
ORANGE DÉLICE   *27% CALORIES FROM FAT*

CARROT-WALNUT SALAD
SALMON WITH SORREL SAUCE
ROASTED NEW POTATOES
SWEET WONTON CRISPS WITH STRAWBERRIES   *599 CALORIES*
    AND FROZEN YOGURT   *21% CALORIES FROM FAT*

RED ONION, GRAPEFRUIT AND TOMATO SALAD
HONEYED HAM STEAKS
PEA, MUSHROOM AND CORN MEDLEY   *533 CALORIES*
MELON WITH LIME SAUCE   *28% CALORIES FROM FAT*

MIDDLE EASTERN LETTUCE PACKAGES
CHICKEN IN LIME AND YOGURT MARINADE
LENTIL AND CARROT STEW   *738 CALORIES*
APRICOT WHIP   *25% CALORIES FROM FAT*

GAZPACHO
GRILLED HERBED TUNA ON SPINACH SALAD
BASIL COUSCOUS WITH RED PEPPER AND SUNFLOWER SEEDS   *1,035 CALORIES*
STRAWBERRY GRANOLA PARFAITS   *30% CALORIES FROM FAT*

Vegetable Soup with Basil Pistou
Broiled Chicken Salad
Corn Tortillas with Peppers,
    Onions and Cheese
Pineapple in Maple Syrup

709 CALORIES
17% CALORIES FROM FAT

Dried Mushroom Soup with Tofu
Turkey Meat Loaf in Tomato-Mushroom Sauce
Puree of Lima Beans
Applesauce Cake

697 CALORIES
24% CALORIES FROM FAT

Eggplant Oriental on Tomato Rounds
Pepper Steak
Baked Stuffed Potatoes
Sautéed Apple Rings in Honey and Maple Sauce

875 CALORIES
21% CALORIES FROM FAT

Squid Salad with Cucumber and Mint
Curried Scallops Oriental
Black Bean Stew
Apricot Whip

880 CALORIES
20% CALORIES FROM FAT

Crêpe Purses with Mushroom Duxelles
Sea Scallops Grenobloise
Carottes Provençale
Strawberries in Strawberry Sauce

402 CALORIES
30% CALORIES FROM FAT

Stuffed Mushrooms with Raisins and Cilantro
Veal Scallopini with Snow Peas and Asparagus
Basic Couscous
Banana Ricotta Cream with Fresh Fruits

825 CALORIES
21% CALORIES FROM FAT

Microwave Potato Chips with Salsa Cruda
Carbonnade of Beef
Basic Rice
Cold Fruit Compote

817 CALORIES
15% CALORIES FROM FAT

Egg Whites Stuffed with Bulgur
Sautéed Chicken and Fruit Curry
Basic Rice
Meringue Shells
Banana-Strawberry Sherbet

718 CALORIES
13% CALORIES FROM FAT

Jalapeño Dip
Blackened Swordfish
Hominy, Cilantro and Cumin Stew
Oranges in Yogurt Cream

703 CALORIES
24% CALORIES FROM FAT

Ratatouille Dip with Endive
Warm Shrimp Salad with Fennel
   and Potatoes
Hot Orange Soufflés with Orange Segments

473 CALORIES
17% CALORIES FROM FAT

Fettuccine in Bitter Salad
Pan-Seared Veal Chops with
   Herbes de Provence
Seared Tomatoes with Bread Topping
Pears in Red Wine

725 CALORIES
27% CALORIES FROM FAT

Roasted Red Peppers in Red Wine Vinegar
Penne in Clam Sauce
Cold Sweet Strawberry Soup

749 CALORIES
18% CALORIES FROM FAT

Cannellini Bean Hummus

Broiled Lamb Kabobs

Brown Rice with Celery and Onions

Orange Floating Islands with
    Orange-Yogurt Sauce

611 CALORIES
20% CALORIES FROM FAT

Corn and Leek Soup

Braised Stuffed Trout with Herb Crust

Lime Peas in Tomato Cups

Raspberry Soufflés in Raspberry Sauce

840 CALORIES
22% CALORIES FROM FAT

Orzo à la Puttanesca

Garlic-Studded Roast Monkfish in Ratatouille

Puree of Lima Beans

Poached Oranges

817 CALORIES
19% CALORIES FROM FAT

Minty Cream of Butternut Squash Soup

Sautéed Chicken Legs with Garlic Slivers
    and Balsamic Vinegar

Pasta and Escarole

Poached Pears in Lemon-Apricot Sauce

570 CALORIES
19% CALORIES FROM FAT

Hot Thai Soup with Noodles

Chicken Stir-Fry

Basic Rice

Plum Stew with Pecans

624 CALORIES
20% CALORIES FROM FAT

Tomato Potage with Basil

Veal Roast with Shiitake Mushrooms
    and Onions

Mashed Potatoes and Carrots

Sweet Apple Flake Confections

559 CALORIES
23% CALORIES FROM FAT

ROASTED EGGPLANT AND TOMATO SALAD
ROASTED LEG OF LAMB WITH MIREPOIX
POMMES BOULANGÈRE

815 CALORIES
27% CALORIES FROM FAT

STRAWBERRIES IN CREAMY ORANGE SAUCE

ARTICHOKES WITH HOT SALSA
SPICY FLANK STEAK WITH LETTUCE FAJITAS
BLACK BEAN RELISH

752 CALORIES
23% CALORIES FROM FAT

GRATIN OF BANANAS

COLD PEACH SOUP
BROILED RED SNAPPER WITH LEMON-TARRAGON SAUCE
WHOLE-WHEAT COUSCOUS WITH VEGETABLES
ANGEL CAKE

930 CALORIES
16% CALORIES FROM FAT

CHOCOLATE SAUCE

CROUTONS WITH CREAMY RED PEPPER
SAFFRON FISH STEW
BOILED POTATOES
FRUIT SORBETS

753 CALORIES
15% CALORIES FROM FAT

MERINGUE SHELLS

BEET SALAD IN YOGURT SAUCE
SALMON STEAKS WITH CRUDITÉ SAUCE
WHITE BEAN FRICASSÉE WITH CURRY

544 CALORIES
23% CALORIES FROM FAT

YOGURT CAKE

SPINACH MINI-FRITTATAS
POACHED SHRIMP AND POTATOES IN VEGETABLE STOCK
GARLIC BROCCOLI

603 CALORIES
17% CALORIES FROM FAT

BANANA-STRAWBERRY SHERBET

Basic Staples

Stocks, Sauces, dressings, and more ...

Brown Chicken Stock

Yield: 2½ quarts

he difference between white stock and brown stock is not only the color but also the flavor, which is more assertive in a brown stock because of the browning of the bones. When a brown stock is reduced, it's sometimes called demi-glace *in French and is often the base of delicate sauces served in expensive restaurants. It can be flavored with mushrooms, truffles, red wine, shallots or other ingredients. As the flavoring changes, the name of the sauce changes. I've added some dark soy sauce to my stock to give it a deeper color and a sharper taste. You may substitute light soy sauce for a milder taste and lighter color.*

- 5 pounds chicken bones (preferably necks, backs and gizzards), with most of the fat and skin removed
- 2 medium onions (about 12 ounces), unpeeled but washed and quartered
- 2 large carrots (about 8 ounces), washed, trimmed and cut into chunks
- 2 gallons water
- 4 large stalks celery (about 8 ounces), washed, trimmed and cut into chunks
- 1 ounce (about ½ cup) dried mushrooms (black Polish, shiitake or another dry variety)
- 1 bay leaf
- 1 teaspoon dried thyme
- 1 teaspoon whole black peppercorns
- 1 teaspoon dried herbes de Provence (see opposite page)
- 1 tablespoon dark soy sauce

Preheat the oven to 425°.

Spread the chicken bones out in an even layer in a large roasting pan and bake them for 1½ hours, stirring occasionally so they don't burn. Scatter the onions and carrots around the bones and bake for an additional 30 minutes, or until the bones and vegetables are well browned.

Using a slotted spoon to minimize picking up fat, transfer the bones and vegetables from the pan to a stockpot. Discard the accumulated fat from the roasting pan and pour 1 cup of the water into the pan. Bring the water to a boil on top of the stove and scrape the bottom of the pan with a wooden spatula to help dislodge the solidified juices. Stir until these melt. Add this liquid and the remaining water to the stockpot.

Bring the mixture to a boil, uncovered, over high heat. Then reduce the heat and boil gently for 1 hour, removing any impurities and fat that rise to the surface, preferably with a fine-mesh skimmer.

Add the celery, mushrooms, bay leaf, thyme, peppercorns and herbes de Provence. Boil the stock gently, uncovered, for about 3 hours longer.

Strain the stock through a fine strainer into a large bowl and measure. You should have about 2½ quarts of stock. If you have more, boil it until it is reduced to 2½ quarts; if you have less, add water to bring the stock to 2½ quarts. Add the soy sauce and mix it in well.

Cool to room temperature. Cover and refrigerate overnight. The next day skim off and discard any solidified fat from the surface.

Cover and refrigerate for use within 4 to 5 days or freeze in 2-cup containers for use as needed.

Per 1 cup: 5 calories, 0 g. fat (0% of calories), 0 g. saturated fat, 0 mg. cholesterol, 106 mg. sodium.

Herbes de Provence is a mixture of herbs commonly found in the south of France. Thyme, savory, marjoram and oregano are generally present. Sometimes fennel seeds, sage, rosemary and lavender flowers are included. Look for the mixture in the spice section of well-stocked supermarkets.

You can make your own mixture by combining 1 tablespoon dried thyme, 1 tablespoon dried savory, 1 tablespoon dried marjoram and 1 tablespoon dried oregano. If you like, add 1 tablespoon ground fennel seeds, 1 teaspoon dried sage, 1 teaspoon dried rosemary and 1 teaspoon dried lavender flowers. Store the mixture in a tightly sealed container.

White Chicken Stock

Yield: 3 quarts

You can extend the life of refrigerated stock and prevent it from souring after four or five days by bringing it back to a boil, cooling it and refrigerating it again.

- 5 pounds chicken bones (preferably necks, backs and gizzards), with most of the fat and skin removed
- 2 gallons cold water
- 2 medium onions (about 12 ounces), peeled and cut into 1″ pieces
- 4 large stalks celery (about 8 ounces), washed, trimmed and cut into chunks
- 2 large carrots (about 8 ounces), washed, trimmed and cut into chunks
- 1 ounce (about ½ cup) dried mushrooms (black Polish, shiitake or another dry variety)
- 2 bay leaves
- 1 teaspoon whole black peppercorns
- 1 teaspoon dried herbes de Provence (see page 13)

Place the chicken bones and water in a large stockpot. Bring to a strong boil, uncovered, over high heat, then reduce the heat to low and boil the mixture gently for 1 hour, removing any impurities and fat that rise to the surface, preferably with a fine-mesh skimmer.

Add the onions, celery, carrots, mushrooms, bay leaves, peppercorns and herbes de Provence. Continue to boil the mixture gently, uncovered, for another 3 hours.

Strain the stock through a fine strainer into a bowl and measure. You should have about 3 quarts of stock. If you have more, boil it until it is reduced to 3 quarts; if you have less, add water to bring the stock to 3 quarts.

Cool to room temperature. Cover and refrigerate overnight. The next day skim off and discard any solidified fat from the surface.

Cover and refrigerate for use within 4 to 5 days or freeze in 2-cup containers for use as needed.

Per 1 cup: 3 calories, 0 g. fat (0% of calories), 0 g. saturated fat, 0 mg. cholesterol, 2 mg. sodium.

Clear Vegetable Stock

Yield: 2 quarts

ade without any meat products, this stock is a good vegetarian substitute for chicken or other meat stocks.

- 1 ounce (½ cup) dried mushrooms, preferably a boletus variety (*cèpes* in French, *porcini* in Italian)
- 2 medium onions (about 8 ounces), peeled and thinly sliced (2 cups)
- 4 medium carrots (10–11 ounces), trimmed, peeled and chopped (2 cups)
- 1 medium leek (7–8 ounces), trimmed, thinly sliced and washed (2 cups)
- 3 stalks celery (about 6 ounces), washed, trimmed and thinly sliced (1½ cups)
- 5–6 cloves garlic, peeled and thinly sliced (1 tablespoon)
- 1 teaspoon herbes de Provence (see page 13)
- 10 cups water

Rinse the mushrooms briefly under cold running water to remove any dirt, then place them in a large stockpot with the onions, carrots, leeks, celery, garlic, herbes de Provence and water. Bring the mixture to a strong boil, reduce the heat to low, cover and boil gently for 1 hour.

Strain the mixture through a fine strainer into a large bowl, pressing on the solids to extract as much liquid as possible. You should have about 2 quarts. If you have more, boil it until reduced; if you have less, add water.

Cool to room temperature. Cover and refrigerate for use within 4 to 5 days or freeze in 2-cup containers for use as needed.

Per 1 cup: 5 calories, 0 g. fat (0% of calories), 0 g. saturated fat, 0 mg. cholesterol, 13 mg. sodium.

To cool hot stock quickly, strain it into a metal container and place in a sink or large pot of ice water. Leave it uncovered and stir often until the liquid has cooled. Transfer to smaller containers and seal tightly. Refrigerate or freeze. If you thaw frozen stock and then do not use it all, bring the remainder to a full boil before refreezing.

Poultry Brown Base Sauce

Yield: 2 cups

*T*his syrupy, concentrated liquid, called demi-glace *in French, is the base of many classic brown sauces flavored in different ways—with truffles, red wine, Madeira or vinegar.*

    1 quart Brown Chicken Stock (page 12)
    2 teaspoons cornstarch
    1 tablespoon cold water

Boil the stock in a medium saucepan until the liquid is reduced to 2 cups. Remove the pan from the heat.

In a cup, dissolve the cornstarch in the water. Whisk the mixture into the stock. Return the pan to the stove and bring the mixture to a boil, stirring occasionally to avoid scorching. The mixture will thicken as it reaches a boil. Set the sauce aside to cool.

Cover and store for up to a week in the refrigerator or freeze in 1-cup containers. Use as directed in other recipes.

Per 1 cup: 20 calories, 0 g. fat (0% of calories), 0 g. saturated fat, 0 mg. cholesterol, 212 mg. sodium.

Never add cornstarch directly to a hot liquid, or it will lump. Mix it first with a small amount of cold liquid to dissolve it and then stir it into the hot liquid. If you make the cornstarch mixture ahead, it will separate. Be sure to stir it well before adding it to the hot liquid.

Poultry White Base Sauce

Yield: 3 cups

his sauce is handy for giving a certain richness and smoothness to a finished dish or even to extend a salad dressing. It substitutes for the classic velouté, or cream sauce, used in most professional kitchens.

- 1 quart White Chicken Stock (page 14) or lower-salt canned chicken broth
- 2 tablespoons cornstarch
- 2 tablespoons cold water
- 1 cup skim milk

Boil the stock or broth in a medium saucepan until the liquid is reduced to 2 cups. Remove the pan from the heat.

In a cup, dissolve the cornstarch in the water. Whisk the mixture into the stock or broth. Return the pan to the stove and bring the mixture to a boil, stirring occasionally to avoid scorching. The mixture will thicken just before it reaches a boil. Add the milk, bring again to a boil and set the sauce aside to cool.

Cover and store for up to a week in the refrigerator or freeze in 1-cup containers. Use as directed in other recipes.

Per 1 cup: 53 calories, 0.2 g. fat (3% of calories), 0.1 g. saturated fat, 1 mg. cholesterol, 46 mg. sodium.

Tomato Sauce

Yield: 3 cups

his basic tomato sauce is as good with pasta as it is with dumplings (see Scallop Wontons with Tomato Sauce, page 132) or veal (see Fricadelles of Veal in Tomato Sauce, page 192). The sauce can be made ahead and reheated at serving time.

1 tablespoon virgin olive oil

1 medium onion (about 4 ounces), peeled and coarsely chopped (1 cup)

2 large cloves garlic, peeled, crushed and finely chopped (1 teaspoon)

½ teaspoon dried thyme

1 pound plum tomatoes (6–10), quartered

1 cup water

1 tablespoon tomato paste

½ teaspoon freshly ground black pepper

½ teaspoon salt

Heat the oil in a medium stainless steel saucepan until it is hot but not smoking. Add the onions, garlic and thyme and sauté for 1 to 2 minutes. Add the tomatoes and sauté for 1 minute, then add the water, tomato paste, pepper and salt. Bring the mixture to a boil, cover and boil gently for 10 minutes.

Transfer the mixture to the bowl of a food processor or blender and process until smooth (or, for an even smoother result, push through a food mill fitted with a fine-mesh screen).

Per ½ cup: 47 calories, 2.6 g. fat (48% of calories), 0.1 g. saturated fat, 0 mg. cholesterol, 207 mg. sodium.

Onion Sauce

Yield: 1½ cups

his onion sauce makes grilled meat or poultry more elegant and more flavorful, especially when you're serving guests.

   6 ounces caramelized onions (see Onion Papillote, page 245)
   1 cup Poultry Brown Base Sauce (page 16)

Place the onions in the bowl of a food processor or blender and puree until smooth. Pour the puree into a small saucepan, add the base sauce and mix well. Bring the mixture to a boil. Remove from the heat. Use as directed in other recipes.

Per ½ cup: 33 calories, 0.7 g. fat (17% of calories), 0 g. saturated fat, 0 mg. cholesterol, 72 mg. sodium.

Salsa Cruda

Salsa Cruda

his piquant salsa can be served with potato chips (see Microwave Potato Chips with Salsa Cruda, page 66), poached fish or broiled chicken. Or use it as a seasoning for salad.

1 large or 2 medium tomatoes (8–9 ounces), peeled, seeded and chopped (about 1¾ cups)

1 cup loosely packed chopped fresh cilantro leaves

1 medium onion (about 4 ounces), peeled and chopped (¾ cup)

1 small cucumber (about 8 ounces), trimmed, peeled, seeded and chopped (¾ cup)

4 scallions, washed, trimmed and finely chopped (½ cup)

¼ cup red wine vinegar

5–6 cloves garlic, peeled, crushed and finely chopped (1 tablespoon)

1 small jalapeño pepper, seeded, if desired (to eliminate some of its hotness), and finely chopped (1 tablespoon)

½ teaspoon salt

¼ teaspoon freshly ground black pepper

In a medium bowl, mix the tomatoes, cilantro, onions, cucumbers, scallions, vinegar, garlic, jalapeño peppers, salt and black pepper. (For a smooth salsa, especially if it is to be used as a salad dressing, puree the ingredients in a food processor or blender.)

Cover and store in the refrigerator for up to 2 weeks.

Per ½ cup: 30 calories, 0.3 g. fat (8% of calories), 0 g. saturated fat, 0 mg. cholesterol, 208 mg. sodium.

Oriental Sauce

this sauce is very versatile and can be served with artichokes (see Artichokes with Oriental Sauce, page 75), grilled fish or steamed or grilled chicken. Combined with a small amount of oil, it also makes an excellent dressing for green salads.

- 4 scallions, washed, trimmed and minced (about ½ cup)
- ⅓ cup water
- 1 large radish, chopped (2 tablespoons)
- 2 tablespoons rice wine vinegar
- 1 tablespoon Vietnamese fish sauce
- 2 teaspoons canola or safflower oil
- 2–3 cloves garlic, peeled, crushed and finely chopped (1 teaspoon)
- 1 small piece fresh ginger, peeled and finely chopped (1 teaspoon)
- 1 teaspoon sugar
- ¼ teaspoon Tabasco hot-pepper sauce

In a small bowl, mix the scallions, water, radishes, vinegar, fish sauce, oil, garlic, ginger, sugar and hot-pepper sauce.

Cover and store in the refrigerator for up to 2 weeks.

Per 1 tablespoon: 10 calories, 0.8 g. fat (66% of calories), 0 g. saturated fat, 0 mg. cholesterol, 88 mg. sodium.

Vietnamese fish sauce is available in most Asian markets and in the ethnic food section of some supermarkets. If you can't locate any, replace it with light soy sauce.

Creamy French-Style Dressing

Yield: 2 cups

*his dressing gets its beautiful pink color from paprika and fresh tomatoes.
Balsamic vinegar gives it a distinctive taste. Prepared in a food processor or
blender, it has a creamy texture. Use about 1½ to 2 tablespoons of dressing per
each serving of about 1½ cups of greens.*

1 cup Poultry White Base Sauce (page 17)

1 small tomato (3 ounces), peeled, seeded and coarsely chopped
(½ cup)

3 tablespoons balsamic vinegar

3 tablespoons canola, corn or virgin olive oil

1 scallion, washed, trimmed and finely chopped
(about 2 tablespoons)

1 tablespoon red wine vinegar

2 teaspoons sugar

1 small piece fresh ginger, peeled and finely chopped
(1½ teaspoons)

1 teaspoon paprika

1 teaspoon dry mustard

½ teaspoon freshly ground black pepper

½ teaspoon salt

Place the base sauce, tomatoes, balsamic vinegar, oil, scallions, wine vinegar,
sugar, ginger, paprika, mustard, pepper and salt in a blender or food processor
and process until smooth. Transfer the dressing to a jar with a tight-fitting lid
and refrigerate for up to 10 days. Shake well before using.

*Per 1½ tablespoons: 25 calories, 2 g. fat (72% of calories), 0 g. saturated fat, 0 mg.
cholesterol, 52 mg. sodium.*

Creamy Caramelized Garlic Dressing

Yield: about 2½ cups

*H*ere the soft flesh of baked garlic heads is pressed out and combined with *tarragon, vinegar and nonfat yogurt to make a creamy garlic dressing. Serve the dressing on salad greens. The baked garlic also can be served on its own or as a garnish for roasted meat or poultry.*

   4 tablespoons plus 1 teaspoon canola oil
   2 heads garlic (6 ounces), cut in half crosswise
   3 tablespoons cider vinegar
   2 tablespoons chopped fresh tarragon leaves
   ½ teaspoon salt
   ¼ teaspoon freshly ground black pepper
   2 cups plain nonfat yogurt

Preheat the oven to 400°.

Coat one side of an 8″ to 10″ length of aluminum foil with 1 teaspoon of the oil. Arrange the garlic heads, cut side down, side by side on the foil and wrap the foil around them to encase them completely. Place the foil package on a cookie sheet or in a small pan and bake for 40 minutes. Then set the garlic heads aside, still wrapped, for 10 minutes to cool slightly.

Open the package and press the cooked flesh from the garlic heads into the bowl of a food processor. Add the vinegar, tarragon, salt and pepper. Process for 4 to 5 seconds, stopping the motor and scraping down the sides of the bowl with a spatula once during the processing.

Add the yogurt and process the mixture for about 30 seconds until it is creamy. Add the remaining 4 tablespoons oil and process until blended, about 15 seconds.

Store, tightly covered, in the refrigerator for up to a week.

Per 2 tablespoons: 52 calories, 3 g. fat (51% of calories), 0.2 g. saturated fat, 0 mg. cholesterol, 72 mg. sodium.

Clockwise from top: Creamy Caramelized Garlic Dressing (page 24);
Creamy French-Style Dressing (page 23) and Sesame Dressing (page 26)

Sesame Dressing

his is an exotic dressing that tastes good on basic salads as well as on hearty ones (see Broiled Chicken Salad, page 160).

- 1 tablespoon dark soy sauce
- 1 tablespoon Worcestershire sauce
- 1 tablespoon dark sesame oil
- 1 tablespoon canola or virgin olive oil
- 1 tablespoon lemon juice
- 1 tablespoon balsamic vinegar
- 1 teaspoon sugar
- 2–3 cloves garlic, peeled, crushed and finely chopped (1 teaspoon)
- ½ teaspoon dry mustard
- ¼ teaspoon freshly ground black pepper

Place the soy sauce, Worcestershire sauce, sesame oil, canola or olive oil, lemon juice, vinegar, sugar, garlic, mustard and pepper in a jar with a tight-fitting lid. Mix well by shaking the jar.

Store, tightly covered, in the refrigerator for up to a week. Shake well before using.

Per 1 tablespoon: 52 calories, 4.6 g. fat (78% of calories), 0.5 g. saturated fat, 0 mg. cholesterol, 197 mg. sodium.

Cucumber-Scallion Dressing

Yogurt gives this refreshing dressing its creamy texture and slightly sour taste, which is pleasantly offset by a little sugar. Making the dressing in a blender creates a smoother texture than is possible with a food processor.

1 small cucumber (about 8 ounces), trimmed, peeled, seeded and coarsely chopped (¾ cup)

2 scallions, washed, trimmed and coarsely chopped (about ¼ cup)

2 tablespoons chopped fresh dill

3 cloves garlic, peeled

1½ cups plain nonfat yogurt

2 tablespoons lemon juice

2 tablespoons virgin olive oil

2 teaspoons sugar

½ teaspoon salt

Place the cucumbers, scallions, dill and garlic in a blender and blend until the mixture is creamy. Add the yogurt, lemon juice, oil, sugar and salt. Pulse a few seconds, just until the dressing is smooth.

Store, tightly covered, in the refrigerator for up to 1 week.

Per 2 tablespoons: 32 calories, 1.8 g. fat (47% of calories), 0.3 g. saturated fat, 0 mg. cholesterol, 84 mg. sodium.

Mustard-Vinaigrette Dressing

Yield: 2 cups

his vinaigrette dressing is accented with Poultry Brown Base Sauce. The dressing develops more flavor after a few hours and can be stored for up to ten days. Use about 2 tablespoons of dressing for each serving of 1½ cups of greens.

- 1 cup Poultry Brown Base Sauce (page 16)
- ½ cup red wine vinegar
- 3 tablespoons virgin olive oil
- 2 tablespoons Dijon mustard
- 5–6 cloves garlic, peeled, crushed and finely chopped (1 tablespoon)
- 1 teaspoon chopped fresh parsley leaves
- 1 teaspoon freshly ground black pepper

Place the base sauce, vinegar, oil, mustard, garlic, parsley and pepper in a jar with a tight-fitting lid and mix well by shaking the jar.

Store, tightly covered, in the refrigerator for up to 10 days. Shake well before using.

Per 2 tablespoons: 28 calories, 2.7 g. fat (81% of calories), 0.5 g. saturated fat, 0 mg. cholesterol, 39 mg. sodium.

Tomato-Vinaigrette Dressing

Yield: 2¼ cups

his salad dressing contains very few calories and is practically fat-free, so it can be served on salad greens as an extra dish with every meal. Make a large quantity of the dressing; it keeps well. Use 1½ to 2 tablespoons on each serving of lettuce or other greens.

- 1   cup White Chicken Stock (page 14) or lower-salt canned chicken broth
- 2   teaspoons cornstarch
- 1   tablespoon cold water
- 1   ripe large tomato (about 8 ounces), halved and seeded
- 2   scallions, washed, trimmed and coarsely chopped (about ¼ cup)
- 3   tablespoons balsamic vinegar
- 3   tablespoons red wine vinegar
- 2   tablespoons Dijon mustard
- 1   teaspoon paprika
- 1   teaspoon salt (adjust if canned broth is used)
- 3   cloves garlic, peeled and crushed
- ½   teaspoon freshly ground black pepper
- ¼   teaspoon Tabasco hot-pepper sauce

Bring the stock or broth to a boil in a small saucepan. Remove from the heat.

In a cup, dissolve the cornstarch in the water. Whisk into the stock or broth to thicken it lightly. Bring the mixture to a boil, then set it aside to cool.

Cut the tomato into 1″ chunks and place them in the bowl of a food processor. Add the scallions, balsamic vinegar, wine vinegar, mustard, paprika, salt, garlic, pepper and hot-pepper sauce. Process until smooth. Add the thickened stock or broth and process briefly, until incorporated.

Transfer the dressing to a jar with a tight-fitting lid. Store, tightly covered, in the refrigerator for up to a week. Shake well before using.

Per 2 tablespoons: 10 calories, 0.2 g. fat (15% of calories), 0 g. saturated fat, 0 mg. cholesterol, 143 mg. sodium.

First Courses

Cold Peach Soup

Asparagus in Sesame Sauce

Apple and Mushroom Salad

and more . . . .

Onion Soup Gratinée

Yield: 6 servings

*S*oup *is probably one of the best vehicles for cutting back on calories
because it can be made almost fat-free without any real loss of flavor.*

*In this country-style onion soup, I cook the onions until they turn a rich, dark
color and take on an intense flavor. Then I puree a little of the finished soup and
stir it into the remainder to slightly thicken it. If you prefer, all of the finished
soup can be pureed in a food processor to give it the texture of a light onion
puree. Or you can serve the soup plain (not pureed and without the cheese and
final browning in the oven), with a garnish of croutons.*

*In the gratinée version, the finished soup should have a beautiful golden crust
of bread and cheese, achieved here with only a quarter of the cheese used in conventional recipes for this classic soup. This is a satisfying dish, and the mixture of
lean mozzarella and good Swiss (Gruyère) cheese makes a nice combination.*

1	tablespoon virgin olive oil
6–8	medium onions (about 2 pounds), peeled and thinly sliced (about 8 cups)
5	cups Brown Chicken Stock (page 12) or lower-salt canned chicken broth
2	cups water
	Freshly ground black pepper, to taste
16–18	thin slices bread (about 1½ ounces total from a French-style baguette bread loaf weighing about 9 ounces)
½	cup shredded part-skim mozzarella cheese
¼	cup shredded Gruyère cheese

Heat the oil in a large heavy pot. When it is hot, add the onions. Cover and
cook over high heat for 5 minutes. Uncover and cook over medium heat for
15 minutes, until the onions are well browned. Add the stock or broth, water
and pepper. Cover and cook for 20 minutes.

Meanwhile, preheat the oven to 400°.

Arrange the bread slices in a single layer on a baking tray. Bake for
10 minutes, or until the bread is brown. Set aside for use as croutons while
you finish the soup.

Transfer about ⅓ of the cooked soup to the bowl of a food processor and
puree it. Add the puree to the remaining soup in the pot.

To serve the soup, pour it into a large crock (or divide it among 6 individual

Onion Soup Gratinée

crocks). Top with the croutons, then sprinkle on the mozzarella and Gruyère. Place the crock on a baking sheet and bake for 35 minutes. If needed, place under the broiler for 5 minutes to brown the cheeses and create a crusty top on the soup. Serve immediately.

Per serving: 145 calories, 5.8 g. fat (36% of calories), 2.4 g. saturated fat, 10 mg. cholesterol, 192 mg. sodium.

Vegetable Soup with Basil Pistou

Vegetable Soup with Basil Pistou

Yield: 6 servings

his soup containing a variety of vegetables can be made ahead. Pistou, a mixture found in the Provençal cooking of southern France, is similar to an Italian pesto. It's added at the last moment here to season the soup and give it the fresh taste of herbs, garlic and cheese. You can also serve the pistou over pasta.

SOUP

- 1 medium leek (6–7 ounces), trimmed, thinly sliced and washed (1½ cups) or 8–9 scallions (about 6 ounces), washed, trimmed and thinly sliced (1½ cups)
- 1 small piece eggplant (about 4 ounces), unpeeled but trimmed and cut into 1″ dice (1½ cups)
- 1 kohlrabi (about 8 ounces), peeled and cut into ½″ dice (1 cup)
- 1 medium onion (4 ounces), peeled and cut into ½″ dice (¾ cup)
- 1–2 stalks celery, including leafy tops (about 4 ounces), washed, trimmed and cut into ½″ dice (¾ cup)
- 3 medium carrots (7–8 ounces), trimmed, peeled and cut into ½″ dice (¾ cup)
- 1 small piece butternut squash (6 ounces), peeled, seeded and cut into ½″ dice (about 1 cup)
- 1 medium potato (6–7 ounces), peeled and cut into ½″ dice (¾ cup)
- 1 small zucchini (4 ounces), washed, trimmed and cut into ½″ dice (1 cup)
- ½ cup cut green beans
- ½ teaspoon salt (adjust if canned broth is used)
- 5 cups White Chicken Stock (page 14) or lower-salt canned chicken broth
  About 3 ounces spinach, trimmed, washed and torn into slightly smaller pieces (2 cups)

PISTOU

- ¾ cup loosely packed fresh basil leaves
- ½ cup loosely packed fresh parsley leaves
- 4 cloves garlic, peeled
- 3 tablespoons White Chicken Stock (page 14) or lower-salt canned chicken broth
- 3 tablespoons grated Parmesan cheese

To make the soup: In a large pot, combine the leeks or scallions, eggplant, kohlrabi, onions, celery, carrots, squash, potatoes, zucchini, beans, salt and stock or broth. Bring the mixture to a boil, reduce the heat to low, cover and boil gently for 35 minutes. Add the spinach and cook, uncovered, for another 10 minutes. Meanwhile, prepare the pistou.

To make the pistou: Puree the basil, parsley, garlic, stock or broth and Parmesan in the bowl of a food processor, blender or mini-chop until very smooth. Transfer the mixture to a bowl and set it aside.

When the soup is cooked, remove about 3 cups of it from the pot and puree it in a food processor or blender. Return the pureed soup to the pot and mix it in well to thicken the soup somewhat and give it a richer, denser taste.

To serve, ladle the hot soup into soup bowls and top each serving with 1 to 2 tablespoons of the pistou. (Alternatively, add all the pistou to the pot of soup just before serving, stir the mixture well and pour it into a large soup tureen. Bring the tureen to the table and ladle the soup into individual bowls.)

Per serving: 125 calories, 1.5 g. fat (10% of calories), 0.7 g. saturated fat, 2 mg. cholesterol, 287 mg. sodium.

Leeks are grown in sandy soil and can hold a lot of dirt. One way to remove it is to slice the leeks and place the pieces in a large bowl of cold water. Swish the leeks around and then allow them to stand for a few minutes to release the dirt. Carefully lift the leeks out of the water so that the dirt will remain in the bottom of the bowl.

You can peel ginger with a paring knife or a vegetable peeler. Another very effective way to remove the peel is to hold the ginger in one hand and scrape the surface away with a teaspoon. The spoon makes it easy to get into all the crevices that a piece of fresh ginger has.

Spinach and Chicken Soup

Yield: 6 generous servings

he most important thing to remember when preparing this quick soup is not to overcook the chicken. It takes only a few minutes for the raw strips of skinless, boneless chicken breast to cook. This is ideal as a light supper main course as well as a delicious first course.

6	cups White Chicken Stock (page 14) or lower-salt canned chicken broth
1	cup water
6	scallions (4 ounces), washed, trimmed and thinly sliced (1 cup)
3	ounces small pasta, preferably farfalline or small bow ties (1 cup)
8	ounces spinach, trimmed, washed and coarsely cut (6 cups)
3	ounces domestic mushrooms, washed and chopped (1 cup)
2	skinless, boneless chicken breasts (12 ounces), trimmed of all surrounding fat and cut crosswise into fine julienne strips
½	teaspoon salt (adjust if canned broth is used)
¼	teaspoon freshly ground black pepper
1	medium tomato (6 ounces), halved, seeded and cut into ½″ dice (about 1 cup)

Bring the stock or broth, water and scallions to a boil in a pot. Add the pasta and bring the mixture back to a full boil. Then reduce the heat to low, cover and boil gently for 5 minutes.

Add the spinach and mushrooms, mix well, bring back to a strong boil and boil for 1 minute. Add the chicken, separating the pieces, and the salt and pepper. Mix well and bring back to a boil. Cover and set aside off the heat for 5 minutes. Add the tomatoes, stir and serve immediately.

Per serving: 118 calories, 1.4 g. fat (11% of calories), 0.3 g. saturated fat, 23 mg. cholesterol, 225 mg. sodium.

Corn and Leek Soup

Yield: 6 generous servings

ade with low-fat milk, leeks and onions, this soup has a surprisingly creamy appearance and rich flavor. If you want to thicken the soup a little, you can add some creamed corn along with the fresh corn kernels.

- 6 cups 1% low-fat milk
- 1 medium leek (5–6 ounces), trimmed, thinly sliced and washed (1½ cups)
- 1 medium onion (5 ounces), peeled and chopped (1 cup)
- 5–6 cloves garlic, peeled, crushed and finely chopped (1 tablespoon)
- 1 teaspoon salt
- ½ teaspoon freshly ground black pepper
- 4 ears sweet corn (2 pounds), husked with kernels cut off the cobs (3 cups)

Place the milk, leeks, onions, garlic, salt and pepper in a large saucepan and bring the mixture to a boil, watching closely so it doesn't boil over. Boil for 2 minutes. Add the corn and return the mixture to a boil. Remove the pan from the heat and let it sit for 5 minutes before serving. Serve in bowls or on soup plates.

Variation: For a slightly thicker soup, add a 16½-ounce can of creamed corn along with the fresh corn kernels and proceed according to the recipe instructions.

Per serving: 197 calories, 2.8 g. fat (12% of calories), 1.6 g. saturated fat, 10 mg. cholesterol, 488 mg. sodium.

Mushroom-Barley Soup

Yield: 6 servings

*S*ince it takes time to cook this soup, you may want to double the recipe *and freeze half for future use. For best results, defrost it in the refrigerator or in a microwave oven and then return it to a boil before serving. A very earthy, satisfying soup, it includes both fresh and dried mushrooms.*

½ cup barley

5 cups water

1 tablespoon virgin olive oil

5–6 cloves garlic, peeled, crushed and finely chopped (1 tablespoon)

2 medium carrots (5½–6 ounces), trimmed, peeled and thinly sliced (2 cups)

1 medium onion (4 ounces), peeled and very thinly sliced (1 cup)

6 ounces domestic mushrooms, washed and very thinly sliced (about 3 cups)

About 1 ounce dried mushrooms (½ cup), crushed into small pieces in a mini-chop or with a mortar and pestle

2 cups White Chicken Stock (page 14) or lower-salt canned chicken broth

½ teaspoon freshly ground black pepper

¾ teaspoon salt (adjust if canned broth is used)

¼ cup chopped fresh parsley leaves

Place the barley in a saucepan with 3 cups of the water. Bring the mixture to a boil, cover, reduce the heat to low and boil very gently for 50 to 60 minutes. The barley should be tender but not mushy. Set aside.

Heat the oil in a large pot, add the garlic and cook for 1 minute. Add the carrots and onions and cook over high heat for 1 minute. Add the domestic mushrooms, dried mushrooms, stock or broth and the remaining 2 cups water. Bring to a boil, reduce the heat to low and boil gently for 10 minutes. Add the pepper, salt and barley with its liquid. Bring back to a boil. Stir in the parsley.

Variations: Process 2 cups of the finished soup in a food processor and return it to the pot as a thickening agent for the soup. Or process all the soup.

Per serving: 149 calories, 3 g. fat (17% of calories), 0.5 g. saturated fat, 0 mg. cholesterol, 282 mg. sodium.

Spinach-Dumpling Soup

Yield: 6 servings

his recipe features little matzo-meal dumplings containing club soda, which lightens the dumplings considerably. I cook the dumplings on the side— since they would cloud the soup if cooked in it—and then add them to the soup just before serving it.

DUMPLINGS
- ½ cup matzo meal
- 2 egg whites, lightly beaten with a fork
- 1–2 scallions, washed, trimmed and finely chopped (¼ cup)
- 3 tablespoons club soda
- 1 tablespoon peanut or canola oil
- ⅛ teaspoon freshly ground black pepper
- ⅛ teaspoon salt

SOUP
- 6 cups White Chicken Stock (page 14) or lower-salt canned chicken broth
- 6 ounces spinach, trimmed, washed and torn into slightly smaller pieces (5 cups)
- ½ teaspoon salt (adjust if canned broth is used)

To make the dumplings: Mix the matzo meal, egg whites, scallions, soda, oil, pepper and salt in a medium bowl. Set the mixture aside to rest and thicken for 15 to 20 minutes.

Bring a large pot of water to a boil. Using a spoon and your hands, form the matzo mixture into 12 balls or dumplings. Drop the dumplings into the boiling water, reduce the heat to low and cook the dumplings at a very gentle boil for 12 to 15 minutes. Remove them from the water with a slotted spoon and set them aside on a tray or plate.

To make the soup: Bring the stock or broth to a boil in a pot and add the spinach, pushing it down into the liquid. Bring the liquid back to a boil and boil the spinach for 2 minutes. Add the salt and the matzo balls. Heat through.

Per serving: 78 calories, 2.5 g. fat (28% of calories), 0.4 g. saturated fat, 0 mg. cholesterol, 267 mg. sodium.

Clockwise from top: Spinach-Dumpling Soup (page 40);
Mushroom-Barley Soup (page 39) and Corn and Leek Soup (page 38)

Cornmeal and Vegetable Soup

Yield: 6 servings

his fresh, nourishing soup can be prepared in just a few minutes. The cornmeal gives it a satisfying rich taste and provides the dense texture needed for this type of soup. If leeks are not available, substitute scallions or a mixture of scallions and onions. Herbs from the garden—parsley, chervil, basil, tarragon—are always welcome and make nice additions.

        1   tablespoon peanut oil
     1½   teaspoons unsalted butter
        2   large leeks (about 10 ounces), trimmed, thinly sliced and washed
             (2½ cups)
        2   medium carrots (about 5½ ounces), trimmed, peeled and cut into
             ¼″ dice (1 cup)
        2   medium turnips (about 6 ounces), peeled and cut into ¼″ slices
        2   stalks celery (about 5 ounces), washed, trimmed and thinly sliced
             (1 cup)
        7   cups White Chicken Stock (page 14) or lower-salt canned
             chicken broth
       ½   cup yellow cornmeal
       ¼   teaspoon salt (adjust if canned broth is used)

Heat the oil and butter until hot in a large saucepan. Add the leeks and cook for 2 to 3 minutes over medium to high heat. Add the carrots, turnips, celery and stock or broth. Bring to a boil over high heat. Reduce the heat to low, cover halfway with a lid and boil gently for 15 minutes. Add the cornmeal and salt. Cook at a very gentle boil, stirring occasionally, for 5 minutes. Serve immediately.

Per serving: 118 calories, 3.9 g. fat (30% of calories), 1.2 g. saturated fat, 6 mg. cholesterol, 148 mg. sodium.

Vegetable, Leek and Oatmeal Soup

Yield: 6 servings

C anned vegetable broth is available now in supermarkets, but you can make it easily at home: Place an assortment of raw vegetables and herbs— try carrots, celery, onions, leeks, scallions, potatoes and parsley, for example— in a large saucepan or pot, add enough water to cover them and bring the water to a boil. Reduce the heat and boil gently until the vegetables are tender. Drain, reserving the cooking liquid for use in this recipe and others that call for vegetable stock.

5 cups homemade vegetable stock (see above or page 15) or canned vegetable broth

1 medium to large leek (7–8 ounces), trimmed, chopped and washed (2 cups)

1¼ cups old-fashioned rolled oats

1½ cups skim milk

Salt, to taste

Bring the stock or broth to a boil in a large saucepan. Add the leeks and oats and bring the mixture back to a boil. Boil gently for 7 to 8 minutes. Add the milk and stir well. Add salt, if needed. Serve immediately.

Per serving: 168 calories, 2.5 g. fat (13% of calories), 0.5 g. saturated fat, 1 mg. cholesterol, 45 mg. sodium.

Dried Mushroom Soup with Tofu

Yield: 6 servings

his soup contains two varieties of dried mushrooms: intensely flavored shiitake mushrooms and tree ear mushrooms, which are liked more for their chewy texture than for their taste. After reconstituting the mushrooms, remove the shiitake stems, which tend to be tough, and cut off and discard the fibrous, often sandy "foot" from the tree ears. Chunks of tofu enhance the flavor of this delicious, quickly cooked soup.

18 dried shiitake mushrooms (1½ ounces)

1½ ounces dried tree ear mushrooms

3 cups boiling water

3 cups White Chicken Stock (page 14), Brown Chicken Stock (page 12) or lower-salt canned chicken broth

8 scallions (about 5 ounces), washed, trimmed and finely chopped (1 cup)

2 stalks celery (4 ounces), washed, trimmed and coarsely chopped (⅔ cup)

4 tablespoons soy sauce

2 tablespoons rice wine vinegar

2 tablespoons chili sauce with garlic

14 ounces firm tofu, cut into 1″ squares (3 cups)

Hot chili oil or dark sesame oil (optional)

Place the shiitake mushrooms and tree ear mushrooms in a large bowl and add the water. Soak the mushrooms for 15 to 20 minutes, then remove from the water. Reserve the mushrooms and soaking liquid separately.

Cut off the shiitake mushroom stems, which tend to be tough, and reserve them for use in a stock. Set aside the caps.

Trim the roots from the tree ear mushrooms and discard. Then stack the tree ears, roll them together and cut them into thin strips.

Place the stock or broth in a large saucepan and carefully add the reserved mushroom soaking liquid, leaving behind and discarding any sandy residue in the bottom of the bowl.

Add the shiitake mushrooms and tree ear mushrooms. Bring the mixture to a boil. Then reduce the heat to low, cover and boil gently for 5 minutes. Add the scallions, celery, soy sauce, vinegar and chili sauce to the pan and boil the mixture, uncovered, over medium to high heat for 5 minutes longer. Stir in the tofu and cook the mixture over low heat for 1 minute without boiling to warm it through.

Ladle the soup into bowls. If desired, sprinkle with the oil.

Per serving: 162 calories, 6 g. fat (30% of calories), 0.9 g. saturated fat, 0 mg. cholesterol, 781 mg. sodium.

If any of the ingredients for this soup are not available at your grocery store, they will be at an oriental market. Different brands of chili sauce and chili oil may vary in intensity, so start with small amounts and increase them to your taste.

Hot Thai Soup with Noodles

Yield: 6 generous servings

ade with Chinese noodles, this soup is ready to eat in ten minutes. The noodles are sold in compact cakes that should be broken into smaller pieces before you add them to the pot. They cook in just minutes.

Asian flavors are featured in the seasoning mixture that is stirred into the soup just before it is served. The mixture has a piquant flavor I like, although you can change the ingredients at will to accommodate your personal taste preferences. Tomatoes, not common in Chinese cooking, do appear in other Far Eastern cuisines and make a nice addition here.

THAI SEASONING MIXTURE

1 lime
1 cup loosely packed fresh cilantro leaves, coarsely chopped (⅔ cup)
3 tablespoons soy sauce
2 tablespoons red wine vinegar
1 tablespoon dark sesame oil
1–2 small serrano peppers, seeded, if desired (to eliminate some of the hotness), and finely chopped (1 tablespoon)
2 cloves garlic, peeled, crushed and finely chopped (1 teaspoon)

SOUP

6 cups White Chicken Stock (page 14) or lower-salt canned chicken broth
3 cups water
4 ounces plain, dry Chinese noodles
1 medium tomato (7 ounces), peeled, seeded and cut into ½" dice (1 cup)

To make the Thai seasoning mixture: Cut the lime lengthwise into ¼" slices; stack the slices and cut them into ¼" dice. (You should have ½ cup.) Place the lime pieces in a small bowl. Add the cilantro, soy sauce, vinegar, oil, peppers and garlic. Mix well and set aside.

To make the soup: Bring the stock or broth and water to a boil in a large pot. Add the noodles, breaking them into chunks, and bring the mixture to a full boil. Then reduce the heat to low, cover and boil gently for 4 minutes.

Hot Thai Soup with Noodles

Add the reserved seasoning mixture and the tomatoes, bring the mixture to a boil and ladle into bowls. Serve immediately.

Per serving: 111 calories, 2.5 g. fat (19% of calories), 0.4 g. saturated fat, 0 mg. cholesterol, 525 mg. sodium.

Winter Vegetables and Grits Soup

Yield: 6 generous servings

When I want soup in a hurry but have no homemade stock available to use as a base, I occasionally use water and chicken bouillon cubes. The cubes make a fine base, provided you use them sparingly, as they tend to dominate the flavor of a soup. Here, a search of my refrigerator turned up pieces of cabbage, yellow turnips, butternut squash and some beet greens. I cooked these with bouillon cubes in water until the vegetables were tender, then added some grits to thicken the mixture. No salt is needed here, since the bouillon cubes are salty. If substituting unsalted chicken stock for the bouillon cubes and water, add salt to taste.

12	ounces savoy cabbage, cut into 2″ pieces (4 cups)
12	ounces yellow turnips, peeled and cut into ½″ pieces (1½ cups)
1¼	pounds butternut squash, peeled, seeded and cut into ½″ dice (3 cups)
14	ounces leaves and ribs from a bunch of beets, cut into 2″ pieces and washed (about 7 cups)
4	chicken bouillon cubes
8	cups water
⅓	cup grits

Place the cabbage, turnips, squash, beet leaves and ribs, bouillon cubes and water in a large pot, preferably stainless steel. Bring the mixture to a boil, then cover, reduce the heat to low and boil gently for 45 minutes.

Sprinkle the grits into the pot, stirring the mixture as you add them. Bring the soup back to a boil, reduce the heat to low, cover and cook for 10 minutes. Stir and serve.

Per serving: 87 calories, 0.4 g. fat (4% of calories), 0.1 g. saturated fat, 0 mg. cholesterol, 781 mg. sodium.

Chunky Lentil Soup

Yield: 6 servings

his is one of those earthy, leguminous soups that taste so good on cold winter days. In my rendition of this classic dish, I add julienne strips of corn tortillas, which give the soup a specific taste that I find appealing. If you object to the intense flavor of corn tortillas, use flour tortillas or eliminate the garnish altogether.

8	ounces lentils (1½ cups)
1	medium potato (8 ounces), peeled and cut into ½″ dice (about 1 cup)
1	onion (4 ounces), peeled and thinly sliced (about 1 cup)
1	carrot (2 ounces), trimmed, peeled and cut into ½″ dice (½ cup)
½	teaspoon dried thyme
4	cups White Chicken Stock (page 14) or lower-salt canned chicken broth
3	cups water
2–3	cloves garlic, peeled, crushed and finely chopped (1 teaspoon)
¾	teaspoon salt (adjust if canned broth is used)
¼	teaspoon Tabasco hot-pepper sauce
2	corn tortillas (6″ in diameter; 2 ounces each), cut in half and then into julienne strips

Sort the lentils, discarding any damaged lentils or stones. Wash the lentils in a sieve held under cold tap water.

Place the lentils, potatoes, onions, carrots, thyme, stock or broth and water in a pot and bring the mixture to a boil over high heat. Stir well, reduce the heat to very low, cover and boil gently for 50 minutes.

Combine the garlic, salt and hot-pepper sauce in a small bowl. Add this mixture to the cooked soup with the corn tortillas. Bring the soup back to a boil and serve.

Per serving: 197 calories, 0.9 g. fat (4% of calories), 0.1 g. saturated fat, 0 mg. cholesterol, 553 mg. sodium.

Minty Cream of Butternut Squash Soup

Yield: 6 servings

For this beautifully smooth and creamy soup, I cook butternut squash until tender and then puree it. I season it with a dash of curry powder and fresh mint. Rich and flavorful, it makes a good first-course party dish.

- 1 butternut squash (2¾ pounds), peeled, seeded and cut into 2″ pieces
- 1 medium onion (4 ounces), peeled and sliced (1 cup)
- 2 cups water
- ½ teaspoon curry powder
- ½ teaspoon ground cumin
- 3 cups White Chicken Stock (page 14) or lower-salt canned chicken broth
- 2 sprigs fresh mint
- 1 medium carrot (4 ounces), trimmed and peeled
- 1 small leek or piece of leek (3 ounces), trimmed
- ¾ teaspoon salt (adjust if canned broth is used)
- ¼ teaspoon freshly ground black pepper

Place the squash, onions, water, curry powder, cumin and 2 cups of the stock or broth in a pot. If the mint sprigs have woody stems, strip off the leaves and add them to the pot; otherwise, add the whole sprigs. Bring the mixture to a full boil, reduce the heat to low, cover and cook for 45 minutes.

Meanwhile, cut the carrot lengthwise into ¼″ slices. Halve the slices crosswise so they are about 3″ long. Stack the pieces and cut them lengthwise into thin julienne strips.

Cut the leek lengthwise in half, then cut each half lengthwise into thin julienne strips. Wash the leeks under cold running water.

Place the carrots and leeks in a medium saucepan with the remaining 1 cup stock or broth. Bring to a boil, reduce the heat to medium and boil for 10 minutes. Set aside off the heat.

When the soup has cooked for 45 minutes, puree it in the pot with a hand blender. (Or puree it in batches in a blender.) Stir in the salt, pepper, carrots and leeks. Bring the mixture back to a boil. Serve immediately.

Per serving: 80 calories, 0.3 g. fat (3% of calories), 0 g. saturated fat, 0 mg. cholesterol, 276 mg. sodium.

*Minty Cream of Butternut Squash Soup (page 50)
and Tomato Potage with Basil (page 53)*

Vegetable and Clam Chowder

Yield: 6 generous servings

C lams give this soup a flavor similar to Manhattan clam chowder. If you eliminate the clams, this is a hearty vegetable stew.

 1 pound chopped clams
 1 small eggplant (8 ounces), unpeeled but trimmed and cut into 1″ dice (3 cups)
 6 ounces Chinese cabbage, cut into 1″ pieces (3 cups)
 2 small zucchini (8 ounces), washed, trimmed and cut into ½″ dice (2 cups)
 1 medium potato (8 ounces), peeled and coarsely chopped (1 cup)
 1 red bell pepper (4 ounces), halved, cored, seeded and cut into ½″ pieces (1 cup)
 1 medium onion (4 ounces), peeled and thinly sliced (1 cup)
 2 stalks celery (4 ounces), washed, trimmed and thinly sliced (1 cup)
 1 medium carrot (3 ounces), trimmed, peeled and coarsely chopped (½ cup)
 ½ small leek (2 ounces), trimmed, sliced and washed (½ cup)
 1 teaspoon dried thyme
 5 cups water
 ½ teaspoon freshly ground black pepper
 1 tablespoon Vietnamese or Thai fish sauce
 3–4 cloves garlic, peeled, crushed and finely chopped (2 teaspoons)
 ½ teaspoon salt

Place the clams (with their juice), eggplant, cabbage, zucchini, potatoes, red peppers, onions, celery, carrots, leeks, thyme, water and ¼ teaspoon of the black pepper in a pot. Bring the mixture to a full boil over high heat, cover, reduce the heat to low and cook at a very gentle boil for 1 hour.

Combine the fish sauce, garlic, salt and the remaining ¼ teaspoon black pepper in a small bowl.

Insert a hand blender into the pot and blend the mixture for 8 to 10 seconds. (Or partially puree in a blender.) Add the garlic mixture to the pot and serve.

Per serving: 141 calories, 1.1 g. fat (7% of calories), 0.1 g. saturated fat, 25 mg. cholesterol, 280 mg. sodium.

Tomato Potage with Basil

Yield: 6 servings

this recipe is particularly good if you make it when tomatoes are in full season. You may serve the soup cold as well as hot.

- 1 tablespoon virgin olive oil
- 2 medium onions (12 ounces), peeled and sliced (about 3 cups)
- 1 carrot (4 ounces), trimmed, peeled and cut into ¼″ dice (¾ cup)
- 3 sprigs fresh thyme or 1 teaspoon dried thyme
- 4 cloves garlic, peeled and crushed
- 6–10 ripe tomatoes (3 pounds)
- 4 cups White Chicken Stock (page 14) or lower-salt canned chicken broth
- 1 teaspoon salt (adjust if canned broth is used)
- 1 teaspoon freshly ground black pepper
- 1 teaspoon sugar
- 1 large sprig fresh mint
- 1½ teaspoons unsalted butter
- ¼ cup fresh basil leaves, sliced into a fine chiffonade (see page 100)
- ¼ cup coarsely chopped fresh parsley leaves

Heat the oil in a large stainless steel saucepan. When it is hot, add the onions, carrots, thyme and garlic. Cook for 3 to 4 minutes over high heat, until the onions are lightly browned. Remove the pan from the heat and set it aside.

Remove the skin from 1 tomato with a knife and add the skin to the saucepan. Cut the peeled tomato in half crosswise. Press out the seeds and juice; add them to the saucepan. Cut the tomato flesh into ¼″ dice and reserve it to serve as a garnish with the soup.

Cut the remaining tomatoes into chunks and add them to the saucepan. Add the stock or broth, salt, pepper, sugar and mint.

Cover the saucepan and bring to a boil. Then reduce the heat to low and boil the mixture gently for 10 minutes. Remove the pan from the heat and press the contents through a food mill fitted with a fine-mesh screen.

Return the soup to the saucepan and whisk in the butter. Serve hot or cold, garnishing each serving with about 2 tablespoons of the reserved diced tomatoes, some of the basil and some of the parsley.

Per serving: 118 calories, 4.1 g. fat (27% of calories), 1.1 g. saturated fat, 6 mg. cholesterol, 388 mg. sodium.

Gazpacho

Yield: 6 servings

Gazpacho is made from raw vegetables that are pureed and served as a soup or "liquid salad." Refreshing and healthful, it is the ideal hot-weather soup. You can adjust the ingredients to suit your own tastes, adding more or less cucumber, tomato or onion, for example, or even eliminating vegetables or seasonings that you don't find appealing. You may prepare this soup up to 12 hours ahead, but don't prepare it too far ahead, because it may ferment if it stands for several days.

2	slices bread, cut into ½" dice
2	large cucumbers (about 2 pounds), trimmed, peeled and seeded
3	medium tomatoes (about 1¼ pounds), halved and seeded
1	medium onion (5 ounces), peeled and sliced (1½ cups)
1	medium green bell pepper (4 ounces), halved, cored and seeded
3	cloves garlic, peeled
½	small jalapeño pepper, seeded, if desired (to eliminate some of its hotness), and finely chopped (2 teaspoons)
1	small piece fresh ginger, peeled and finely chopped (½ teaspoon)
¼	teaspoon freshly ground black pepper
⅓	cup cold water
1½	cups unsalted tomato juice
2	tablespoons red wine vinegar
1	tablespoon virgin olive oil
½	teaspoon Tabasco hot-pepper sauce
¼	teaspoon salt

Preheat the oven to 400°.

Spread the bread on a cookie sheet and bake for 8 to 10 minutes. Set aside for use as croutons.

Cut enough of the cucumbers and tomatoes into ½" dice to have about ⅔ cup of each. Set aside as garnishes; reserve the remainder for the soup.

Cut enough onion and green pepper into ¼" dice to have ⅓ cup of each. Set aside as garnishes; reserve the remainder for the soup.

54   FIRST COURSES

Coarsely chop the remaining cucumbers, tomatoes, onions and green peppers and place them in the bowl of a food processor or blender along with the garlic, jalapeño pepper, ginger, black pepper and water. Blend until smooth, then add the tomato juice, vinegar, oil, hot-pepper sauce and salt. Blend again, just until the mixture is smooth. Refrigerate until serving time.

To serve, ladle the soup into bowls. Sprinkle some of the reserved garnishes on top before serving or let the guests help themselves to the garnishes at the table.

Per serving: 108 calories, 3.2 g. fat (24% of calories), 0.5 g. saturated fat, 0 mg. cholesterol, 163 mg. sodium.

An easy way to remove seeds from any type of pepper—sweet or hot—is to cut the pepper in half through the core. Pull out the core, seed area and inner membranes. Often they'll come out in a single piece. Rather than scraping out whatever seeds remain, hold the pepper half (cut side down) and hit the back of it with your hand. That will dislodge the loose seeds.

Vegetarian Borscht with Creamy Horseradish

This bright red borscht is both sweet and sour, with the combined flavors of beets, yogurt and horseradish. It is an ideal cold soup for an elegant dinner in summer, when beets are in full season—at their most flavorful, most nutritious and most economical. I make the soup with water because stock tends to dull its intense vegetable taste.

- 1 tablespoon canola, corn or virgin olive oil
- 1 medium onion (4 ounces), peeled and shredded on the slicing disc of a food processor (1¼ cups)
- 2 small carrots (4 ounces), trimmed, peeled and shredded on the slicing disc of a food processor (1 cup)
- 6 cups hot water
- 6 beets (1½ pounds), trimmed, peeled and shredded on the slicing disc of a food processor (4 cups)
- 2 tablespoons lemon juice
- 2 tablespoons red wine vinegar
- 1 tablespoon sugar
- 1 teaspoon salt
- ¾ teaspoon freshly ground black pepper
- 1 cup plain nonfat yogurt
- 1 tablespoon grated horseradish, preferably fresh
- 1 tablespoon chopped fresh dill

Heat the oil until hot in a large pot. Add the onions and carrots and sauté them over high heat for 2 minutes. Add the water, bring it to a boil and boil for 5 minutes. Add the beets and bring the mixture back to a boil. Boil for 6 to 8 minutes and add the lemon juice, vinegar, sugar, salt and pepper. Set aside to cool, then cover and refrigerate.

Mix the yogurt and horseradish in a small bowl.

At serving time, divide the cold soup among individual bowls and add a dollop of the yogurt-horseradish mixture to each portion. Sprinkle with the dill and serve.

Per serving: 92 calories, 2.5 g. fat (23% of calories), 0.2 g. saturated fat, 1 mg. cholesterol, 458 mg. sodium.

Cold Tzatziki Soup

Yield: 6 generous servings

*T*zatziki is the name of a classic Turkish salad that features cucumber, dill, garlic and mint. Here, with the addition of nonfat yogurt, I transform these ingredients into a refreshing summer soup. Attractively garnished just before serving with a mixture of diced cucumber and dill, it is an ideal starter for a summer dinner party.

- 6 medium cucumbers (4 pounds), trimmed, peeled, seeded and cut into chunks
- ¼ cup loosely packed chopped fresh dill
- 1 small onion (1–2 ounces), peeled and chopped (⅓ cup)
- ¼ cup loosely packed fresh mint leaves
- 3 tablespoons rice wine vinegar
- 5–6 cloves garlic, peeled, crushed and finely chopped (1 tablespoon)
- 1 teaspoon salt
- ¾ teaspoon Tabasco hot-pepper sauce
- 3 cups plain nonfat yogurt

Cut enough of the cucumber chunks into ⅛″ to ¼″ dice to measure 1 cup. Place the diced cucumbers in a small bowl, add the dill and mix well. Set aside.

Place the remaining cucumber chunks in the bowl of a food processor and process them into a puree. (You should have 5 cups.) Add the onions, mint, vinegar, garlic, salt and hot-pepper sauce. Process the mixture for 30 seconds, until it is creamy. Add the yogurt and process for 10 to 15 seconds longer.

Transfer the soup to a serving bowl, cover and refrigerate until chilled. To serve, divide the soup among bowls and garnish each serving with a generous tablespoonful of the cucumber and dill mixture.

Per serving: 112 calories, 0.7 g. fat (5% of calories), 0.2 g. saturated fat, 2 mg. cholesterol, 453 mg. sodium.

Cold Peach Soup

Cold Peach Soup

Yield: 6 servings

his is the ideal soup to serve in late summer, when peaches are very ripe, plentiful and inexpensive. For variety, substitute apricots or nectarines for the peaches and garnish the soup with currants, blackberries or raspberries instead of blueberries. This fruit soup can double as a dessert sauce for ice cream or pound cake.

½ cup sugar
4 whole cloves
1 cinnamon stick, broken into small pieces
1¾ cups water
1½ tablespoons cornstarch
1 cup dry white wine
8 ripe peaches (2¾ pounds)
¾ cup fresh blueberries, washed, drained and patted dry

Place the sugar, cloves, cinnamon and 1½ cups of the water in a saucepan. Bring the mixture to a boil, reduce the heat to low, cover and boil very gently for 10 minutes to create a syrup.

Dissolve the cornstarch in the remaining ¼ cup water. Stir it into the saucepan with a whisk to blend it with the syrup. Bring the mixture back to a boil and set it aside to cool. When it is cold, strain it through a fine mesh strainer into a bowl and discard the cinnamon pieces and cloves. Add the wine, stir well, cover and refrigerate until cold.

Peel 2 of the peaches (use a sharp knife or vegetable peeler or submerge the peaches in boiling water for 30 seconds to loosen the skin); discard the skin. Pit the peeled peaches and cut the flesh into ¼″ dice (about 1½ cups total). Add to the cold syrup.

Cut the remaining 6 peaches in half lengthwise and remove and discard their pits. Cut the flesh coarsely and puree it in the bowl of a food processor or blender. Add to the cold syrup. Refrigerate for at least 1 hour, or as long as overnight.

To serve, divide the soup among bowls and garnish with the blueberries.

Per serving: 195 calories, 0.3 g. fat (1% of calories), 0 g. saturated fat, 0 mg. cholesterol, 4 mg. sodium.

Appetizer Wonton Crisps

Yield: 36 crisps

hese are good to have on hand for unexpected guests. Although I've flavored them here with herbes de Provence in one variation and Parmesan cheese in another, you could mix the herbs and cheese or create your own seasonings with other combinations of spices, cheeses and herbs. I sometimes also sprinkle the wonton wrappers with sugar for use in desserts (see Sweet Wonton Crisps with Strawberries and Frozen Yogurt, page 296). The crisps keep almost indefinitely if stored in a tin or plastic container with a tight-fitting lid, and they can also be frozen. Usually found in the produce area of supermarkets, wonton wrappers or skins come in 12-ounce packages. They're each about 3" square, and there are about 48 wrappers in a package.

HERB WONTON CRISPS

18 wonton wrappers, each 3" square (4½ ounces)
   Vegetable cooking spray or 2 teaspoons canola oil
 2 teaspoons herbes de Provence (see page 13)
¼ teaspoon salt

PARMESAN WONTON CRISPS

18 wonton wrappers, each 3" square (4½ ounces)
   Vegetable cooking spray or 2 teaspoons canola oil
 2 tablespoons grated Parmesan cheese

Preheat the oven to 375°.

To make the herb wonton crisps: Bring about 2 quarts of water to a boil in a large pot. Add 9 of the wonton wrappers, dropping them into the water 1 at a time. Cook for 1½ minutes, then remove them from the water carefully with a skimmer and transfer them to a large bowl of cold water.

Coat a 16" × 14" cookie sheet with the vegetable cooking spray or brush it with ½ teaspoon of the oil. Place your hands in the bowl containing the wrappers and carefully unfold them 1 at a time under the water. Transfer them, still wet, to the cookie sheet, arranging them side by side.

Spray the surface of the wrappers lightly with the cooking spray, or brush or lightly rub them with another ½ teaspoon oil. Sprinkle with 1 teaspoon herbes de Provence and ⅛ teaspoon salt. Bake for 16 to 18 minutes, or until dry and brown.

Repeat with the remaining wonton wrappers, oil, salt and herbs.

To make the Parmesan wonton crisps: Follow the directions above, re-placing the herbs and salt with 1 tablespoon grated Parmesan for each batch of 9 wontons.

Per 3 herb crisps: 69 calories, 0 g. fat (0% of calories), 0 g. saturated fat, 0 mg. cholesterol, 146 mg. sodium.

Per 3 Parmesan crisps: 79 calories, 0.6 g. fat (7% of calories), 0.4 g. saturated fat, 2 mg. cholesterol, 185 mg. sodium.

Wonton crisps are delicious with a variety of dips. Use them in place of potato chips, corn chips and crackers, which are often higher in fat.

Cannellini Bean Hummus

Yield: 2¼ cups

I use a can of cannellini beans—a fairly large white variety—for this last-minute dip. You can, of course, cook any dried white beans—limas, perhaps— and substitute them for the canned beans. Serve the hummus with toast, pita bread or Appetizer Wonton Crisps (page 60).

- 1 **cup lightly packed fresh basil leaves**
- 1 **cup lightly packed fresh parsley leaves**
- 4 **cloves garlic, peeled**
- ½ **teaspoon salt**
- ¼ **teaspoon freshly ground black pepper**
- 1 **can (19 ounces) cannellini beans, drained (see note)**
- 2 **tablespoons extra-virgin olive oil**
  Tabasco hot-pepper sauce, to taste

Bring about 5 cups of water to a boil in a saucepan. Add the basil and parsley, pushing the herbs down into the water, and cook for 10 seconds.

Drain the herbs in a sieve, pressing on them lightly to extract excess moisture, and place them in the bowl of a food processor with the garlic, salt and pepper. Process the mixture for a few seconds to combine the ingredients, then scrape down the sides of the bowl with a rubber spatula to gather the ingredients in the bottom of the bowl.

Add the beans and process for about 1 minute, again stopping the motor once or twice and scraping down the sides of the bowl with a rubber spatula, until the mixture is smooth with flecks of green visible throughout. Add the oil and hot-pepper sauce and process for about 5 seconds, or until they are incorporated. Transfer the mixture to a serving bowl.

Variation: You can use the hummus as a pasta sauce. Reserve about ½ cup canning liquid from the beans and add to the finished dip, along with 1 cup water, 1 tablespoon olive oil and ¼ teaspoon salt. You'll have about 3 cups.

Per 2 tablespoons: 40 calories, 1.8 g. fat (32% of calories), 0.2 g. saturated fat, 0 mg. cholesterol, 120 mg. sodium.

Clockwise from top: Ratatouille Dip with Endive (page 64);
Cannellini Bean Hummus (page 62) and Jalapeño Dip (page 65)

Ratatouille Dip with Endive

Yield: 6 servings

classic dish of Provence, ratatouille is a mixture of eggplant, zucchini, tomato, garlic and onion. These ingredients are diced here to create a dip. If you prefer, you can roll the ratatouille in lettuce leaves for serving.

- 2 teaspoons canola, corn or virgin olive oil
- 1 large onion (about 8 ounces), peeled and cut into ½" dice (about 2 cups)
- 1 small eggplant (about 10 ounces), unpeeled but trimmed and cut into ½" dice (3 cups)
- 2 small zucchini (about 8 ounces), washed, trimmed and cut into ½" dice (2 cups)
- ½ cup water
- 5–6 cloves garlic, peeled, crushed and finely chopped (1 tablespoon)
- ½ small jalapeño pepper, seeded, if desired (to eliminate some of its hotness), and finely chopped (2 teaspoons)
- 2 medium tomatoes (10 ounces), seeded and cut into ½" dice (1½ cups)
- 1½ tablespoons white wine vinegar
- ½ teaspoon sugar
- ¼ teaspoon salt
- 6 large pieces leaf lettuce
- 30 spears Belgian endive
- ¼ cup fresh basil leaves, sliced into a fine chiffonade (see page 100)
- 6 slices bread, toasted and cut into 4 triangles each

Heat the oil in a large saucepan. When it is hot, add the onions and sauté them over high heat for 3 minutes. Add the eggplant, zucchini, water, garlic and peppers. Cover the pan, bring the mixture to a boil over high heat, then reduce the heat and cook gently for 15 minutes. Stir in the tomatoes and bring the mixture back to a boil. Cook for 5 minutes, then set aside to cool.

Mix the vinegar, sugar and salt in a small bowl and combine with the cooled ratatouille. Line each of 6 plates with a large piece of leaf lettuce and arrange 5 spears of endive on top in a star pattern, with the tips extending to the edge of the plate. Place a ½-cup scoop of ratatouille in the center of each plate and sprinkle with the basil. Serve with the toast triangles.

Per serving: 122 calories, 2.8 g. fat (20% of calories), 0.4 g. saturated fat, 0 mg. cholesterol, 214 mg. sodium.

Jalapeño Dip

Yield: 6 servings

*J*alapeño pepper gives this dip a very spicy flavor. You can create a hotter or milder version by adding more or less of it. The mixture will develop more flavor if refrigerated overnight. Serve the dip with cucumber and carrot sticks, celery ribs and endive leaves. Or use it as a type of relish to accent the taste of poached fish or boiled chicken or meat.

2	slices bread, toasted
5–6	ounces domestic mushrooms, washed and cut into ¼″ dice (1¼ cups)
1	large tomato (8 ounces), seeded and chopped (1 cup)
½	cup loosely packed chopped fresh cilantro leaves
3	tablespoons white wine vinegar
2	tablespoons lemon juice
5–6	cloves garlic, peeled, crushed and finely chopped (1 tablespoon)
1	tablespoon sugar
2	teaspoons corn or canola oil
1	small piece jalapeño pepper, seeded and chopped (½ teaspoon)
1	teaspoon chili powder
¼	teaspoon Tabasco hot-pepper sauce
⅛	teaspoon salt

Break the toast into pieces and place it in the bowl of a food processor. Process until the bread is crumbed. Transfer to a large bowl.

Add the mushrooms, tomatoes, cilantro, vinegar, lemon juice, garlic, sugar, oil, peppers, chili powder, hot-pepper sauce and salt. Mix well.

Per serving: 66 calories, 2.2 g. fat (27% of calories), 0.4 g. saturated fat, 0 mg. cholesterol, 99 mg. sodium.

Microwave Potato Chips with Salsa Cruda

Yield: 6 servings

*I*t is amazing how potato slices dry and brown in a microwave oven without the addition of any fat or salt. It is important to cut the potatoes into very thin slices in a food processor fitted with a slicer disc attachment or with a hand-held potato slicer. The only drawback to this recipe is that you can cook just 10 to 15 potato slices at a time (depending on your microwave's size).

To make larger batches of the chips, lightly coat a large jelly-roll pan or cookie sheet with vegetable cooking spray. Arrange the slices in a single layer, without overlapping, and spray the surface of the slices. Bake the slices at 400° for 16 to 18 minutes, watching closely and removing slices as they become brown and crisp.

> 3 large potatoes (about 2¼ pounds), peeled
> 3 cups Salsa Cruda (page 21)

Using either a 2-millimeter slicing disc fitted on a food processor or a conventional potato slicer, cut the potatoes into ¹⁄₁₆″ slices. Wash the slices in a large bowl of cool water and dry them thoroughly with paper towels.

Arrange some of the potatoes in 1 layer on a waffled microwave tray and microwave on high heat for 5 minutes, or until crisp. Remove. Repeat until the remaining potato slices are cooked. Serve with the Salsa Cruda.

Per serving: 198 calories, 0.5 g. fat (2% of calories), 0.1 g. saturated fat, 0 mg. cholesterol, 220 mg. sodium.

Microwave Potato Chips with Salsa Cruda

Croutons with Creamy Red Pepper

Yield: 6 servings

hese make colorful, tasty hors d'oeuvres. Each person gets an ounce of bread, which amounts to seven or eight thin slices if you make your croutons from a long, thin, French-style baguette loaf.

- 1 medium clove garlic, peeled
- 1 jar (5 ounces) red peppers, drained
- 2 ounces low-fat cream cheese (¼ cup)
- 2 tablespoons 1% low-fat cottage cheese
- 1 teaspoon minced fresh dill
- 2 teaspoons lemon juice
- ⅛ teaspoon freshly ground black pepper
- 1 very thin French-style baguette bread loaf (6 ounces)
  Fresh dill sprigs

Place the garlic in the bowl of a food processor. Add the red peppers, cream cheese, cottage cheese, dill, lemon juice and black pepper. Process the mixture until it is smooth. Set aside.

Preheat the oven to 400°.

To make the croutons, cut the bread into 42 to 48 slices. Arrange the slices on a cookie sheet and bake them for 10 minutes, or until crisp.

Spread the croutons with the pepper spread and garnish each with a small sprig of fresh dill.

Per serving: 111 calories, 2.9 g. fat (23% of calories), 1.2 g. saturated fat, 4 mg. cholesterol, 230 mg. sodium.

Kim Chee

Yield: 3 cups

his is the quintessential Korean dish. Poor families in Korea consider it a meal with plain rice. Versions of the dish, some of which are extremely hot, are served as a condiment in most Korean restaurants in this country.

- 1 Chinese cabbage (1½ pounds), cut crosswise into 2″ sections and then into 2″ pieces (14 cups lightly packed)
- 2 tablespoons salt
- 2 tablespoons sugar
- ¼ cup rice wine vinegar
- ¼ cup hot tap water
- 3 tablespoons Vietnamese fish sauce (see page 22)
- 1 small piece fresh ginger, peeled and coarsely chopped (1½ tablespoons)
- 1 tablespoon paprika
- 5–6 cloves garlic, peeled, crushed and finely chopped (1 tablespoon)
- ½ teaspoon Tabasco hot-pepper sauce
- ¼ teaspoon ground red pepper

Place the cabbage in a large food-safe plastic bag with the salt and 1 tablespoon of the sugar. Close the bag securely; shake and turn it several times to mix the ingredients together well. Set the bag aside for 2 hours.

Empty the contents of the bag into a sieve and rinse the cabbage thoroughly under cold tap water. Drain and then press the leaves gently between your palms to remove excess water.

In a bowl large enough to hold the cabbage, mix the vinegar, water, fish sauce, ginger, paprika, garlic, hot-pepper sauce, red pepper and the remaining 1 tablespoon sugar. Add the cabbage and toss well.

Cover and refrigerate for at least 24 hours before serving to allow the mixture to ferment and develop that sour, pungent taste peculiar to kim chee. Store tightly covered in the refrigerator for as long as several weeks.

Per ½ cup: 54 calories, 0.4 g. fat (5% of calories), 0.1 g. saturated fat, 0 mg. cholesterol, 456 mg. sodium.

Pickled Vegetables

Yield: about 3 quarts

his is a great way to use up odds and ends of vegetables; the selection here reflects the excess in my refrigerator vegetable bin one day when I decided to prepare this dish. You can make vegetable substitutions based on what you have on hand. And you can change the choice of marinade spices to suit your tastes. The pickled vegetables are a great accompaniment for cold cuts or roasts, and they're a good, healthful snack on their own. They'll keep, refrigerated, for several weeks.

3	medium carrots (12 ounces), trimmed, peeled, halved lengthwise and cut into sticks 2"–3" long × 1½" thick
1	piece cauliflower (12 ounces), divided into small florets (about 1½" across)
1	large zucchini (12 ounces), washed, trimmed, halved lengthwise and cut into sticks about 2" long × ½" thick
1–2	small red bell peppers (8 ounces), halved, cored, seeded and cut lengthwise into ½" sticks
1	piece fennel (8 ounces), cut into 2" pieces
1	turnip (6 ounces), peeled and cut into sticks 2" × ½" × ½"
4	ounces green beans, trimmed
11–12	cloves garlic, peeled and thinly sliced
3	large sprigs fresh tarragon
5	cups water
2	cups distilled white vinegar
3	tablespoons salt
3	tablespoons sugar
12	whole cloves
1	teaspoon allspice berries
1	teaspoon juniper berries

Using a 3-quart jar (or several smaller jars), pack in alternating layers of the carrots, cauliflower, zucchini, peppers, fennel, turnips, beans and garlic, arranging them so the various colors create an attractive pattern. Add the tarragon sprigs, pushing them in along the sides of the jar.

Combine the water, vinegar, salt, sugar, cloves, allspice berries and juniper berries in a large saucepan. Bring the mixture to a boil over high heat. Reduce the heat to low, cover and boil gently for 5 minutes. Pour the hot liquid over the

Pickled Vegetables

vegetables in the jar. Make sure the vegetables are totally covered with the liquid. Cover the jar loosely and refrigerate. When the vegetables are cold, cover the jar securely and refrigerate for at least 48 hours before serving.

Per serving: 24 calories, 0.2 g. fat (5% of calories), 0 g. saturated fat, 0 mg. cholesterol, 287 mg. sodium.

Artichokes with Hot Salsa

Yield: 6 servings

*P*repare this dish when large artichokes are available inexpensively at the market. The best way to determine when artichokes are cooked is to pull a lower leaf from the base of each. When they are done, the leaves will pull out easily, and the flesh inside will be tender. The piquant salsa that is spooned in the hollows created by the removal of the chokes contains a minimum of oil and so is not too caloric.

- 6 medium artichokes (3 pounds)
- 1 medium tomato (about 7 ounces), peeled, seeded and cut into 1″ pieces (1 cup)
- 1 small onion (about 2 ounces), peeled and chopped (¼ cup)
- 2 scallions (about 2 ounces), washed, trimmed and finely chopped (¼ cup)
- ½ cup loosely packed fresh cilantro leaves, chopped (¼ cup)
- 2 tablespoons cider vinegar
- 2 tablespoons water
- 2 tablespoons canola oil
- 1 jalapeño pepper, seeded, if desired (to eliminate some of its hotness), and finely chopped (4 teaspoons)
- ½ teaspoon salt

Place the artichokes on their sides and trim 2″ from the pointed top of each with a large, sharp knife. Then trim off the thorny tips of the remaining leaves with scissors. Leave the stems attached but peel off the fibrous outer layer of each stem with a small, sharp knife.

Bring about 6 cups of water to a boil in a large saucepan. Add the artichokes and place a small pan lid (smaller than the saucepan) on top of them to keep them immersed in the water. Bring the water back to a boil and cook the artichokes for 35 to 45 minutes, depending on their size. Test for doneness by pulling out one leaf from the base of each artichoke; if the leaf pulls out easily, the artichoke is cooked.

Drain off the hot water and add cold water and ice to the pan. Set aside until the artichokes are completely cooled.

To make the salsa, combine the tomatoes, onions, scallions, cilantro, vinegar, water, oil, peppers and salt in a small bowl. Mix well.

When the artichokes are cool, drain, then squeeze them gently between your palms to remove as much water from them as possible. Cut each artichoke in half lengthwise, cutting through the center of the stem. Remove and discard the fuzzy choke from each half and arrange the halves, cut side up, on a platter.

Spoon about 2 tablespoons of the tomato salsa into the hollows created by the removal of the chokes. Serve 2 halves per person as a first course.

Per serving: 114 calories, 4.9 g. fat (34% of calories), 0.4 g. saturated fat, 0 mg. cholesterol, 324 mg. sodium.

Cilantro is also known as fresh coriander or Chinese parsley. It has a distinctive flavor that can't be duplicated. But if you can't find any, substitute Italian (flat-leaf) parsley. The dish will look the same but have a more subtle taste.

After working with hot peppers, be certain to wash your hands well. If you don't, the compound that gives peppers their hotness can easily be transferred to your eyes, lips and other sensitive parts of the body. Some people take the extra precaution of covering their hands with plastic gloves, rubber gloves or even small plastic bags when cutting and otherwise handling hot peppers.

Artichokes with Oriental Sauce

Artichokes with Oriental Sauce

Yield: 6 servings

B uy very firm, deep-green artichokes for this dish. The artichoke stems are edible if their fibrous outer layer is removed before cooking.

6 large artichokes (about 3½ pounds)
¾ cup Oriental Sauce (page 22)

Place the artichokes on their sides and trim 2″ from the pointed top of each with a large, sharp knife. Then trim off the thorny tips of the remaining leaves with scissors. Leave the stems attached but peel off the fibrous outer layer of each stem with a small, sharp knife.

Bring about 6 cups of water to a boil in a large saucepan. Add the artichokes and place a small pan lid (smaller than the saucepan) on top of them to keep them immersed in the water. Bring the water back to a boil and cook the artichokes for 35 to 45 minutes, depending on their size. Test for doneness by pulling out one leaf from the base of each artichoke; if the leaf pulls out easily, the artichoke is cooked.

Drain off the hot water and add cold water and ice to the pan. Set aside until the artichokes are completely cooled.

When the artichokes are cool, drain, then squeeze them gently between your palms to remove as much water from them as possible. Cut each artichoke in half lengthwise, cutting through the center of the stem. Remove and discard the fuzzy choke from each half.

Arrange 2 artichoke halves, cut side up, on each of 6 plates. Spoon about 2 tablespoons of the sauce into the cavity created in the center of each by the removal of the choke. Serve.

Variation: You can substitute Tomato-Vinaigrette Dressing (page 29) for the Oriental Sauce in this recipe.

Per serving: 127 calories, 1.9 g. fat (11% of calories), 0.2 g. saturated fat, 0 mg. cholesterol, 378 mg. sodium.

Asparagus in Sesame Sauce

Yield: 6 servings

i think the best asparagus are the fat specimens with very tight heads. Contrary to popular belief, the size of the spears isn't an indicator of age; larger spears emerge that way from the ground and may grow right alongside smaller, thinner spears. When selecting asparagus, look for firm stalks and tight heads, the best evidence that the vegetable is young. Be sure to peel the lower 3" of the stalks; this section is covered with fibrous skin and would be inedible otherwise. Removing the skin with a vegetable peeler is not a difficult job and makes the entire spear edible. The tangy sesame sauce can also be used as salad dressing.

2 bunches asparagus (2 pounds; about 30–36 spears total)
1 small or ½ medium tomato (about 2 ounces), peeled, seeded and coarsely chopped (⅓ cup)
3 tablespoons soy sauce
3 tablespoons red wine vinegar
2 tablespoons dark sesame oil
1 tablespoon chopped fresh chives
1 small piece fresh ginger, peeled and finely chopped (1 tablespoon)
2 cloves garlic, peeled, crushed and finely chopped (1 teaspoon)
1 teaspoon sesame seeds
½ teaspoon sugar
¼ teaspoon freshly ground black pepper

Lay 1 asparagus spear flat on your work surface and grasp it as close to the base as possible with one hand. Use a vegetable peeler to remove a strip of peel about 3" long at the bottom of the spear. Repeat until you've peeled the stalk all the way around. Then cut or break off the base of the spear. Repeat with the remaining spears and wash them in cold water.

Bring about 1½ cups of water to a boil in a wide stainless steel saucepan. Add the asparagus in no more than 2 layers. (The asparagus might not be completely covered with water.) Bring the water back to a boil, cover and cook the asparagus for 5 to 7 minutes, depending on their size and how tender you like them. Most of the water should have evaporated at this point; drain off any that remains. Remove the asparagus spears from the pan with a large spatula and arrange them on a platter, spreading them out so they cool quickly.

Meanwhile, to make the sauce, combine the tomatoes, soy sauce, vinegar, oil, chives, ginger, garlic, sesame seeds, sugar and pepper in a small bowl.

Asparagus in Sesame Sauce

When the asparagus has cooled to room temperature, drain any water from the platter and arrange the spears in slightly overlapping rows. Stir the sauce again (to mix in the ginger, which tends to settle) and spoon it over the asparagus. Serve.

Per serving: 89 calories, 5.3 g. fat (48% of calories), 0.7 g. saturated fat, 0 mg. cholesterol, 522 mg. sodium.

Eggplant Oriental on Tomato Rounds

Eggplant Oriental on Tomato Rounds

Yield: 6 servings

he combination of ingredients in this recipe gives it a Chinese flavor. A peppery dish that really wakes up your taste buds, its flavor develops further after a few days in the refrigerator, and the dish can be prepared several days ahead. I serve the eggplant mixture on slices of tomato, which is a lower-calorie choice than bread or toast rounds.

- 2 eggplants (2 pounds)
- 1 large piece fresh ginger, peeled and finely chopped (3½ tablespoons)
- 3 tablespoons chopped fresh cilantro leaves
- 2 tablespoons soy sauce
- 5–6 cloves garlic, peeled, crushed and finely chopped (1 tablespoon)
- 1 tablespoon rice wine vinegar
- 1 tablespoon dark sesame oil
- ½ teaspoon sugar
- ¼ teaspoon hot chili oil or Tabasco hot-pepper sauce
- 2 medium tomatoes (about 12 ounces), each cut crosswise into 6 slices

Preheat the oven to 400°.

Place the whole eggplants on a cookie sheet and bake them for 1 hour. Set them aside to cool. When they are cool enough to handle, peel them and cut them into ½" dice. (You should have 3½ cups.)

Mix the ginger, cilantro, soy sauce, garlic, vinegar, sesame oil, sugar and chili oil or hot-pepper sauce in a large bowl. Add the eggplant and mix well.

Arrange 2 tomato slices on each of 6 plates. Spoon the eggplant mixture evenly on top of the tomato slices and serve.

Per serving: 77 calories, 2.8 g. fat (29% of calories), 0.4 g. saturated fat, 0 mg. cholesterol, 354 mg. sodium.

Egg Whites Stuffed with Bulgur

Yield: 6 servings

ulgur is steamed and dried cracked wheat that is reconstituted by soaking in cold water. This salad contains both lemon juice and raisins, giving it tart and sweet taste accents. Although I use the salad as a stuffing for hard-cooked egg whites here, it is excellent served on its own or with salad greens. For best flavor, serve at room temperature.

- ⅔ cup bulgur wheat
- 3 cups cold water
- ½ cup finely chopped fresh parsley leaves
- 2 scallions (1–2 ounces), washed, trimmed and finely chopped (¼ cup)
- 2 tablespoons lemon juice
- 2 tablespoons raisins
- 1 tablespoon finely chopped fresh mint leaves
- 1–2 cloves garlic, peeled, crushed and finely chopped (1 teaspoon)
  About 6 strips lemon rind (removed with a vegetable peeler), finely chopped (1 teaspoon)
- 1 small piece jalapeño pepper, seeded, if desired (to eliminate some of its hotness), and finely chopped (½ teaspoon)
- ½ teaspoon salt
- ¼ teaspoon Tabasco hot-pepper sauce
- 1 small tomato
- 9 eggs

Place the bulgur in a large bowl and cover it with the water. Let stand for 1 hour. Drain well in a sieve.

Return the bulgur to the bowl. Add the parsley, scallions, lemon juice, raisins, mint, garlic, lemon rind, peppers, salt and hot-pepper sauce.

Use a vegetable peeler to peel the tomato; reserve the peel. Seed the tomato and dice the flesh; add to the bowl. Mix well.

Bring about 3 cups of water to a boil in a saucepan. Lower the eggs gently into the water and allow the water to return to a boil. Reduce the heat to low and cook the eggs very gently for 9 minutes. Drain the water from the pan and shake the pan to crack the shells of the eggs. Fill the pan with ice and let the eggs cool completely in the ice.

Shell the eggs, cut them in half lengthwise and remove and discard the egg yolks. Fill each half with approximately 4 teaspoons of the bulgur mixture.

Cut the reserved tomato peel into thin julienne strips and garnish each stuffed egg white with a few pieces of the peel. Serve 3 halves per person.

Per serving: 96 calories, 0.3 g. fat (3% of calories), 0 g. saturated fat, 0 mg. cholesterol, 265 mg. sodium.

When using any citrus rind, scrub the fruit first with a cloth and warm water to remove any protective wax that may be on the rind. Be sure to use only the colored part of the rind and not the underlying white pith, which tends to be bitter.

Middle Eastern Lettuce Packages

Middle Eastern Lettuce Packages

Yield: 6 servings

I use lettuce as wrappers for these edible packages instead of the conventional choice, Chinese pancakes. Of course, that makes them much lower in calories. The refreshing sweet and salty stuffing makes this an ideal first course in the summer.

- 1 cup bulgur wheat
- 1 cup boiling water
- 1 grapefruit (1 pound)
- 3 ounces dried apricot halves (½ cup), each half cut into 6 pieces
- 2 ounces walnuts, broken into ¼″ pieces (½ cup)
- 3 scallions, washed, trimmed and finely chopped (½ cup)
- ½ cup lightly packed fresh dill, chopped (¼ cup)
- 2 tablespoons lemon juice
- 2 tablespoons peanut oil
- ½ teaspoon salt
- ¼ teaspoon freshly ground black pepper
- 1 head iceberg lettuce (with loose leaves, if possible)

Place the bulgur in a large bowl and add the water. Cover and set aside for 30 minutes.

Using a sharp knife, peel the grapefruit, removing all the skin and the underlying white pith so the flesh of the fruit is totally exposed. Then cut between the membranes on each side of every segment and remove the flesh in wedgelike pieces. Cut the flesh into ½″ dice. (You should have 1½ cups.)

Add the grapefruit to the soaked bulgur. Add the apricots, walnuts, scallions, dill, lemon juice, oil, salt and pepper. Toss to mix.

Core the head of lettuce, then insert your thumbs in the resulting hole; gently pull the head open to expand it and loosen the leaves. Pull off 12 of the largest outside leaves (reserving the remainder of the head for another use).

Wash the leaves, if needed, dry them thoroughly and arrange them side by side on a platter. Spoon about ⅓ to ½ cup of the bulgur stuffing mixture into the center of each lettuce leaf. If desired, roll up the lettuce to enclose the filling.

Per serving: 261 calories, 10.6 g. fat (34% of calories), 1.2 g. saturated fat, 0 mg. cholesterol, 194 mg. sodium.

Roasted Eggplant and Tomato Salad

Yield: 6 servings

or this delicious first course or salad course, I roast thin slices of eggplant in the oven. This is a healthier way to prepare it than in a skillet, where eggplant absorbs a lot of oil. A tomato salad seasoned with garlic, scallions and shallots makes an appealing topping for the slices.

EGGPLANT

1   medium eggplant (1¼ pounds), unpeeled but trimmed and cut lengthwise into 6–8 slices about ½" thick

½   teaspoon salt

TOMATO SALAD

4   scallions (about 3 ounces), washed, trimmed and finely chopped (½ cup)

¼   cup white wine vinegar

3   tablespoons extra-virgin olive oil

1   small to medium shallot (about 1 ounce), peeled, trimmed and finely chopped (2 tablespoons)

2   tablespoons loosely packed fresh oregano leaves

1   large clove garlic, peeled, crushed and finely chopped (1 teaspoon)

½   teaspoon salt

½   teaspoon freshly ground black pepper

4   medium tomatoes (about 2 pounds), peeled, seeded and cut into ¼" dice

To make the eggplant: Preheat the oven to 400°.

Lightly coat a baking tray with vegetable cooking spray. Arrange the eggplant slices side by side on the sheet. Lightly coat the top of the slices with more cooking spray and sprinkle them with the salt. Bake for 25 minutes, turn the slices over and bake them for 10 minutes longer. Set aside until cool.

To make the tomato salad: Combine the scallions, vinegar, oil, shallots, oregano, garlic, salt and pepper in a bowl. Add the tomatoes and toss well.

Arrange the eggplant on a platter and mound the tomato salad on top.

Per serving: 124 calories, 7.5 g. fat (50% of calories), 1 g. saturated fat, 0 mg. cholesterol, 373 mg. sodium.

Spinach Mini-Frittatas

Yield: 6 servings

hese easy-to-make frittatas are strongly accented with spinach and Parmesan cheese. You can make them ahead, freeze them and then reheat them briefly in a microwave just before serving.

- ½ package (10-ounce size) frozen chopped spinach, thawed and drained
- ¾ cup part-skim ricotta cheese
- ½ cup grated Parmesan cheese
- 2–3 domestic mushrooms (1–2 ounces), washed and chopped (½ cup)
- 1 egg
- ¼ teaspoon dried oregano
- ⅛ teaspoon salt

Preheat the oven to 375°.

Mix the spinach, ricotta, Parmesan, mushrooms, egg, oregano and salt in a medium bowl.

Coat 18 miniature muffin cups lightly with vegetable cooking spray. Divide the egg mixture among the cups. Bake for 25 minutes. Unmold the frittatas and serve.

Per serving: 101 calories, 5.8 g. fat (52% of calories), 3.4 g. saturated fat, 51 mg. cholesterol, 269 mg. sodium.

Crêpe Purses with Mushroom Duxelles

his is an impressive first-course dish for parties. The crêpes, made with egg whites instead of whole eggs, are low in fat and quite flavorful. The mixture of mushrooms, pine nuts and onions makes a very satisfying crêpe filling that can also be used as a stuffing for fish or meat.

6	long strips scallion greens (to tie the purses)
1	tablespoon canola, corn or virgin olive oil
½	small onion (1–2 ounces), peeled and chopped (¼ cup)
¼	cup pine nuts
1½	pounds domestic mushrooms, washed and finely chopped in a food processor (about 2¼ cups)
3	tablespoons chopped fresh chives
½	teaspoon Tabasco hot-pepper sauce
½	teaspoon sugar
¼	teaspoon salt
6	fresh shiitake mushrooms, washed and with stems removed
2	tablespoons water
1	tablespoon soy sauce
6	crêpes (page 338)

Bring a small pot of water to a boil. Add the scallion greens and boil them for about 10 seconds, just until the greens are softened. Drain, pat dry and set aside.

Heat 2 teaspoons of the oil over medium-high heat in a large nonstick skillet. When the oil is hot, add the onions and pine nuts and cook until the onions are softened and the nuts are browned, about 2 minutes. Add the domestic mushrooms and cook the mixture until the liquid evaporates, about 4 minutes. Add the chives, hot-pepper sauce, sugar and salt.

In a small skillet, heat the remaining 1 teaspoon oil over medium-high heat. When the oil is hot, add the shiitake mushrooms and 2 tablespoons water. Cover the pan and cook for 2 minutes. Remove the cover and continue to cook the mushrooms until all the water has evaporated and the mushrooms are browned. Brush the mushroom tops with the soy sauce and cut each into thirds.

Drape 1 crêpe in a small cup or ramekin and place a heaping tablespoon of the mushroom mixture in the center. Bring up all sides of the crêpe and tie it closed at the top with a scallion green. (The packet should resemble a small

Crêpe Purses with Mushroom Duxelles

money sack or purse.) Repeat to use the remaining crêpes, mushroom mixture and scallion greens. Divide among 6 plates, garnish with the shiitake pieces and serve.

Per serving: 139 calories, 6.9 g. fat (40% of calories), 0.3 g. saturated fat, 0 mg. cholesterol, 288 mg. sodium.

Stuffed Mushrooms with Raisins and Cilantro

Yield: 6 servings

i use very large mushrooms and serve only two per person in this recipe, but you could use smaller ones and serve three apiece. Notice that I scoop out some of the mushroom gills to produce a larger receptacle, and that I use the stems and trimmings in the stuffing. The combination of flavors—sweet from the raisins, spicy from the Tabasco and pepper—is unusual and delightful with the mushrooms and onions. Serve the mushrooms warm or at room temperature, as they lose flavor when they're cold.

12	large domestic mushrooms (about 1½ pounds), washed
1½	tablespoons virgin olive oil
1	medium onion (about 4 ounces), peeled and chopped (1 cup)
2	cloves garlic, peeled, crushed and finely chopped (1 teaspoon)
2	slices bread, processed into crumbs in a food processor (1 cup)
½	cup golden raisins
1	tablespoon chopped fresh cilantro leaves
¼	teaspoon salt
¼	teaspoon freshly ground black pepper
⅛	teaspoon Tabasco hot-pepper sauce

Remove the mushroom stems, breaking them off as close as possible to where they join the cap; reserve them. Using a metal measuring teaspoon (because these spoons have sharp edges), scoop out some of the mushroom gills to make the caps into larger receptacles. Place all the trimmings and the mushroom stems in the bowl of a food processor and chop them coarsely. Set the chopped pieces aside.

Preheat the oven to 400°.

Arrange the caps, hollow side down, in a single layer in a gratin dish and bake them for 12 to 15 minutes, or until the caps soften and release some of their juices. Discard the juices and set the caps aside.

Heat the oil in a heavy skillet. When it is hot, add the onions and sauté them for 2 minutes. Then add the garlic and sauté the mixture for 30 seconds. Add the chopped mushrooms and cook them for 3 to 4 minutes over high heat. Some liquid will seep out of the mushrooms; continue to cook the mixture until enough of the mushroom liquid has evaporated so that the mixture is just moist. Stir in the bread crumbs, raisins, cilantro, salt, pepper and hot-pepper sauce.

Divide the stuffing mixture evenly among the mushroom caps and arrange the stuffed caps side by side in a gratin dish.

Preheat the broiler.

Place the dish on the middle shelf of the oven and broil the mushrooms for 3 to 4 minutes, until the stuffing mixture is nicely browned on top. Cool the caps slightly and serve them warm or at room temperature.

Per serving: 139 calories, 5.4 g. fat (32% of calories), 0.8 g. saturated fat, 0 mg. cholesterol, 136 mg. sodium.

It is always useful to have fresh bread crumbs on hand. And crumbs make good use of bread that's begun to go stale. Tear slices into pieces and grind them in a food processor. Store the crumbs in plastic bags in the freezer. If you're buying bread specifically to make crumbs, look for day-old bread at the grocery store or bakery.

Beet Salad in Yogurt Sauce

Yield: 6 servings

lthough I still sometimes cook beets by boiling them or baking them, I've come to prefer doing them in a microwave. They can take as long as 1½ hours to get tender when cooked conventionally, but in the microwave, they require only 20 minutes or less. In this recipe, the creamy yogurt-based dressing takes on a beautiful pink color from the beets.

6 medium to large beets with tops removed (2 pounds)
½ cup water
½ cup plain nonfat yogurt
2 tablespoons chopped fresh dill or cilantro leaves
1 tablespoon red wine vinegar
2 teaspoons sugar
¾ teaspoon salt
¼ teaspoon freshly ground black pepper

Place the beets and water in a microwave-safe plastic bag. Set the bag in a glass bowl, loosely close the bag and place the bowl in a microwave oven. Cook on high for 18 to 20 minutes, until the beets are tender when pierced with the point of a sharp knife. (Alternatively, place the beets in a saucepan with cool tap water to cover and bring the water to a boil over high heat. Cover, reduce the heat to low and cook the beets for 1¼ hours, or until they are tender when pierced with the point of a sharp knife.) Set aside until cool enough to handle.

Peel the beets and cut into slices ⅜″ thick.

Combine the yogurt, dill or cilantro, vinegar, sugar, salt and pepper in a bowl large enough to hold the beets. Add the beet slices while they are still lukewarm and mix thoroughly. Serve at room temperature.

Per serving: 51 calories, 0.2 g. fat (3% of calories), 0 g. saturated fat, 0 mg. cholesterol, 333 mg. sodium.

To protect your hands from stains when handling cut raw or cooked beets, slip on plastic gloves or small plastic bags.

Clockwise from top: Carrot-Walnut Salad (page 93);
Apple and Mushroom Salad (page 92) and Beet Salad in Yogurt Sauce (page 90)

Apple and Mushroom Salad

his crunchy, pungent mixture of apples and mushrooms with cucumber dressing makes an unusual but refreshing hors d'oeuvre or a good first course during the hot summer months. It is also excellent served in a large bowl for a buffet. The salad is best made no more than a few hours before serving, as both the mushrooms and apples will render some liquid if mixed with the dressing too far ahead. Should that occur, drain off most of the accumulated liquid before plating the dish.

10–12 ounces domestic mushrooms, washed and cut into ½″ dice (about 2½ cups)

1 pound Rome Beauty apples, unpeeled but halved, cored, cut lengthwise into ¼″ slices and then crosswise into sticks

1 cup Cucumber-Scallion Dressing (page 27)

½ teaspoon salt

6 large lettuce leaves

Place the mushrooms, apples, dressing and salt in a bowl and mix them together well. Line each of 6 plates with a lettuce leaf and spoon about 1⅓ cups of the salad on each of the leaves. Serve.

Per serving: 101 calories, 2.8 g. fat (23% of calories), 0.4 g. saturated fat, 1 mg. cholesterol, 293 mg. sodium.

Carrot-Walnut Salad

Yield: 6 servings

he ingredients in this salad are available year-round, but since carrots tend to be woody in the winter, make sure that the ones you select for this dish are of good quality. The salad develops flavor in the refrigerator and can be kept, properly covered, for up to two days. Serve as a first course for dinner or as a luncheon accompaniment.

3–4	large carrots (1 pound), trimmed and peeled
½	cup coarsely chopped fresh parsley leaves
¼	cup walnut pieces
1	tablespoon wine vinegar
4	teaspoons corn or canola oil
1	teaspoon salt
1	teaspoon coarsely ground black pepper
6	lettuce leaves

Using the grater attachment on a food processor or a hand grater (on the side with the large holes), shred the carrots.

Transfer the carrots to a bowl and add the parsley, walnuts, vinegar, oil, salt and pepper. Toss well to thoroughly saturate the carrots with the seasonings.

Divide the lettuce among 6 plates. Mound the salad mixture on the lettuce leaves and serve it cool, not cold, so as not to lose the delicate flavor of the dish.

Per serving: 97 calories, 6.3 g. fat (54% of calories), 1.4 g. saturated fat, 0 mg. cholesterol, 386 mg. sodium.

Red Onion, Grapefruit and Tomato Salad

Yield: 6 servings

o peel the tomatoes for this recipe, plunge them into boiling water for 10 to 15 seconds; the skin should peel off easily. The tomatoes are also seeded here, leaving only the tomato flesh, which is combined with the flesh of grapefruit, red onions and basil and tossed with a classic sherry vinaigrette dressing.

1   **Ruby Red grapefruit (1 pound)**

3   **medium tomatoes (about 1 pound), peeled, seeded and cut into 1″ pieces (3 cups)**

1   **medium red onion (6 ounces), peeled and cut into ¼″ dice (1¼ cups)**

⅓   **cup fresh basil leaves, sliced into a fine chiffonade (see page 100)**

2   **tablespoons extra-virgin olive oil**

1   **tablespoon sherry vinegar**

½   **teaspoon salt**

½   **teaspoon freshly ground black pepper**

1   **bunch watercress (about 2 ounces)**

Using a sharp knife, peel the grapefruit, removing all the skin and the underlying white pith so the flesh of the fruit is totally exposed. Then cut between the membranes on each side of every segment and remove the flesh in wedgelike pieces. Cut each grapefruit wedge in half and place the pieces in a large bowl. Then, holding the membranes over the bowl, squeeze them over the grapefruit flesh to extract any remaining juice before discarding them. (You should have about 1 cup of grapefruit flesh and 3 tablespoons of juice.)

Add the tomatoes, onions and basil to the bowl. Mix well.

Mix the oil, vinegar, salt and pepper in a small bowl. Toss with the grapefruit mixture.

When ready to serve, cut the bottom 2″ of stems from the watercress and discard. Wash and thoroughly dry the rest of the bunch. Arrange the watercress attractively around the periphery of a platter and mound the salad in the center.

Per serving: 95 calories, 4.9 g. fat (43% of calories), 0.7 g. saturated fat, 0 mg. cholesterol, 190 mg. sodium.

Red Onion, Grapefruit and Tomato Salad

Squid Salad with Cucumber and Mint

Yield: 6 servings

nice feature of this salad is that it can be made ahead, since it will keep, refrigerated, for three or four days. Squid are blanched here and combined with cucumbers and a number of seasonings. The dominating herb flavors are mint and cilantro. In combination with commercial fish sauce, available in most Asian markets, these herbs give the dish a wonderfully assertive flavor.

2½ pounds squid, bodies cut crosswise into ½" rings and each tentacle cut into 2–3 pieces

2 medium cucumbers (1 pound), trimmed, peeled, seeded and thinly sliced (3½ cups)

2 medium onions (about 8 ounces), peeled and thinly sliced (2 cups)

2 medium tomatoes (about 14 ounces), chopped (2 cups)

1 cup loosely packed fresh mint leaves, sliced into a fine chiffonade (see page 100)

1 cup loosely packed fresh cilantro leaves and stems, coarsely chopped

¼ cup Vietnamese fish sauce (see page 22)

¼ cup red wine vinegar

1 jalapeño pepper, seeded, if desired (to eliminate some of its hotness), and finely chopped (1–1½ tablespoons)

5–6 cloves garlic, peeled, crushed and finely chopped (1 tablespoon)

½ teaspoon sugar

½ teaspoon salt

Wash the squid in cold water and drain it well. Set aside.

Bring about 2 quarts of water to a boil in a large pot.

Meanwhile, combine the cucumbers, onions, tomatoes, mint, cilantro, fish sauce, vinegar, peppers, garlic, sugar and salt in a large bowl.

When the water in the pot comes to a boil, add the squid, stir and cook over high heat for 2 to 3 minutes (the water will not come back to a boil). Drain the squid well and add it to the mixture in the bowl. Cool to room temperature, cover and refrigerate for at least 1 hour or as long as overnight.

Squid Salad with Cucumber and Mint

To serve, return the salad to room temperature and divide it among 6 plates.

Per serving: 232 calories, 3.1 g. fat (12% of calories), 0.8 g. saturated fat, 440 mg. cholesterol, 399 mg. sodium.

Main Courses

Chicken African Style

Navarin of lamb

Carbonnade of beef

Pasta Primavera

and more ...

Salmon with Sorrel Sauce

Yield: 6 servings

he tart flavor of sorrel cuts the richness of the salmon and produces an excellent dish. If sorrel is not available, you can prepare the same chiffonade mixture with Boston lettuce. If you use lettuce, however, add ½ teaspoon of lemon juice to the sauce just before serving it to simulate the tartness of sorrel.

  6 salmon fillets (5–6 ounces each and ½″–¾″ thick)
  ½ cup dry white wine
  ¾ cup Poultry White Base Sauce (page 17)
 12–15 large sorrel leaves, cut into a chiffonade (see below)
  ¼ teaspoon freshly ground black pepper
  ½ teaspoon salt

Preheat the oven to 400°.

Place the salmon fillets in a single layer in a baking dish suitable for stovetop use. Add the wine and bring to a boil on top of the stove. Place the dish in the oven and bake the fillets for 5 to 6 minutes.

Use a metal spatula to transfer the fish to a serving platter; reserve the juices in the dish. Cover the fish with aluminum foil and keep warm while you prepare the sauce.

Pour the salmon cooking juices into a saucepan and boil them until they are reduced to 2 tablespoons. Add the base sauce, sorrel and pepper; bring the mixture to a boil. Stir in the salt and any juices that have accumulated around the fish.

Arrange the fish on a serving platter and pour the sauce over it. Serve immediately.

Per serving: 159 calories, 4.9 g. fat (28% of calories), 1.2 g. saturated fat, 27 mg. cholesterol, 251 mg. sodium.

  Note: Chiffonade is a French term that refers to thin strips or shreds of herbs or vegetables. Basil, sorrel and lettuce are often cut that way. To make chiffonade, stack the leaves together and roll them tightly end to end. Cut the bundle crosswise into thin slices with a sharp knife and unroll into long, narrow strands.

Salmon with Sorrel Sauce (page 100) and Roasted New Potatoes (page 264)

Salmon Sausage with Chipotle Sauce

Yield: 6 servings

*he salmon is butterflied for this dish, so the center cut—being of almost
equal size and thickness throughout—produces the best result. You can
make the stuffing, containing spinach and both wild and domestic mushrooms,
ahead and stuff the salmon a day ahead of cooking. The finished "sausage" is
wrapped in plastic wrap and then in aluminum foil for poaching.*

*The sauce served with the salmon roll features chipotle peppers, a semi-hot,
smoked variety. It can be prepared in a food processor instead of a food mill, as
indicated in the recipe, but then must be strained afterward.*

PEPPERS

5 dried chipotle peppers (about 1 ounce)

1 cup water

STUFFING

4 ounces fresh shiitake mushrooms, washed and with
stems removed

1 tablespoon unsalted butter

1 tablespoon virgin olive oil

2 medium shallots (2 ounces), peeled, trimmed and finely chopped
(⅓ cup)

½ small leek, both white and green parts (about 2 ounces),
trimmed, chopped and washed (½ cup)

5–6 domestic mushrooms (3–4 ounces), washed and chopped
(1 cup)

½ cup water

10 ounces spinach, trimmed, washed and cut into 2″ pieces

1 tablespoon chopped fresh tarragon leaves

¼ teaspoon salt

¼ teaspoon freshly ground black pepper

SALMON

1 salmon fillet (1¾ pounds), center cut or with tail removed,
so the piece is of equal thickness throughout

¼ teaspoon salt

¼ teaspoon freshly ground black pepper

CHIPOTLE SAUCE

- 2 tablespoons virgin olive oil
- 1 small onion (3 ounces), peeled and chopped (½ cup)
- ½ stalk celery (1 ounce), washed, trimmed and thinly sliced (¼ cup)
- 1 teaspoon dried summer savory
- ½ teaspoon salt
- 4 medium tomatoes (1½ pounds), cut into 2″ pieces
- 3–4 cloves garlic, peeled, crushed and finely chopped (2 teaspoons)
- 1 tablespoon unsalted butter

ASSEMBLY

- 2 tablespoons chopped fresh dill or parsley leaves

To make the peppers: Place the peppers in a small bowl and add the 1 cup water. Cover and set aside to soak for at least 6 hours, but preferably overnight.

To make the stuffing: Slice the shiitake caps and place in the bowl of a food processor; pulse them 10 times, until they are coarsely chopped. (You should have 1¼ cups.) Set aside.

Heat the butter and oil in a large skillet. When it is hot, add the shallots and leeks and sauté them for 1 minute. Add the shiitake mushrooms to the skillet. Stir in the domestic mushrooms and ½ cup water. Cover the skillet and cook the mixture for 2 minutes over high heat. Then remove the lid and add the spinach, pushing it down into the mixture.

Reduce the heat to medium, cover and cook for 2 minutes. Add the tarragon, salt and pepper and mix well. Set aside until cooled to room temperature.

To make the salmon: Place the fillet, skin side down, on a cutting board and, using clean tweezers or pliers, pull out and discard the line of small bones that runs down the center of the fillet. Then remove and discard the salmon skin, any sinews and the fatty tissue that lies under the skin.

With the fillet skin side down on the board, position your knife so the blade is almost parallel to the board. Beginning about 1″ in from the thinnest lengthwise edge, butterfly the fillet, stopping when you come within ½″ of the other side. Then open the fillet like a book.

You now have a large, almost square piece of salmon of about equal thickness throughout. To assure that it is of equal thickness, place it between 2 large sheets of plastic wrap and, using a meat pounder, pound the fillet gently in any areas where it is thicker to make it of uniform thickness throughout.

(continued)

Remove the top sheet of plastic wrap and sprinkle the surface of the fillet with the salt and pepper. Pile the stuffing on top and spread it to within 1" of the edges of the fillet.

Starting at a long edge, roll up the fillet to encase the filling; roll it as tightly as possible, using the plastic wrap underneath to help you guide it as you roll. When you are finished, wrap the rolled salmon tightly in the plastic wrap and twist the wrap at both ends to enclose it securely. Then wrap the salmon in aluminum foil, twisting the foil at both ends. (The salmon roll should be about 9½" × 3".)

Bring about 2 quarts of water to a boil in a 10" or 12" saucepan deep enough to hold the salmon roll with room to spare. Place the roll in the pan (it should be submerged in the water) and put a small pan lid (smaller than the saucepan) on top of the roll to hold it down under the water. Cook the roll at just under the boiling point (190° to 200°) for about 20 minutes.

To make the chipotle sauce: While the salmon is cooking, remove the peppers from the soaking water (reserve the water). Halve the peppers; remove and discard the seeds.

Heat the oil in a large saucepan. When the oil is hot, add the onions, celery, savory and salt; sauté for 1 to 2 minutes. Add the tomatoes, garlic and the peppers with their reserved soaking liquid. Bring the mixture to a strong boil. Then reduce the heat to low, cover and boil gently for 15 minutes.

Strain the mixture through a food mill fitted with a fine-mesh screen and stir in the butter. (You should have 2¾ to 3 cups.) For a smoother sauce, emulsify the mixture with a hand blender.

To assemble: Use an instant-read thermometer to check the salmon. When it has reached an internal temperature of 137° to 140°, set it aside off the heat for 15 minutes (still in the pan of water). Then unwrap it and wipe off any white liquid (protein) accumulation from the top of the roll with paper towels.

Line a platter with the sauce and place the salmon roll on top, in the center of the platter. For an attractive presentation, cut a few 1½" slices from the roll and arrange them in front of the uncut portion of the roll. Sprinkle with the dill or parsley. Cut the remainder of the salmon slices at the table and serve 1 slice per person with additional sauce.

Per serving: 299 calories, 16 g. fat (47% of calories), 4.5 g. saturated fat, 35 mg. cholesterol, 521 mg. sodium.

Salmon Sausage with Chipotle Sauce (page 102)
and Pea, Mushroom and Corn Medley (page 249)

Salmon Steaks with Crudité Sauce

Yield: 6 servings

lthough salmon is a fatty fish, it is less fatty than most meats and has a very delicate flavor. I serve it here with a crudité sauce that is fresh, crunchy, delicious and elegant. Be certain that the fishmonger who cuts your steaks removes all the skin, bones and sinews. To save time, you could prepare the vegetables ahead. The fish poaching liquid forms the base for the light, appealing sauce.

1½ teaspoons grated lime rind
¾ teaspoon freshly ground black pepper
6 boneless, skinless salmon steaks (4 ounces each)
1 cup water
3 plum tomatoes (about 6 ounces total), halved, seeded and cut into ¼″ dice (1½ cups)
1 medium zucchini (6 ounces), washed, trimmed and cut into ¼″ dice (about 1½ cups)
6 radishes, cleaned and cut into ⅛″-thick julienne strips
3 tablespoons chopped fresh chives
¾ teaspoon salt
1 tablespoon virgin olive oil
1 tablespoon unsalted butter

Sprinkle the lime rind and pepper on 1 side of the salmon steaks. Heat a very large skillet (or 2 smaller ones) until hot. Place the salmon in the hot skillet with the water and cook the steaks over high heat for 45 seconds. Then turn the steaks over and cook them for 45 seconds on the other side. Cover the skillet, remove it from the heat and let the steaks sit for 2 to 3 minutes before transferring them to a tray and setting them aside in a warm place. Reserve the juices in the skillet. (You should have about 1 cup.)

Bring the reserved juices to a strong boil. Add the tomatoes, zucchini, radishes, chives and salt and cook over high heat for 1 minute (the juices might not return to a boil), just until the vegetables are slightly softened. Add the oil and butter, bring the mixture to a strong boil and boil for about 30 seconds to emulsify the mixture. Pour the sauce over the salmon and serve.

Per serving: 153 calories, 8.3 g. fat (49% of calories), 2.4 g. saturated fat, 26 mg. cholesterol, 324 mg. sodium.

Sole Fillets with Stewed Tomatoes

Yield: 6 servings

t is best to cook these fillets at the last moment and serve the dish as soon as it is ready. If you are rushed, however, you can prepare the dish a half-hour ahead, cooking the fillets for only seven to eight minutes and then setting them aside in a 180° oven for 30 minutes to finish cooking while you make the sauce. You may use Dover, lemon or gray sole or even flounder.

- 1 medium onion (4 ounces), peeled and finely chopped (½ cup)
- 6 sole fillets (about 5 ounces each)
- ½ cup dry white wine
- 1 small tomato (3–4 ounces), peeled, seeded and cut into ½" dice (½ cup)
- 1 teaspoon salt
- 2 tablespoons virgin olive oil

Preheat the oven to 400°.

Place the onions in a sieve and rinse them thoroughly under cold tap water to remove their acidic, bitter taste and make them milder in flavor.

Arrange the fillets in a single layer in a large gratin dish and sprinkle the onions over them. Add the wine, tomatoes and salt. Place a piece of wax paper on top and bake in the center of the oven for 10 to 12 minutes, until the fillets are tender and just cooked through.

Transfer the fillets to a serving platter. Pour the juice from the gratin dish into a skillet and boil it until it is reduced to about ⅔ cup. Add the oil and bring the mixture to a boil. Immediately pour the sauce over the fillets. Serve.

Per serving: 155 calories, 5.8 g. fat (34% of calories), 0.9 g. saturated fat, 53 mg. cholesterol, 440 mg. sodium.

Fillets of Sole in Salad Casings

Yield: 6 servings

his dish is ideal for a party because the fish stays quite moist wrapped in lettuce leaves. You can wrap and cook the fillets and make the sauce up to an hour ahead; if you do, however, cut the cooking time of the fillets to two to three minutes and place them (separate from the sauce), covered, in a 180° oven until serving time. At serving time, bring the sauce to a boil, discard any liquid that has collected around the fillet packages and serve as directed.

- 1 very large head iceberg lettuce (with loose leaves, if possible)
- 6 ounces domestic mushrooms, washed and finely chopped (about 2 cups)
- ½ teaspoon salt (adjust if canned broth is used)
- 1½ pounds sole fillets (about 4 ounces each)
- 1 large carrot (3–4 ounces), trimmed and peeled
- 1 small leek (3–4 ounces), trimmed and cut lengthwise into 3–4 slices
- ½ teaspoon freshly ground white pepper
- 1 cup dry white wine
- 2 tablespoons corn oil
- 1 tablespoon all-purpose flour
- ½ cup White Chicken Stock (page 14), lower-salt canned chicken broth or water

  A few drops lemon juice (optional)
- 2 tablespoons chopped fresh parsley leaves

Bring a large pot of water to a boil.

Meanwhile, core the lettuce, then insert the tips of your fingers in the resulting hole and carefully spread the leaves apart to help loosen the large outside leaves. Separate the leaves, taking care to leave them whole, and pick out 6 of the largest leaves. (Reserve the rest of the lettuce for another use.)

Drop the lettuce leaves into the boiling water and gently push them down into the water as they wilt. Bring the water back almost to a boil; at this point the leaves will be soft. Place the whole pot in the sink and let cold water run in it until the leaves are cold. Then carefully lift the leaves from the water and drain them individually on paper towels.

Place the mushrooms in a large skillet set over medium heat and cook them until all the liquid they release evaporates. Season with ¼ teaspoon of the salt and divide the mixture among the leaves, spooning it into the center of each.

Fold the pieces of the fish in half, fleshy side out (skin side in, so they don't unfold during cooking), and place 1 fillet on top of the mushroom mixture on each leaf. Fold the lettuce leaves around the fish to create neat packages.

Cut the carrot lengthwise into ¼″ slices, then halve the slices crosswise. Stack the slices and cut them lengthwise into thin julienne strips. (You should have about 1 cup.)

Stack the leek slices and fold them in half end to end. Then cut them lengthwise into thin julienne strips. Wash the strips in a sieve held under cold water.

Sprinkle a large skillet with the pepper and the remaining ¼ teaspoon salt. Cover with the carrots and leeks. Then place the fillet packages in a single layer on top of the vegetables.

Pour the wine over the packages and cover the skillet tightly with a lid. Bring the wine to a boil and simmer the mixture gently for about 8 minutes (slightly longer if the packages are packed very tightly together in the skillet).

To make the sauce, heat 1 tablespoon of the oil in a heavy saucepan and add the flour. Cook the mixture over medium heat, stirring it with a whisk, for about 30 seconds. Holding the fillets in place with the skillet lid, pour the fish cooking liquid from the skillet into the flour-oil mixture. Mix thoroughly with the whisk, bring to a boil and whisk continuously until the mixture thickens. Let simmer gently for about 2 minutes. (You should have about ¾ cup of sauce.)

Add the stock, broth or water. Bring the mixture to a boil and add the remaining 1 tablespoon oil. Boil for 2 to 3 minutes, until the mixture is reduced to about 1 cup.

Remove the packages from the skillet and arrange the vegetables on a serving platter. Place the packages on top of them and set the platter in a 180° oven until serving time.

At serving time, pour out or blot up with paper towels any juice that has accumulated around the fillets so it will not dilute the sauce.

Heat the sauce, stirring in a few drops of lemon juice for flavor, if desired, and pour the sauce over the fillets. Sprinkle with the parsley.

Per serving: 198 calories, 6.1 g. fat (28% of calories), 0.9 g. saturated fat, 53 mg. cholesterol, 280 mg. sodium.

An alternate way to cook the packages is to bring the wine to a boil on top of the stove, then transfer the skillet to a 425° oven for 8 to 10 minutes.

Catfish Sauté with Vegetable Medley

Catfish Sauté with Vegetable Medley

Yield: 6 servings

*C*atfish, a very white, fleshy and firm fish, is available at most fish markets. Be sure that the fillets you buy are absolutely fresh and as clean as possible. There is always a layer of dark, strong-flavored fat on top of catfish fillets; if your fishmonger doesn't remove this, you should. Likewise, when you cut the fillets into strips, be sure to trim off any remaining visible fat. If catfish is not available, substitute another firm fish, such as monkfish or swordfish; you could even use scallops.

2¼	pounds trimmed catfish fillets
2	tablespoons canola, corn or virgin olive oil
1	small stalk celery, washed, trimmed and cut into ¼″ dice (⅓ cup)
½	small onion (1½ ounces), peeled and cut into ¼″ dice (⅓ cup)
½	small red bell pepper (2 ounces), halved, cored, seeded and cut into ¼″ dice (⅓ cup)
10	medium domestic mushrooms (6 ounces), washed and cut into 2″ dice (2½ cups)
2	small zucchini (5 ounces), washed, trimmed and cut into ½″ dice (2½ cups)
¾	teaspoon salt
¼	teaspoon freshly ground black pepper
1	small lime, peeled and the flesh cut into ¼″ dice (3 tablespoons)
1	tablespoon balsamic vinegar
6	tablespoons fresh basil leaves sliced into a fine chiffonade (see page 100)

Trim all fat from the catfish fillets and cut them into strips approximately 4″ long × 1″ wide. (You should have about 2 cups.)

Heat a very large skillet (or 2 smaller ones) and add the oil. When the oil is hot, add the celery, onions and red peppers and sauté them for 1½ minutes. Add the mushrooms and zucchini and sauté the mixture for 1 minute longer.

Add the catfish, salt and black pepper; cook the mixture for 3½ minutes. Toss in the lime and vinegar. Arrange on a platter and top with the basil.

Per serving: 252 calories, 11.9 g. fat (44% of calories), 2 g. saturated fat, 98 mg. cholesterol, 382 mg. sodium.

Garlic-Studded Roast Monkfish in Ratatouille

Yield: 6 servings

his recipe from the South of France features monkfish, a firm, white fish that can be roasted like a piece of meat. It is studded here, like a roast of lamb, with thin slivers of garlic. If monkfish is not available, buy a thick fillet of cod instead and prepare it the same way; it will cook faster (10 minutes rather than 15 minutes) and tend to flake, so it can be served in chunks rather than slices. Remember that the fresher the fish, the better the dish. I serve the fish here on ratatouille, a mixture of vegetables that is good served on its own cold as well as warm.

- 2 trimmed monkfish fillets (1 pound each; see note)
- 3 large cloves garlic, peeled, each cut lengthwise into 4–6 slivers (12–18 slivers total)
- 2 small eggplants (1¼ pounds), unpeeled but trimmed and cut into 1″ dice (about 7 cups)
- 2 medium zucchini (10 ounces), washed, trimmed and cut into 1″ dice (about 3 cups)
- 2 medium onions (12 ounces), peeled and cut into 1″ dice (about 3 cups)
- 1 cup water
- ½ teaspoon fennel seeds
- 2 teaspoons dried oregano
- 1 teaspoon freshly ground black pepper
- 2 tablespoons virgin olive oil
- 1½ pounds plum tomatoes, cut into 1″ dice (about 4 cups)
- 6–8 medium cloves garlic, peeled, crushed and finely chopped (1½ tablespoons)
- 1 teaspoon salt
- 1 tablespoon chopped fresh tarragon leaves

Cut small slits in the flesh of the monkfish fillets and insert the slivers of garlic into the slits. Set aside.

Place the eggplant, zucchini, onions and water in a large stainless steel saucepan. Bring the mixture to a boil, cover and cook for 4 minutes, or until the water evaporates. Transfer the vegetables to a platter and sprinkle them with the fennel seeds.

Sprinkle the fish with the oregano and ½ teaspoon of the pepper. Heat the oil in the saucepan you used to cook the vegetables. When the oil is hot, add the fish and brown it on each side for 1 minute. Add the tomatoes, chopped garlic, salt, the remaining ½ teaspoon pepper and the reserved vegetables. Cover the pan, reduce the heat to low and cook for 15 minutes.

Transfer the fish to a platter. Increase the heat under the vegetables and cook them for 3 to 4 minutes, or until most of the moisture surrounding them has evaporated. (Retain only enough liquid to keep the vegetables moist.)

Mound the vegetable mixture on another platter. Slice the fish on the diagonal and arrange the slices over the vegetables. Sprinkle with the tarragon and serve.

Per serving: 237 calories, 7.6 g. fat (28% of calories), 0.7 g. saturated fat, 37 mg. cholesterol, 401 mg. sodium.

Always trim monkfish well before cooking it. As there is often a fair amount of membrane attached, you should buy about 2½ pounds of fillet for this recipe to get the 2 pounds of cleaned fish required.

When buying fresh garlic, choose loose bulbs rather than the boxed ones so you can handle them. Look for firm, tightly closed heads without any visible sprouting or bruising. Store garlic in a dry place but do not refrigerate.

Broiled Red Snapper
with Lemon-Tarragon Sauce

Yield: 6 servings

It is always important to use fresh fish, especially so when the fish is simply cooked. Broiled snapper fillets are served here with a light, fresh-flavored sauce tasting of lemon and tarragon.

6	snapper fillets (8 ounces each and about ¾″ thick at its thickest part)
½	teaspoon plus 2½ tablespoons virgin olive oil
2	tablespoons water
1	tablespoon grated lemon rind
1	tablespoon chopped fresh tarragon leaves
1	tablespoon balsamic vinegar
1	small shallot, peeled, trimmed and finely chopped (1 tablespoon)
½	teaspoon salt
¼	teaspoon freshly ground black pepper
1	small clove garlic, peeled, crushed and finely chopped (¼ teaspoon)

Score the fillets, cutting through the skin of each with 6 shallow diagonal cuts (3 running across the width and 3 down the length of each fillet). Lightly brush the fillets on both sides with ½ teaspoon of the oil and arrange them, skin side up, in a single layer on a foil-lined cookie sheet.

To make the sauce, place the water, lemon rind, tarragon, vinegar, shallots, salt, pepper, garlic and the remaining 2½ tablespoons oil in a small bowl. Mix well. (You should have about ½ cup.)

Preheat the broiler.

Place the fillets under the broiler so they are no more than 2″ from the heat. Broil for 5 minutes (making appropriate adjustments if your fillets are thinner or thicker than specified). Remove from the oven, cover and set aside for 2 minutes.

To serve, place a fillet on each of 6 plates. Drizzle about 1½ tablespoons of sauce on each fillet. Serve.

Per serving: 286 calories, 9 g. fat (30% of calories), 1.5 g. saturated fat, 83 mg. cholesterol, 279 mg. sodium.

Broiled Red Snapper with Lemon-Tarragon Sauce

Blackened Swordfish (page 117) with Hominy, Cilantro and Cumin Stew (page 232)

Blackened Swordfish

Yield: 6 servings

I *t is particularly important that you use a heavy nonstick pan here—and in most of my sauté recipes—so less fat is needed. A mixture of thyme, oregano, cumin and black and red peppers coats the fish and gives it a wonderfully hot taste. The fish is best if seared in a very hot pan and not cooked too long. Fish that is approximately 1" thick should be slightly undercooked in the center so it remains moist throughout.*

1½	teaspoons dried thyme
1½	teaspoons dried oregano
1	teaspoon ground cumin
¾	teaspoon freshly ground black pepper
½	teaspoon salt
¼	teaspoon ground red pepper
6	swordfish fillets (5 ounces each and 1" thick)
2	tablespoons corn or canola oil
	Juice from ½ lemon (about 1 tablespoon)

Mix the thyme, oregano, cumin, black pepper, salt and red pepper in a bowl, then spread the mixture out on a plate. Press the fillets into the mixture, coating them well on both sides.

Heat the oil in a very large nonstick skillet (or 2 smaller ones). When it is very hot, add the fish in a single layer and brown it for 1 minute on each side. Reduce the heat to low, cover and cook the fish for an additional 3 minutes.

Arrange the fish on a serving platter, sprinkle the lemon juice over it and serve immediately.

Per serving: 217 calories, 10.4 g. fat (44% of calories), 2.2 g. saturated fat, 56 mg. cholesterol, 306 mg. sodium.

Swordfish with Oriental Sauce or Salsa

Yield: 6 servings

ake sure that the fish you use in this dish is super fresh—your nose will tell you—and have it cut as close to ¾" thick as possible. If it is thicker or thinner, adjust the cooking time accordingly. If you do not have a grill at your disposal, broil the fish close to the heat source in a conventional oven for about the same amount of time as indicated in the recipe.

If cooking the fish on a barbecue grill, be certain that the grill rack is very clean so the fish doesn't stick to it. The grill should also be extremely hot, so the fish is nicely marked and has a distinct charcoal flavor. Transfer the fish to a 180° oven for five to ten minutes while you finish preparing other dishes on the menu; the fish will continue to cook at this low temperature, releasing its juices and becoming more moist and delicate.

- 1 tablespoon chopped fresh tarragon leaves
- 1 tablespoon soy sauce
- 1½ teaspoons dark sesame oil
- 6 swordfish steaks (6 ounces each and ¾" thick)
  Rice wine vinegar (optional)
- 1½ cups Salsa Cruda (page 21) or ¾ cup Oriental Sauce (page 22)

Mix the tarragon, soy sauce and oil in a small bowl. Rub the mixture into the flesh of the fish on both sides.

Preheat a grill until very hot.

Place the fish on a clean rack and cook for about 2 minutes on one side. Using a large metal spatula, turn the steaks gently and grill them for another 2 minutes on the other side. (At this point, the fish should still be undercooked in the center.) Transfer the steaks to a 180° oven for 5 to 10 minutes to rest and continue cooking.

Arrange the steaks on a serving platter and, if desired, sprinkle with a little vinegar. Pass the salsa or oriental sauce for diners to add as they please.

Per serving: 235 calories, 8.2 g. fat (32% of calories), 2.1 g. saturated fat, 67 mg. cholesterol, 429 mg. sodium.

Braised Stuffed Trout with Herb Crust

Yield: 6 servings

*t**rout is nutritious, delicious, a good buy and available year-round. Buy your trout in a store that carries whole fresh trout (some stores have them alive in fish tanks), and have your fishmonger cut them into fillets. You will need about two 3-ounce fillets of completely cleaned fish per person, which is the yield from a 10-ounce trout. Use dried shiitake or porcini mushrooms, which are usually much more flavorful than the fresh varieties. The liquid these are soaked in is used to cook the fish in this recipe.*

1 ounce dried shiitake or porcini mushrooms (1 cup)

1½ cups hot water

6 ounces domestic mushrooms, washed and sliced (2½–3 cups)
  Vegetable cooking spray or ½ teaspoon canola oil

1 small leek (3–4 ounces), trimmed, chopped and washed (1 cup)

1 medium onion (4 ounces), peeled and chopped (¾ cup)

½ teaspoon freshly ground black pepper

1 teaspoon salt

6 whole trout (10 ounces each), filleted, skin removed and split in half to make 12 fillets

2 slices bread, processed into crumbs in a food processor (1 cup)

2 tablespoons virgin olive oil

2 tablespoons chopped fresh chives

Place the dried mushrooms in a bowl, add the water and soak the mushrooms until they are softened, about 30 minutes. Remove the mushrooms from the water. Pour the liquid into another bowl, discarding any sand or dirt that has collected at the bottom, and reserve the liquid.

Remove and discard the stems from the dried mushrooms (which tend to be tough) and place the caps in the bowl of a food processor with the domestic mushrooms. Chop coarsely.

Heat a large nonstick skillet and coat it lightly but evenly with vegetable cooking spray or brush it lightly with the canola oil. Add the leeks and onions and sauté them for 1 minute. Add the chopped mushrooms, pepper and ½ teaspoon of the salt. Sauté the mixture for 3 minutes longer. Set the skillet aside off the heat.

Preheat the oven to 400°.

(continued)

Place 6 of the fish fillets in a single layer in a baking dish. Divide the mushroom mixture evenly over the fillets, then cover with the remaining 6 fillets, arranging them in the opposite direction of the fillets underneath. Pour the reserved mushroom soaking liquid over them.

Mix the bread crumbs with the olive oil, chives and the remaining ½ teaspoon salt in a small bowl. Sprinkle this mixture over the fish. Bake the fillets for 15 minutes, then broil them for 1 to 2 minutes directly under the heat, if needed, to brown the crumbs nicely on top. Serve within the next 15 minutes.

Per serving: 284 calories, 10.4 g. fat (33% of calories), 1.7 g. saturated fat, 90 mg. cholesterol, 441 mg. sodium.

To clean fresh mushrooms, wipe them off with a damp towel. If they need more than that, wash them briefly in cold water. Dry them with paper towels. If you're going to cook them, don't worry about getting off all the moisture. The excess will evaporate as the mushrooms cook.

Braised Stuffed Trout with Herb Crust (page 119)
and Lime Peas in Tomato Cups (page 250)

Grilled Herbed Tuna on Spinach Salad

Yield: 6 servings

i *t is difficult to grill fish properly at home because the grills designed for home use often don't get as hot as those in professional kitchens. A very clean, hot grill is required here and if one is not available, broil the tuna instead, placing it no more than 2" from the heat. Don't overcook the fish; it should be served slightly underdone with a pink center.*

- 2 tablespoons sherry vinegar
- 1 small shallot (about 1 ounce), peeled, trimmed and chopped (2 tablespoons)
- 1 tablespoon chopped fresh tarragon leaves
- ¼ teaspoon freshly ground black pepper
- 3 tablespoons extra-virgin olive oil
- ¾ teaspoon salt
- 7 medium domestic mushrooms (4 ounces), washed and cut into ½" dice (1½ cups)
- 1 medium tomato (7 ounces), peeled, seeded and cut into ½" pieces (1 cup)
- 12 ounces spinach
- 1 tablespoon whole black peppercorns, crushed (see opposite page)
- 1 tablespoon herbes de Provence (see page 13)
- 6 center-cut tuna steaks (6 ounces each and about ¾" thick)

In a very large bowl, mix the vinegar, shallots, tarragon, ground pepper, 2 tablespoons of the oil and ¼ teaspoon of the salt. Add the mushrooms and tomatoes, toss well and set aside.

Trim, wash and dry the spinach. Break the leaves into slightly smaller pieces. (You should have about 7 cups.) Set aside.

Pat the crushed pepper and herbes de Provence into the tuna. Sprinkle both sides of the steaks with the remaining 1 tablespoon oil and the remaining ½ teaspoon salt.

Preheat a grill until very hot.

Arrange the tuna on a clean rack and cook for 1½ minutes for rare (or 2 minutes for medium) on each side. Transfer to a large platter and cover with a domed lid.

Add the spinach to the bowl with the dressing mixture; toss well. Divide the salad among 6 plates.

Grilled Herbed Tuna on Spinach Salad

Cut each tuna steak on the diagonal into 3 pieces and arrange the equivalent of 1 steak on each plate. Serve immediately.

Per serving: 357 calories, 16.3 g. fat (41% of calories), 3.3 g. saturated fat, 71 mg. cholesterol, 389 mg. sodium.

The easiest way to crush whole peppercorns is with the bottom of a heavy pan. Place the peppercorns in a single layer on a flat surface, such as a cutting board. Press down on them with the pan to crack them to the coarseness desired.

Saffron Fish Stew

Yield: 6 servings

Scallops and codfish are poached here in a flavorful stock that forms the base of this dish. The stew is seasoned with saffron, an expensive addition that's well worth the investment.

    3 tablespoons virgin olive oil
    1 small leek or piece of a larger leek (3–4 ounces), trimmed,
       thinly sliced and washed (1 cup)
    2 carrots (4 ounces), trimmed, peeled, thinly sliced and cut into
       ⅛"–¼" dice (¾ cup)
    1 small onion (about 3 ounces), peeled and chopped (½ cup)
    ⅓ cup leafy fennel greens
    ½ stalk celery (about 2 ounces), washed, trimmed and thinly sliced
       (¼ cup)
  5–6 cloves garlic, peeled, crushed and finely chopped (1 tablespoon)
    1 large tomato (about 8 ounces), peeled, seeded and chopped
       (1½ cups)
    1 cup dry white wine
    1 cup cold water
    1 teaspoon salt
    ½ teaspoon freshly ground black pepper
    3 medium domestic mushrooms, washed and cut into ½" dice (½ cup)
    ½ cup warm water
    1 tablespoon chopped fresh tarragon leaves
    1 teaspoon loosely packed saffron threads
    1 teaspoon grated lemon rind
   1½ pounds mussels (about 48)
    1 pound scallops (about 36)
    6 codfish steaks (1¼ pounds)

Heat the oil in a large saucepan. When it is hot, add the leeks, carrots and onions; sauté for 2 minutes over medium to high heat. Add the fennel, celery and garlic to the saucepan and sauté for 1 minute.

Add the tomatoes, wine, cold water, salt and pepper. Bring the mixture to a boil. Add the mushrooms, bring the mixture back to a boil and cook for 2 minutes.

(continued)

Saffron Fish Stew

Meanwhile, combine the warm water, tarragon, saffron and lemon rind in a small bowl. Set aside.

Add the mussels to the saucepan and bring the mixture back to a strong boil. Stir and cook for 2 to 3 minutes, until the mussels open.

Pour about 2 cups of the stew liquid into another saucepan and add the saffron mixture and the scallops and cod. Bring the mixture to a boil, cover and cook over high heat for 1 minute. Set aside for 4 to 5 minutes.

Divide the seafood mixtures among 6 large soup plates, evenly apportioning the mussels, scallops and cod.

Per serving: 325 calories, 9.5 g. fat (27% of calories), 1.1 g. saturated fat, 99 mg. cholesterol, 720 mg. sodium.

Saffron is a very expensive ingredient, but a little goes a long way. It comes from a certain species of crocus and is actually the dried stigma of the flower. Each crocus contains three stigmas, and about 75,000 crocuses are needed to produce one pound of saffron. The best saffron is red and comes from Spain. Store it tightly capped in a dry place away from light. If your recipe calls for it to be powdered, warm the threads for a few minutes in a dry frying pan or at a low heat in an oven. They'll become brittle and will be easier to pulverize.

Sea Scallops Grenobloise

Yield: 6 servings

he variety of colors represented—white scallops, green zucchini and red pepper—makes the dish very attractive. For best results, be sure to add the croutons at the end; if added sooner, they lose their crunchiness.

- 1½ pounds large sea scallops (about 18)
- 1 tablespoon water
- 2 tablespoons virgin olive oil
- 2 cloves garlic, peeled, crushed and finely chopped (1 teaspoon)
- 1 small zucchini (about 4 ounces), washed, trimmed and cut into ¼″ dice (about 1 cup)
- 1 small red bell pepper (4 ounces), halved, cored, seeded and cut into ½″ dice (about 1 cup)
- ¼ teaspoon freshly ground black pepper
- ¼ teaspoon salt
- 1 small lemon, rind removed with a vegetable peeler and flesh cut into ½″ dice (⅓ cup)
- 2 slices bread, cut into ½″ cubes and browned in the oven (about 1 cup)
- 2 tablespoons chopped fresh chives

Remove and discard the tough sinews attached to the scallops and rinse them in cold water. Drain well.

Place the scallops in a skillet with the water. Bring the water to a boil, cover and cook for 1 minute, until the scallops are firm but still somewhat raw in the center. Transfer the scallops and their cooking juices to a platter and keep them warm in a 180° oven.

Heat the oil in a skillet over medium to high heat. When it is hot, add the garlic and sauté it for 5 to 6 seconds. Then add the zucchini and red peppers; sauté the mixture for 1 to 2 minutes. Drain off and discard the juice around the scallops and add them to the skillet. Season the mixture with the black pepper and salt. Toss the ingredients together and cook them for about 1 minute, until heated through. Stir in the lemon.

Just before serving, add the bread cubes, sprinkle with the chives and transfer the mixture to a serving dish. Serve immediately.

Per serving: 173 calories, 5.8 g. fat (30% of calories), 0.8 g. saturated fat, 37 mg. cholesterol, 312 mg. sodium.

Seared Scallops in Green Pea Sauce (page 129) and Carottes Provençale (page 239)

Seared Scallops in Green Pea Sauce

Yield: 6 servings

*W*hen cooking the scallops, be sure to divide them between two very hot nonstick skillets. They won't sear properly if they are crowded into one pan. After they are lightly browned on both sides, cover them and set them aside to finish cooking in their own residual heat.

I used frozen petite peas for the sauce, but you can substitute fresh peas, provided they are small with thin, tender skins that will liquefy when pressed through a food mill.

2	pounds medium sea scallops (30–36)
2	tablespoons virgin olive oil
¾	teaspoon dried thyme
2	cups water
1⅓	cups fresh or frozen petite peas
⅓	cup loosely packed fresh basil leaves
1	tablespoon unsalted butter
½	teaspoon salt

Remove and discard the tough sinews attached to the scallops and rinse them in cold water. Drain well and pat dry with paper towels.

Spoon 1 tablespoon of the oil onto a platter and turn the scallops in the oil to coat them on all sides. Sprinkle with the thyme. Set aside.

Bring the water to a boil in a medium saucepan over high heat. Add the peas, bring the water back to a boil and cook for 3 minutes. Add the basil and bring the mixture to a boil. Pour 1 cup of the cooking liquid into a bowl and set it aside.

Drain off and discard the rest of the cooking liquid. Place the peas and basil in the bowl of a food processor with ¼ cup of the reserved cooking liquid. Process until smooth, stopping the motor occasionally and scraping down the sides of the bowl with a rubber spatula. Add the remaining ¾ cup reserved liquid and process until it is incorporated.

Then, while the motor is running, add the butter, salt and the remaining 1 tablespoon oil through the feed tube; process until incorporated. Transfer the sauce to a bowl and set it aside in a warm place while you cook the scallops.

Heat 2 large nonstick skillets over high heat until they are very hot. Add the scallops in a single uncrowded layer and cook them for about 1½ minutes on

(continued)

each side (slightly more or less, depending on the scallop size). Remove the pans from the heat, cover and let the scallops rest for 4 to 5 minutes.

To serve, coat the base of each of 6 plates with ¼ cup of the pea sauce. Arrange 5 or 6 scallops in the center of each plate. Serve.

Per serving: 225 calories, 7.8 g. fat (32% of calories), 2 g. saturated fat, 55 mg. cholesterol, 423 mg. sodium.

There is a staggering array of olive oils on the market. Making a choice isn't easy, and price doesn't necessarily indicate quality. Even color and place of origin aren't foolproof guides. Your best bet is to try different brands until you find an oil with a flavor you prefer. Buy the oil in small quantities and store it in a cool, dark place. Oils that come in cans or dark bottles have added protection from light, which can cause the oil to deteriorate.

Curried Scallops Oriental

Yield: 6 servings

his dish can be made very quickly. The trick is to not overcook the scallops. If you are preparing this ahead for a party, cook the scallops only briefly—just until they stiffen—then set them aside to continue cooking in their own residual heat. I begin with a very large quantity of fresh spinach, but it wilts and shrinks to reasonable proportions when cooked. The spinach should be bright green to serve as an attractive base for the scallops.

- 1½   pounds large sea scallops (about 18)
- 1   tablespoon virgin olive oil
- 1½   teaspoons curry powder
- 3   pounds spinach, trimmed and washed (9 quarts)
- ½   teaspoon salt
- ¼   teaspoon freshly ground black pepper
- 1   cup Oriental Sauce (page 22)

Remove and discard the tough sinews attached to the scallops and rinse them in cold water. Drain well. Transfer to a bowl. Add the oil and curry powder.

Coat a very large skillet (or 2 smaller ones) with vegetable cooking spray. Heat until very hot. Add the scallops and sauté them for 3 to 4 minutes, until they are almost cooked. Remove the scallops and set them aside on a platter.

Add the spinach to the drippings in the skillet and cook for 2 to 3 minutes, until it has wilted (work in batches, if necessary). Sprinkle with the salt and pepper.

Divide the spinach among 6 plates and top with the scallops. Drizzle 2 or 3 tablespoons of sauce over each serving.

Per serving: 177 calories, 4.5 g. fat (21% of calories), 0.6 g. saturated fat, 37 mg. cholesterol, 579 mg. sodium.

Scallop Wontons with Tomato Sauce

Yield: 6 servings

*W*onton skins or wrappers, made from high-gluten flour, are available at most supermarkets. They are very thin, flavorful and easy to use. I fill the skins here with a scallop mousse flavored with shiitake mushrooms and scallions.

20	dried shiitake mushrooms (about 2 cups)
2	cups warm water
1¼	pounds sea scallops
3	egg whites
1	teaspoon salt
½	teaspoon freshly ground black pepper
5–6	scallions, washed, trimmed and finely chopped (¾ cup)
48	wonton wrappers, each 3″ square (12 ounces)
3	cups Tomato Sauce (page 18), warmed
	Fresh basil leaves sliced into a fine chiffonade (see page 100)

Soak the mushrooms in the water until soft. Drain (reserving the liquid for use in soup or stock, if desired). Cut off and discard the stems, which are tough. Cut the caps into ¼″ dice. (You should have about 2 cups.)

Remove and discard the tough sinews attached to the scallops and rinse them in cold water. Drain well. Transfer to the bowl of a food processor. Add the egg whites.

Process until smooth, then add the salt and pepper. Combine the scallop mixture in a mixing bowl with the mushrooms and scallions.

Lay 24 wonton wrappers out on a flat work surface and brush them lightly with cold water. Spoon about 2 tablespoons of the filling onto the center of each wrapper, top with a second wrapper and seal by pressing firmly around the edges.

Bring a large pot of water to a boil. Add 8 wonton packages, reduce the heat and cook the packages just under a boil (180°) for 6 to 8 minutes. Remove the packages from the water with a large skimmer and place them on a platter.

To serve, place 4 wonton packages on each plate, top with ½ cup of the tomato sauce and garnish with the basil. Cook the remaining wontons in 2 batches.

Per serving: 381 calories, 5.7 g. fat (14% of calories), 0.8 g. saturated fat, 31 mg. cholesterol, 894 mg. sodium.

Scallop Wontons with Tomato Sauce (page 132)
and Green Beans and Red Onions (page 222)

If you won't be serving the filled wontons right
away, cook them anyway and place them in a bowl of
cold water to cover. To use, drain them and drop into
boiling water for a few seconds to reheat them. Or
place on a plate and microwave briefly.

Mussel Boil

Mussel Boil

Yield: 6 servings

For this recipe, select small mussels that are heavy, indicating fullness and freshness. Commercially grown on nets or lines, mussels don't usually require much cleaning, although it's a good idea to rub them against one another under cold, running water to dislodge any sand and to remove and discard any beards.

4 pounds small mussels, washed and with beards removed

7–8 ounces fresh shiitake mushrooms, washed and with stems removed

1¼ cups dry, fruity white wine

5–6 medium shallots (about 6 ounces), peeled, trimmed and finely chopped (¾ cup)

4–5 scallions (about 3 ounces), washed, trimmed and finely chopped (¾ cup)

7–8 cloves garlic, peeled and thinly sliced (3 tablespoons)

2½ tablespoons balsamic vinegar

¾ teaspoon dried thyme

¾ teaspoon Tabasco hot-pepper sauce

Place the mussels in a very large saucepan or pot, preferably stainless steel.

Slice the mushrooms and add to the mussels. Add the wine, shallots, scallions, garlic, vinegar, thyme and hot-pepper sauce. Bring the mixture to a boil. (This will take 4 to 5 minutes.)

Boil, covered, for 2 minutes. Discard any mussels that have not opened and divide the remainder, along with the vegetables and juice, among 6 plates. Serve.

Per serving: 234 calories, 3.5 g. fat (14% of calories), 0 g. saturated fat, 86 mg. cholesterol, 453 mg. sodium.

Warm Shrimp Salad
with Fennel and Potatoes

Yield: 6 servings

*S*erve this salad lukewarm or at room temperature, but not hot. Slight
cooling enhances the flavor of the various ingredients, with the potatoes,
for example, absorbing some of the taste of the shrimp.

- 2 large potatoes (1 pound), peeled and cut into 1″ pieces
- 1½ cups water
- 1 fennel bulb (¾ pound)
- 2 tablespoons virgin olive oil
- 30 large shrimp (2 pounds), peeled, deveined, rinsed and patted dry
  with paper towels
- ¾ teaspoon salt
- ½ teaspoon freshly ground black pepper
- 1 small onion (about 3 ounces), peeled and chopped (½ cup)
- 1 small piece leek, trimmed, thinly sliced and washed (⅓ cup)
- 2 cloves garlic, peeled, crushed and finely chopped (1 teaspoon)
- ¼ cup dry white wine
- 2 tablespoons balsamic vinegar

Place the potatoes in a medium saucepan with the water. Bring to a boil and
cook over medium to high heat for 5 minutes.

Meanwhile, remove the upper ribs and fuzzy leaves from the fennel,
reserving the leaves for use as a garnish. Cut the bulb into ½″ pieces. (You'll
have about 3¼ cups.) Add the fennel to the saucepan and cook the mixture for
5 minutes longer. Most of the water should be gone; drain off any that remains
and place the vegetables in a bowl large enough to hold the shrimp later. Cover
and set aside.

Heat 1 tablespoon of the oil in a large nonstick skillet. When the oil is hot,
add the shrimp, salt and pepper. Sauté over high heat for 3 minutes. Add to the
bowl containing the fennel and potatoes.

Heat the remaining 1 tablespoon oil in the same skillet. When the oil is hot,
add the onions, leeks and garlic. Sauté for 30 seconds. Add the wine and
vinegar to the skillet, swirl the mixture and heat it for 1 to 2 seconds longer.
Add to the shrimp and vegetable mixture and toss to mix well.

Divide the shrimp and vegetables among 6 plates. Decorate with the reserved fennel leaves. Serve lukewarm or at room temperature.

Per serving: 255 calories, 6.1 g. fat (22% of calories), 1 g. saturated fat, 232 mg. cholesterol, 593 mg. sodium.

Balsamic vinegar is a special aged vinegar that has a unique taste. The best vinegar has been aged a long time, and its price reflects that quality. It has a subtle sweetness and is less acidic than other vinegars. Because of that, you can make delicious dressings using less oil than usual to balance the vinegar.

To devein shrimp, run a paring knife about ⅛" deep into the outside edge of a peeled shrimp. Use the tip of the knife to remove the vein, which can range from barely noticeable to quite prominent.

Top: Poached Shrimp and Potatoes in Vegetable Stock (page 139)
Bottom: Warm Shrimp Salad with Fennel and Potatoes (page 136)

Poached Shrimp and Potatoes in Vegetable Stock

Yield: 6 servings

his dish is similar to the hot crab boils popular in Louisiana and other southern states, except that it features shrimp instead of crab. The shrimp are added to the pot at the end of the cooking period. They're peeled at the table and eaten with the broth and vegetables for a casual, family-style main dish.

6	cups water
12	red potatoes (2 pounds), unpeeled but scrubbed, with blemishes removed
1	large onion (about 7 ounces), peeled and thinly sliced (1½ cups)
2	stalks celery (4 ounces), washed, trimmed and thinly sliced (1 cup)
3	scallions (2 ounces), washed, trimmed and thinly sliced (½ cup)
1	medium carrot (about 2½ ounces), trimmed, peeled and thinly sliced (½ cup)
¼	cup red wine vinegar
5	cloves garlic, peeled and thinly sliced (2 tablespoons)
2–3	bay leaves
1	teaspoon herbes de Provence (see page 13)
1	teaspoon salt
½	teaspoon freshly ground black pepper
½	teaspoon crushed red pepper flakes
2	pounds large unshelled shrimp (about 36)

Place the water, potatoes, onions, celery, scallions, carrots, vinegar, garlic, bay leaves, herbes de Provence, salt, black pepper and pepper flakes in a large pot and bring the mixture to a strong boil. Reduce the heat to low, cover and boil the mixture gently for 20 to 22 minutes, until the potatoes are tender when pierced with the tip of a sharp knife.

Add the shrimp to the pot. Bring the mixture back to a strong boil and boil for 10 seconds. Cover the pot, remove it from the heat and set it aside for at least 15 minutes before serving. Remove and discard the bay leaves. Divide the shrimp and broth among 6 bowls and serve.

Per serving: 278 calories, 1.6 g. fat (5% of calories), 0.4 g. saturated fat, 232 mg. cholesterol, 650 mg. sodium.

Light Double-Fluff Omelet

Yield: 3 servings

his light, fluffy omelet is a good lower-cholesterol alternative to a classic omelet. It contains four egg whites but only two egg yolks and will serve three people for breakfast or brunch. The whites are whipped slightly to add greater volume and lightness to the omelets. I serve the omelet with sautéed mushrooms and tomatoes here, but you can substitute another light garnish—perhaps lean ham and low-fat cheese—if you prefer. If you want to double the recipe, as you will when having guests, mix the ingredients for the two omelets separately. But you may prepare enough garnish for both omelets in one batch.

GARNISH

- 1 teaspoon canola oil
- 2–3 domestic mushrooms (about 2 ounces), washed and sliced (½ cup)
- ⅛ teaspoon salt
- ⅛ teaspoon freshly ground black pepper
- 1 tomato (about 4 ounces), seeded and cut into ½″ pieces (½ cup)
- 1 tablespoon chopped fresh chives

OMELET

- 4 egg whites
- ⅛ teaspoon salt
- 2 egg yolks
- 1 tablespoon chopped fresh chives
- 1 teaspoon unsalted butter
- 1 teaspoon canola oil

To make the garnish: Heat the oil in a nonstick skillet. When it is hot, add the mushrooms, salt and pepper. Cook for about 1 minute over high heat. Add the tomatoes and chives and sauté for 10 seconds. Set aside.

To make the omelet: Place the egg whites and salt in a large stainless steel bowl and beat with a whisk until fluffy (about 1 minute), but not at the soft-peak stage. Add the egg yolks and chives and mix them in well.

Heat the butter and oil in a 10″ nonstick skillet. When they are hot, add the egg mixture. Cook over high heat, stirring with a fork and shaking the pan at the same time, until the mixture is set (45 seconds to 1 minute). Run a spatula or the tines of the fork around the edge of the omelet to loosen it. Arrange half

Light Double-Fluff Omelet

the mushroom mixture in the center of the omelet. Roll the top and bottom edges toward the center to enclose the filling. Invert the omelet onto a 5- to 6-cup oval gratin dish. Decorate at both ends with the remaining mushrooms and tomatoes.

Serve immediately, cutting the omelet into three pieces.

Per serving: 57 calories, 4 g. fat (63% of calories), 1.1 g. saturated fat, 73 mg. cholesterol, 130 mg. sodium.

Chicken Breasts in Creamy Dill Sauce

Yield: 6 servings

*S*kinless, boneless chicken breasts are poached briefly here in a chicken stock flavored with white wine. Then the cooking liquid is reduced, thickened a little with instant potato flakes and finished with dill and lemon juice. Potato flakes work well as a thickening agent, creating a creamy, rich-appearing sauce. Dill is particularly good here, but another herb—chervil or tarragon, for example—could be used instead.

- 2 cups White Chicken Stock (page 14) or lower-salt canned chicken broth
- 1 cup dry white wine
- 1 medium onion (about 4 ounces), peeled and thinly sliced (1 cup)
- 1 teaspoon dried thyme
- ½ teaspoon salt (adjust if canned broth is used)
- ¼ teaspoon freshly ground black pepper
- 6 boneless, skinless chicken breast halves, trimmed of all surrounding fat (2 pounds)
- ½ cup instant potato flakes
- ½ cup loosely packed fresh dill, chopped (¼ cup)
- 2 tablespoons lemon juice

Bring the stock or broth, wine, onions, thyme, salt and pepper to a boil in a large saucepan and simmer the mixture for 2 minutes. Add the chicken breasts in a single layer. (They will be barely covered by the liquid.) Bring the mixture back to a full boil, reduce the heat to low, cover and cook at a very gentle boil for 5 minutes.

Remove the chicken from the saucepan with tongs, place it on a platter and cover while you make the sauce. (The chicken will continue to cook in its own residual heat.)

Bring the liquid in the saucepan back to a boil and boil it for 3 to 4 minutes, until it is reduced to 1¾ cups. Whisk in the potato flakes and bring the mixture back to a boil, then remove it from the heat and emulsify it with a hand blender for a smoother sauce. Stir in the dill and lemon juice. Return the chicken to the pan and warm it through without bringing the sauce to a boil.

To serve, arrange the chicken breasts on a platter and pour the sauce over them (or serve the breasts on individual plates, coating each piece with about ¼ cup of the sauce).

Per serving: 171 calories, 2.7 g. fat (14% of calories), 0.7 g. saturated fat, 61 mg. cholesterol, 243 mg. sodium.

Depending on its size, you should be able to get from 2 to 4 tablespoons of juice from a lemon. For the best yield, the lemon should be at room temperature. Before cutting it, roll it back and forth on the kitchen counter, exerting pressure with your palm. That will help break cell walls so they release more juice.

Sautéed Chicken and Fruit Curry

Yield: 6 servings

*C*hicken legs are featured in this spicy, delicious, unusual dish; dark meat is more flavorful and moist prepared this way than white meat, which tends to dry out. I use six chicken legs, one per person, weighing a total of almost 3½ pounds. By the time you remove the skin, fat and bone ends, the legs will weigh about 2¼ pounds.

If you don't like the assertive flavor of cilantro, substitute parsley. The dish can be made ahead, frozen and then reheated in a microwave oven or on the stove, with a little water added to keep it from burning.

6	chicken legs (about 3½ pounds)
2	Rome Beauty apples, unpeeled, but halved, cored and cut into 1″ dice (2 cups)
2	bananas, peeled and cut into ½″ slices
9–10	cloves garlic, peeled, crushed and finely chopped (2 tablespoons)
2	bay leaves
2	tablespoons curry powder
1	teaspoon cumin powder
1	teaspoon mustard seeds
1	teaspoon salt (adjust if canned broth is used)
½	teaspoon freshly ground black pepper
2	large onions (about 1 pound), peeled and thinly sliced (4 cups)
1½	cups White Chicken Stock (page 14) or lower-salt canned chicken broth
2	tablespoons chopped cilantro leaves

Using a cleaver or a sharp, heavy knife, cut off and discard the tips of the drumsticks and the knobby joint ends. Grasp hold of the chicken skin with a kitchen towel and pull it off. Remove any visible pieces of fat from the meat. Separate each leg into a thigh and drumstick.

In a bowl mix together the apples, bananas, garlic, bay leaves, curry powder, cumin, mustard seeds, salt and pepper. Set aside. Do not worry if the apple and banana pieces discolor slightly as they stand.

Coat a heavy nonstick pot lightly with vegetable cooking spray. Heat until hot. Add the chicken pieces and brown them for 5 to 6 minutes; turn them over,

(continued)

Sautéed Chicken and Fruit Curry

then brown them on the other side for 5 minutes. Transfer the chicken to a platter.

Add the onions to the pot and sauté them for 3 minutes. Stir in the stock or broth and the apple-banana mixture. Cook for 2 to 3 minutes longer.

Return the chicken to the pot, bring the mixture to a boil, cover, reduce the heat to low and boil gently for 25 minutes. Remove and discard the bay leaves. Arrange the chicken and fruit on a platter and sprinkle with the cilantro. Serve a drumstick and a thigh per person with a helping of the curried fruit.

Per serving: 292 calories, 9.1 g. fat (27% of calories), 2.3 g. saturated fat, 89 mg. cholesterol, 449 mg. sodium.

Curry powder is not an actual spice but a mixture of spices. In India, there are probably as many variations as there are cooks. If you want to make your own, here's a good blend. Using a spice mill, blender or mortar and pestle, grind 1 tablespoon coriander seeds, 2 teaspoons black peppercorns, 1 tablespoon cumin seeds, 1 teaspoon mustard seeds, ½ teaspoon cloves and ½ teaspoon hot-pepper flakes until powdered. Stir in 2 teaspoons turmeric and 1 teaspoon ground cinnamon. Store in a tightly covered jar.

Chicken African-Style

his dish is much better if the chicken is marinated in the seasonings for a few hours before it is cooked.

 1 chicken (4 pounds), skin removed from all parts but the wings
 2 medium onions (about 12 ounces), peeled and thinly sliced (3 cups)
 ⅓ cup lime juice
6–8 cloves garlic, peeled, crushed and finely chopped (1½ tablespoons)
 ½ teaspoon crushed red pepper flakes
 1 small piece fresh ginger, peeled and grated (1 tablespoon)
 ½ teaspoon salt
 ¼ teaspoon freshly ground black pepper
 2 tablespoons corn or canola oil

Cut the chicken into 10 pieces. For this recipe, use the legs (separate into thighs and drumsticks), the breasts (cut each in half crosswise) and the wings (remove tips and reserve with the remaining carcass bones for stock).

Combine the onions, lime juice, garlic, pepper flakes, ginger, salt and black pepper in a large bowl or baking dish. Roll the chicken pieces in the mixture. Cover and marinate in the refrigerator for at least for 4 or 5 hours, mixing every hour.

Heat the oil in a large nonstick skillet. When it is hot, add the pieces of chicken and brown them on all sides. Transfer the chicken to a large pot and discard any oil remaining in the skillet. Deglaze the skillet by adding the marinade and bringing it to a boil while stirring to loosen and melt any solidified juices in the skillet.

Pour the hot marinade over the chicken in the pot and bring it back to a boil. Cover, reduce the heat to low and cook the chicken at a very gentle boil for 15 minutes. Then remove the cover, transfer the chicken pieces to a platter and boil the sauce in the pot over high heat for 5 minutes to reduce it and concentrate its flavor.

Serve the meat as is with the sauce or pull it off the bones, shred it into long strips and return it to the sauce until it is warmed through. Serve immediately.

Per serving: 372 calories, 17 g. fat (41% of calories), 5.3 g. saturated fat, 124 mg. cholesterol, 251 mg. sodium.

Sautéed Chicken Legs
with Garlic Slivers and Balsamic Vinegar

Yield: 6 servings

or this recipe, skinless chicken legs are seasoned with herbs and cooked until brown and tender. To give intensity to the dish, the legs are served with a concentrated sauce made from the pan juices mixed with balsamic vinegar, red wine and garlic.

6	chicken legs (3½ pounds)
1	teaspoon dried thyme
1	teaspoon dried marjoram
½	teaspoon salt
½	teaspoon freshly ground black pepper
½	teaspoon virgin olive oil
¼	cup balsamic vinegar
¼	cup dry red wine
3	scallions (2 ounces), washed, trimmed and chopped (⅓ cup)
⅓	cup water
10–12	cloves garlic, peeled and thinly sliced (4 tablespoons)

Using a cleaver or a sharp, heavy knife, cut off and discard the tips of the drumsticks. Grasp hold of the chicken skin with a kitchen towel and pull it off. Remove any visible pieces of fat from the meat.

In a small bowl, combine the thyme, marjoram, ¼ teaspoon of the salt and ¼ teaspoon of the pepper.

Brush a large, heavy saucepan or nonstick skillet with the oil and heat it until hot. Add the chicken legs in a single layer and sprinkle the seasoning mix over them. Cover and cook over medium to low heat for 12 minutes. Turn the legs over, cover again and cook them for 12 minutes on the other side. The chicken should be well browned on all sides. Using tongs, transfer the legs to a serving platter and set them aside in a warm place while you prepare the sauce.

Add the vinegar and wine to the crystallized juices in the pan, bring the mixture to a boil and boil it for 30 seconds. Then add the scallions, water, garlic, the remaining ¼ teaspoon salt and the remaining ¼ teaspoon pepper. Boil for 2 minutes, until the mixture is reduced to ⅔ cup of concentrated liquid.

Sautéed Chicken Legs with Garlic Slivers and Balsamic Vinegar

To serve, discard any juices that have collected around the chicken on the platter and drizzle the sauce over the legs. Serve.

Per serving: 213 calories, 8.5 g. fat (37% of calories), 2.2 g. saturated fat, 89 mg. cholesterol, 270 mg. sodium.

Chicken Sauce Piquant

Yield: 6 servings

his lively chicken dish gets it zip from a sauce accented with red wine vinegar, fresh tomato and Tabasco sauce. These flavors blend well with the oregano and garlic also used as seasonings. The dish takes only a few minutes to cook after the ingredients are assembled and is a good dish to serve at room temperature for a buffet.

- 6 boneless, skinless chicken breast halves (about 6 ounces each), trimmed of all surrounding fat
- 1 teaspoon dried oregano
- ¾ teaspoon salt (adjust if canned broth is used)
- ¾ teaspoon freshly ground black pepper
- 2 tablespoons virgin olive oil
- 5–6 cloves garlic, peeled, crushed and finely chopped (1 tablespoon)
- ⅓ cup red wine vinegar
- 1 cup Brown Chicken Stock (page 12) or lower-salt canned chicken broth
- 2 medium tomatoes (10 ounces), peeled, seeded and coarsely chopped (about 1½ cups)
- 1½ teaspoons cornstarch dissolved in 1 tablespoon water (optional)
- ½ teaspoon Tabasco hot-pepper sauce
- 2 tablespoons chopped fresh chives, tarragon leaves or a mixture of both
- 2 tablespoons chopped fresh parsley leaves

Arrange the chicken in a single layer in a baking dish or pan. Sprinkle it with the oregano, salt, pepper and 1 tablespoon of the oil. Cover with plastic wrap and set it aside at room temperature for 1 hour (or refrigerate and marinate longer).

After the chicken has marinated, heat the remaining 1 tablespoon oil in a very large skillet set over medium-high heat. When the oil is hot, add the chicken pieces in a single layer. (If the chicken pieces are too crowded, they will not brown properly.) Sauté the chicken for 1½ minutes on each side, then transfer it to a platter, cover and keep warm in a 180° oven while you make the sauce.

Add the garlic to the skillet and cook it for about 10 seconds. Add the vinegar and bring the mixture to a strong boil. Continue boiling until the liquid is reduced to only 1 tablespoon. Add the stock or broth and tomatoes, bring the mixture to a boil, then reduce the heat to low and simmer it gently for 2 to 3 minutes. If the sauce is too thin, stir in the dissolved cornstarch. Add the hot-pepper sauce.

Return the chicken pieces to the skillet and cook them just long enough to heat them through.

Arrange the chicken on a platter, spoon the sauce on top and sprinkle with the chives or tarragon and parsley. Serve immediately.

Per serving: 194 calories, 7.6 g. fat (36% of calories), 1.5 g. saturated fat, 69 mg. cholesterol, 351 mg. sodium.

To peel a tomato, remove the core and cut a small X in the bottom end. Drop the tomato in boiling water for 15 to 20 seconds. Remove with a slotted spoon, rinse with cold water until cool enough to handle and peel away the skin.

To seed a tomato, cut it in half crosswise to expose the seeds. Squeeze each half gently to remove the seeds and excess juice. If you like, you may save the seeds and juice for use in stocks or sauces.

Chicken in Mustard Sauce (page 153) and Orechiette Pasta with Red Onion (page 268)

Chicken in Mustard Sauce

Yield: 6 servings

his chicken dish can be prepared quickly and easily, especially since skinless, boneless breasts are used. Quite flavorful cold as well as hot, it is also good served at room temperature for a buffet meal.

- 6 boneless, skinless chicken breast halves (6 ounces each), trimmed of all surrounding fat
- ½ teaspoon salt
- ½ teaspoon freshly ground black pepper
- 1 tablespoon corn, canola or virgin olive oil
- 1 medium onion (4 ounces), peeled and chopped (1 cup)
- 2 tablespoons all-purpose flour
- 1½ cups water
- 1 tablespoon Dijon mustard
- 1½ teaspoons dry mustard
- 1 tablespoon chopped fresh parsley leaves

Sprinkle the chicken with the salt and pepper. Heat the oil in a large, heavy skillet set over medium-high heat. When the oil is hot, sauté the chicken for 1½ minutes on each side, until nicely browned.

Mix in the onions and continue cooking the mixture for 1 minute.

Sprinkle the flour on the chicken pieces, then turn them over in the skillet so they are coated with flour on both sides. Cook for 1 minute to lightly brown the flour. Add the water and stir well to loosen any solidified juices in the bottom of the skillet.

Bring the mixture to a boil, reduce the heat to low, cover and boil gently for 2 minutes. Transfer the meat to a serving platter and keep it warm in a 180° oven while you finish the mustard sauce.

Bring the mixture in the skillet to a boil and add the Dijon mustard and dry mustard, mixing them in well with a whisk. Return the chicken pieces to the skillet and heat gently (just under a boil, so the sauce doesn't separate) for 5 to 6 minutes, or until the chicken is heated through.

Arrange the chicken and sauce on a platter. Sprinkle the parsley on top.

Per serving: 177 calories, 5.6 g. fat (30% of calories), 1.1 g. saturated fat, 69 mg. cholesterol, 272 mg. sodium.

Chicken Stir-Fry

Yield: 6 servings

his dish is prepared very quickly in the traditional Chinese stir-fry manner, but instead of cooking the chicken in a wok, I cook it in a non-stick skillet. Cornstarch and egg white create a light, delicate coating for the chicken pieces, and pepper flakes, sesame oil, garlic and ginger give the dish an assertive flavor that stands up well to the broccoli.

- 10 ounces broccoli
- 1 cup Brown Chicken Stock (page 12) or lower-salt canned chicken broth
- 4 tablespoons dark soy sauce
- ¼ teaspoon crushed red pepper flakes
- 1½ teaspoons cornstarch
- 2–3 skinless, boneless chicken breast halves (1 pound), trimmed of all surrounding fat and cut into 1½" pieces
- 1 egg white, lightly beaten with a fork
- 1½ tablespoons corn or canola oil
- 1 medium onion (about 5 ounces), peeled and thinly sliced (1¼ cups)
- 1 small piece fresh ginger, peeled and grated (1 tablespoon)
- 3–4 cloves garlic, peeled, crushed and finely chopped (2 teaspoons)
- 1½ teaspoons dark sesame oil

Cut the broccoli florets from the stalks and divide them into smaller pieces. Discard the tough stalk ends, then peel the remainder of the stalk pieces; slice them into long, narrow strips, approximately 4" × 1" × ¼".

Mix the stock or broth, soy sauce, pepper flakes and ½ teaspoon of the cornstarch together in a bowl. Set aside.

Place the chicken in another bowl and sprinkle it with the remaining 1 teaspoon cornstarch. Add the egg white and toss the chicken pieces to coat them with the mixture.

Heat the corn or canola oil in a large nonstick skillet. When it is hot, add the chicken pieces and cook them over very high heat for 2½ minutes, turning them as they brown. Remove the chicken from the skillet with a slotted spoon and place it on a plate.

Add the onions to the drippings in the skillet and sauté them for about

Chicken Stir-Fry

30 seconds. Add the broccoli pieces, cover the pan and cook for 2 minutes over medium heat, removing the cover and stirring occasionally.

Return the chicken to the skillet and add the ginger and garlic. Stir in the reserved chicken stock mixture and the sesame oil; cook for 30 seconds longer, until the chicken is heated through. Serve immediately.

Per serving: 137 calories, 6.1 g. fat (39% of calories), 1 g. saturated fat, 30 mg. cholesterol, 753 mg. sodium.

Chicken in a Pot

Chicken in a Pot

Yield: 6 servings

he idea here is to make a stock with chicken necks, backs and gizzards and then poach halved chickens in it. Removing all skin from the chicken reduces the amount of fat in the liquid. The best way to remove the remaining fat is to pour the stock into a tall, narrow container and let it sit undisturbed for a few minutes; the fat will come to the surface and can be skimmed off easily. An appealing assortment of vegetables—turnips, sweet potatoes, carrots, mushrooms and cabbage—is then cooked and served in this almost fat-free stock with pieces of the cooked chicken.

5	quarts water
2	pounds chicken necks, backs and gizzards, with skin removed
3	chicken halves (5 pounds)
2	stalks celery (about 4 ounces), washed, trimmed and thinly sliced (1 cup)
2	teaspoons salt
2–3	bay leaves
1	teaspoon herbes de Provence (see page 13)
1	teaspoon whole black peppercorns
12	whole cloves
3	medium to large leeks (1¾ pounds)
1	medium cabbage (2¼ pounds), halved and cored
2	large sweet potatoes (1½ pounds), peeled and halved
6	small turnips (1¼ pounds), peeled and halved
6	small carrots (about 1 pound), trimmed and peeled
12	dry shiitake mushroom caps

Place the water in a large, heavy pot. Add the chicken necks, backs and gizzards to the pot. Remove the wings from the chicken halves and add the wings to the pot. Bring the water to a boil and boil the mixture for 5 minutes. Then skim the surface of the liquid, removing and discarding fat and scum.

Add the celery, salt, bay leaves, herbes de Provence, peppercorns and cloves.

Wash the leeks and trim them; add the trimmings to the pot and bring the mixture back to a boil. Reduce the heat to low, partially cover (leave the lid ajar) and boil gently for 1 hour.

(continued)

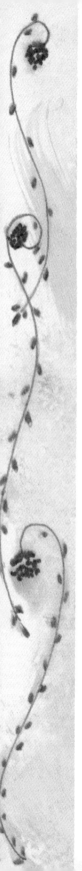

Using a kitchen towel to give you a better grip, grab hold of the skin on the chicken halves, pull it off and discard it. Add the chicken to the pot and place an inverted plate (smaller than the pot) on top to help keep the halves submerged in the stock. Bring the mixture back to a boil (this will take about 10 minutes), reduce the heat to low, cover and boil very gently for 15 minutes. Remove the pot from the heat and set it aside, covered, for 15 minutes. Then remove the chicken from the pot and set it aside on a platter to cool.

Strain the stock into another pot, preferably a tall, narrow one, and discard the solids in the strainer. (You should have about 4 quarts of stock.) Let the stock sit undisturbed for 10 minutes, then skim off and discard as much fat as possible (about ¾ cup) from the surface.

Tie the trimmed leeks into a compact bundle with kitchen string and add them to the defatted stock. Add the cabbage, sweet potatoes, turnips, carrots and mushrooms. Bring the mixture to a boil, reduce the heat to low, cover and boil gently for 30 minutes.

Meanwhile, when the chicken is cool enough to handle, separate each half into 2 pieces (a breast and a leg; if desired, remove the tips of the drumsticks with a cleaver).

When the vegetables have cooked for 30 minutes, return the chicken pieces to the pot and reheat them in the mixture at a gentle boil for 5 minutes.

To serve, remove the chicken pieces from the pot with a slotted spoon and arrange them on a large, deep platter. Still using the slotted spoon, lift out the vegetables and arrange them on the platter; untie the leeks and discard the string. Ladle some of the stock over the chicken and vegetables; pour the remainder into a soup tureen. At the table, serve a piece of chicken and an assortment of vegetables to each guest. Pass the additional stock.

Per serving (breast): 385 calories, 2.4 g. fat (6% of calories), 0.5 g. saturated fat, 68 mg. cholesterol, 455 mg. sodium.

Per serving (leg): 412 calories, 5.9 g. fat (13% of calories), 1.4 g. saturated fat, 104 mg. cholesterol, 490 mg. sodium.

Chicken in Lime and Yogurt Marinade

Yield: 6 servings

his chicken has an exotic taste from both Indian and Russian influences. The acidity of the yogurt goes well with the coriander, cumin and caraway. The chicken is easy to make and can be prepared up to cooking one day ahead; cover and refrigerate it until needed. Try to marinate the chicken in a pan that will fit under your broiler so it can go directly from the refrigerator to the oven.

⅔ cup plain nonfat yogurt

2–3 scallions, washed, trimmed and finely chopped (6 tablespoons)

6 strips lime rind removed with a vegetable peeler, coarsely chopped

2 tablespoons lime juice

4 cloves garlic, peeled and lightly crushed

2 teaspoons coriander seeds, crushed

1 teaspoon cumin powder

½ teaspoon caraway seeds

½ teaspoon freshly ground black pepper

½ teaspoon salt

6 boneless, skinless, chicken breast halves (about 6 ounces each), trimmed of all surrounding fat

In a bowl, combine the yogurt, scallions, lime rind, lime juice, garlic, coriander, cumin, caraway seeds, pepper and salt.

Roll the chicken pieces in the mixture and arrange them in a stainless steel pan that will fit under your broiler. Cover with plastic wrap and marinate at room temperature for 1 hour (or refrigerate and marinate overnight).

At cooking time, preheat the broiler.

Pour all but ¼ cup of the marinade into a small saucepan. Set aside.

Place the pan containing the chicken on the second oven shelf from the top under the broiler. Broil the chicken for 5 minutes on each side, then slice it on the diagonal and serve the equivalent of 1 chicken breast per person.

To serve the leftover marinade as a sauce, bring it to a simmer (160°) to kill any bacteria from the raw chicken marinated in it. Take care not to boil the mixture, as the yogurt in it may curdle. Serve with the chicken.

Per serving: 156 calories, 3.1 g. fat (18% of calories), 0.9 g. saturated fat, 69 mg. cholesterol, 258 mg. sodium.

Broiled Chicken Salad

Yield: 6 servings

his copious dish, served with the lukewarm meat arranged around the cold salad, contains vegetables as well as salad greens. The chicken breasts are flavored with a mixture of thyme, lemon rind and peppercorns before they are broiled. This simple, quick-cooking method (it requires ten minutes at most) keeps the chicken moist and tender. The sesame dressing I use here has a distinctive flavor, which is due largely to the dark sesame oil it contains. If you find this oil objectionable, substitute a milder-tasting oil, perhaps corn or canola.

3–4   medium potatoes (1½ pounds)

2   tablespoons fresh thyme leaves

6   strips lemon rind

½   teaspoon whole black peppercorns

6   boneless, skinless chicken breast halves, trimmed of all surrounding fat

6   cups loosely packed shredded iceberg lettuce

2   cucumbers (1 pound), peeled, seeded and cut into ½" dice (about 3 cups)

6   plum tomatoes (1 pound), cut into ¾" dice (2⅔ cups)

12   medium domestic mushrooms (8 ounces), washed and cut into ½" dice (2–2¼ cups)

12   small radishes, cut into ½" dice (1 cup)

⅓   cup Sesame Dressing (page 26)

2   tablespoons chopped fresh chives or parsley leaves

Scrub the potatoes, place them in a saucepan and add cold water to cover. Bring to a boil and cook until tender when pierced with the tip of a sharp knife. Drain, peel and cut into ½" slices or cubes. Set aside.

Grind the thyme, lemon rind and peppercorns in a mini-chop or coffee grinder and rub the mixture into both sides of the chicken breasts. Then coat the breasts lightly on both sides with vegetable cooking spray.

Preheat the broiler.

Arrange the chicken breasts in a single layer on a broiler rack and place the pan so the chicken is 3" to 4" from the heat. Broil the chicken for approximately 5 minutes on each side. Set it aside to cool slightly while you assemble the salad.

Combine the lettuce, cucumbers, tomatoes, mushrooms and radishes in a large bowl. Toss with the dressing and divide the salad among 6 dinner plates.

Broiled Chicken Salad

Cut each chicken breast on the diagonal into 5 slices and decoratively arrange overlapping slices of chicken and potatoes around the vegetables. Garnish with the chives or parsley. Serve.

Per serving: 333 calories, 8.4 g. fat (22% of calories), 1.5 g. saturated fat, 69 mg. cholesterol, 278 mg. sodium.

Turkey Cassoulet

Turkey Cassoulet

Yield: 6 servings

Cassoulet is an earthy dish from the southwest of France. Traditionally, it contains white beans, poultry and meat or sausage. In my leaner, healthier version, I use turkey breast, adding it at the end of the cooking period so it doesn't overcook and dry out. It is best to let the finished cassoulet sit for a few minutes before serving; this allows time for the flavors to develop, and the dish tastes better if not served too hot.

- 8 ounces dry white beans (pea, navy or great Northern)
- 4 cups White Chicken Stock (page 14) or lower-salt canned chicken broth
- 2 large carrots (about 9 ounces), trimmed, peeled and cut into 1″ pieces (1½ cups)
- 1 stalk celery, washed, trimmed and thinly sliced (½ cup)
- ½ teaspoon salt (adjust if canned broth is used)
- ¼ teaspoon dried thyme
- 2 bay leaves
- 3 whole cloves
- 1 medium onion (about 6 ounces), peeled
- 2 pounds boneless, skinless turkey breast, cut into strips about 2″ × ½″ × ¼″
- 1 small tomato (3 ounces), seeded and coarsely chopped (½ cup)
- ¼ cup chopped fresh parsley leaves
- 2 cloves garlic, peeled, crushed and finely chopped (1 teaspoon)
- ½ teaspoon Tabasco hot-pepper sauce

Sort the beans, discarding any stones or damaged beans. Wash the beans in a sieve under cold water.

Place the beans in a large pot with the stock or broth, carrots, celery, salt, thyme and bay leaves. Push the cloves into the onion and add the onion to the pot.

Bring the mixture to a boil, cover, reduce the heat to low and boil very gently for about 1½ hours (stirring every 15 to 20 minutes to keep the mixture from sticking to the bottom of the pot), until the beans are soft and tender but not mushy and most of the liquid has been absorbed.

(continued)

Remove the onion from the pot. Remove the cloves from the onion and discard them. Coarsely chop the onion and add it to the pot with the turkey, tomatoes, parsley and garlic. Bring the mixture back to a boil and boil it gently for 3 to 5 minutes, or until the turkey is opaque and cooked through.

Remove and discard the bay leaves, then serve, sprinkled with the hot-pepper sauce, within the next hour.

Per serving: 311 calories, 3.8 g. fat (11% of calories), 1.2 g. saturated fat, 66 mg. cholesterol, 270 mg. sodium.

Most of the dry beans sold in stores today are not more than a year old and do not really need to be soaked overnight. If you want to soak them anyway, two or three hours should be sufficient.

Turkey Fricassée with Brown Rice and Cumin

Yield: 6 servings

I use turkey leg meat in this earthy, satisfying dish because it is more moist than white turkey meat. The nutty taste of brown rice goes well with the turkey.

2	turkey legs (about 2½ pounds), with skin and any visible fat removed
5–6	cloves garlic, peeled
1	piece fresh ginger about the same size as the combined cloves of garlic, unpeeled but washed
2¾	cups water
1	teaspoon salt
1	teaspoon freshly ground black pepper
¼	teaspoon crushed red pepper flakes
3	medium onions (12 ounces), peeled and cut into 1″ dice (about 3 cups)
1	teaspoon ground cumin
1	cup uncooked brown rice
½	cup salt-free sun-dried tomatoes, halved and cut into 1–1½″ pieces
1	cup frozen tiny or petite peas, thawed
2	tablespoons chopped fresh parsley leaves

Divide the turkey legs into thighs and drumsticks. Cut the thighs in half.

Place the garlic and ginger in the bowl of a food processor and process until chopped. Transfer to a bowl and add the water, salt, black pepper and pepper flakes. Set aside.

Toss the onions and cumin together in another bowl. Set aside.

Lightly coat a heavy pot with vegetable cooking spray and heat the pot over high heat. When the pot is hot, add the turkey pieces in a single layer and cook them for 5 to 6 minutes per side, until browned all over. Transfer to a platter.

Add the onions to the pot. Sauté them for 10 minutes, until lightly browned. Add the rice and stir it into the onions.

Return the turkey to the pot and add the reserved garlic mixture. Stir in the tomatoes. Bring to a boil, cover, reduce the heat to low and boil gently for 45 minutes. Stir in the peas.

Arrange the turkey, rice and vegetables on a platter. Pull the bones and sinews from the drumsticks, if desired. Sprinkle the dish with the parsley. Serve.

Per serving: 340 calories, 6.6 g. fat (18% of calories), 1.9 g. saturated fat, 70 mg. cholesterol, 444 mg. sodium.

Turkey Steaks with Grape and Currant Sauce

Yield: 6 servings

ere's an elegant dish that makes a good dinner party entrée. You can buy a whole turkey breast and cut it into steaks yourself or you can ask your butcher to do this for you. Use steaks that are as close to ½" thick as possible, making appropriate adjustments in the cooking time to accommodate thicker or thinner ones.

2 tablespoons virgin olive oil
6 turkey breast steaks (6 ounces each and about ½" thick)
1 small leek (3–4 ounces), trimmed, chopped and washed
1 medium onion (4 ounces), peeled and chopped (about ⅔ cup)
¼ cup balsamic vinegar
¼ cup red wine vinegar
1½ cups Poultry Brown Base Sauce (page 16)
2 cups seedless green grapes
¼ cup dried currants
1 teaspoon salt
½ teaspoon freshly ground black pepper
2 tablespoons chopped fresh chives

Heat the oil in a very large heavy skillet set over high heat. When the oil is hot, add the turkey steaks and cook them for 2 to 3 minutes on each side. They will be slightly undercooked at this point; transfer them to a gratin dish and place them in a 180° oven while you make the sauce. (They can wait there for up to 30 minutes.)

Add the leeks and onions to the skillet and sauté them for 2 minutes. Add the balsamic vinegar and red wine vinegar; cook until they have almost evaporated.

Add the base sauce, grapes, currants, salt, pepper and any juices that have accumulated around the turkey steaks in the oven. Boil for 2 to 3 minutes, until the sauce thickens slightly.

Arrange the turkey steaks on a platter, cover them with the sauce and sprinkle the chives on top. Serve.

Per serving: 277 calories, 8.2 g. fat (27% of calories), 1.8 g. saturated fat, 74 mg. cholesterol, 483 mg. sodium.

Turkey Steaks with Grape and Currant Sauce

Turkey Meat Loaf
in Tomato-Mushroom Sauce

Yield: 6 generous servings

*t*urkey breast meat, which is very lean, can be purchased already ground at the supermarket for this recipe. Only one whole egg and an egg white are needed for this moist meat loaf containing fresh bread crumbs and flavorings that range from scallions to garlic, ginger, mushrooms and onion. A tomato sauce made with fresh tomatoes, sliced mushrooms and herbes de Provence is served with the loaf. Any moisture that emerges from the loaf during cooking will be reabsorbed if it is left to sit at room temperature for 20 to 30 minutes before it is served.

TURKEY MEAT LOAF

1½ pounds ground turkey breast

4 slices bread, processed into crumbs in a food processor (2 cups)

8 scallions (5–6 ounces), washed, trimmed and finely chopped (1 cup)

2–3 medium domestic mushrooms, washed and chopped (½ cup)

1 small onion (3 ounces), peeled and chopped (½ cup)

½ cup White Chicken Stock (page 14) or lower-salt canned chicken broth

1 egg

1 egg white

2–3 cloves garlic, peeled, crushed and finely chopped (1 teaspoon)

1 small piece fresh ginger, peeled and finely chopped (1 teaspoon)

1 teaspoon salt (adjust if canned broth is used)

¼ teaspoon freshly ground black pepper

Turkey Meat Loaf in Tomato-Mushroom Sauce (page 168)
and Puree of Lima Beans (page 226)

TOMATO-MUSHROOM SAUCE

4	large tomatoes (2 pounds), cut into 1″ pieces
1	tablespoon virgin olive oil
1	small onion (2–3 ounces), peeled and thinly sliced
1	stalk celery (about 2 ounces), washed, trimmed and chopped (½ cup)
5–6	medium domestic mushrooms (about 3 ounces), washed and thinly sliced (1½ cups)
2–3	cloves garlic, peeled and thinly sliced (1 tablespoon)
1	teaspoon herbes de Provence (see page 13) or Italian seasoning
1	teaspoon sugar
¾	teaspoon salt
¼	teaspoon freshly ground black pepper

To make the turkey meat loaf: Place the turkey, bread crumbs, scallions, mushrooms, onions, stock or broth, egg, egg white, garlic, ginger, salt and pepper in a bowl. Mix well.

Preheat the oven to 350°.

Lightly coat an 8″ × 4″ loaf pan with vegetable cooking spray. Press the meat mixture lightly but firmly into the pan. Cover the surface of the meat with a piece of plastic wrap, pressing it onto the surface of the loaf and making sure it does not extend over the edges of the pan. Cover the pan tightly with aluminum foil.

Bake for 1¼ hours, or until a meat thermometer inserted in the center of the loaf reads 160°. Set the loaf aside, covered, for 20 to 30 minutes.

To make the tomato-mushroom sauce: While the loaf is baking, place the tomatoes in the bowl of a food processor and process them until pureed.

Heat the oil in a saucepan. When it is hot, add the onions and celery; cook over low heat for 3 minutes. Then add the tomato puree, mushrooms, garlic, herbs, sugar, salt and pepper. Simmer for 5 minutes.

To serve, unmold the turkey loaf and cut it into 12 slices. Serve 2 slices per person with the sauce.

Per serving: 247 calories, 6.7 g. fat (24% of calories), 1.5 g. saturated fat, 85 mg. cholesterol, 789 mg. sodium.

Peppered Pork Steaks
with Apple-Vinegar Sauce

Yield: 6 servings

hese delicious pork steaks are prepared like the conventional steak au poivre, except that I add coriander seeds and mustard seeds to the peppercorns, crushing the three together and pressing them into the pork. Although 2 teaspoons of peppercorns may seem excessive, cracked peppercorns are not nearly as strong in flavor as ground pepper.

- 2 teaspoons whole black peppercorns
- 2 teaspoons coriander seeds
- 2 teaspoons mustard seeds
- 6 pieces pork tenderloin (6 ounces each), trimmed of surrounding fat, butterflied and pounded to a thickness of ½″
- 4 Golden Delicious apples (about 1½ pounds), unpeeled but halved, cored and cut into 1½″ chunks (6 cups)
- 1 cup water
- 1½ cups Poultry Brown Base Sauce (page 16)
- 2 tablespoons red wine vinegar
- 2 teaspoons sugar
- ½ teaspoon salt

Place the peppercorns, coriander seeds and mustard seeds together on a cutting board and crush them with a rolling pin or by pressing on them in a forward rolling motion with the base of a heavy skillet. Spread the crushed mixture out on the board and press the steaks into it, coating them evenly on both sides.

Lightly coat a very large nonstick skillet with vegetable cooking spray and heat it over high heat. When it is hot, add the pork and cook for 4 minutes on 1 side. Then turn the steaks over and continue cooking them for 3 to 4 minutes on the other side. Transfer the meat to an ovenproof platter and keep it warm.

Add the apples and the water to the skillet. Bring the mixture to a boil, cover and cook for 1½ minutes. Add the base sauce, vinegar, sugar and salt. Cook, uncovered (to reduce the liquid), for about 5 minutes, until the apples are just tender. Pour the sauce over the pork.

Per serving: 266 calories, 6.1 g. fat (20% of calories), 1.9 g. saturated fat, 101 mg. cholesterol, 305 mg. sodium.

Pork Tenderloin with Apples and Onions

Yield: 6 servings

i use tenderloin in this dish. It is the leanest and most tender portion of pork. It should be trimmed of any sinews or fat, butterflied and pounded to a thickness of about ½". The pork is sautéed for only a short time but continues to cook in its own residual heat, which gives excellent results. The richness of the meat is complemented by the tartness of the apples and vinegar.

- 6 pieces pork tenderloin (6 ounces each), trimmed of surrounding fat, butterflied and pounded to a thickness of ½"
- ½ teaspoon dried thyme
- ¾ teaspoon freshly ground black pepper
- 2 onions (8–9 ounces), peeled and thinly sliced (2 cups)
- ⅓ cup cider vinegar
- ⅓ cup cold water
- 1 teaspoon sugar
- 1 teaspoon ground cumin or caraway seeds
- 1½ pounds Rome Beauty apples, unpeeled but halved lengthwise, cored and thinly sliced crosswise
- ¾ teaspoon salt

Season the pork with the thyme and ¼ teaspoon of the pepper.

Lightly coat 2 nonstick skillets with vegetable cooking spray and place them over high heat. When they are hot, add the pork and cook it for 2 to 3 minutes on each side. Transfer the meat to an ovenproof platter and keep it warm in a 180° oven while you make the sauce.

Divide the onions between the skillets and sauté them for about 3 minutes, until they are softened. Combine all the onions in 1 of the skillets.

Add the vinegar, water, sugar and cumin or caraway seeds to the skillet. Stir in the apples, salt and the remaining ½ teaspoon pepper. Cover and boil the mixture gently over medium heat for 4 to 5 minutes, until the liquid is almost gone and the apples are moist and tender.

Return the pork (and any juices that have accumulated on the platter) to the skillet and reheat for 1 to 2 minutes. Serve immediately.

Per serving: 230 calories, 4.8 g. fat (18% of calories), 1.5 g. saturated fat, 81 mg. cholesterol, 328 mg. sodium.

Pork Tenderloin with Apples and Onions (page 172)
and Mashed Potatoes and Carrots (page 265)

Broiled Pork Loin Chops with Sage

Broiled Pork Loin Chops with Sage

Yield: 6 servings

*S*ince the pork chops for this dish are trimmed of all surrounding fat, it is important to cook them quickly to keep them from drying out. After seasoning the chops with garlic and soy sauce, I broil them for four minutes, then serve them coated with a mixture of chopped sage, lemon juice and lemon rind.

2 cloves garlic, peeled, crushed and finely chopped
   (1 teaspoon)
½ teaspoon soy sauce
¼ teaspoon freshly ground black pepper
6 pork loin chops (about 7 ounces each and ½"–¾" thick),
   trimmed of surrounding fat
¼ teaspoon salt
   About 6 fresh sage leaves, chopped (1 tablespoon)
   Grated rind of 1 lemon (1½ teaspoons)
2 tablespoons lemon juice

Preheat the oven broiler. Line a baking tray with aluminum foil.

Combine the garlic, soy sauce and pepper in a small bowl.

Sprinkle the pork chops with the salt and brush them on 1 side with half of the seasoning mixture. Place the chops, seasoned side down, on the tray and brush them on the other side with the remainder of the seasoning mixture.

Place the chops under the broiler so they are 3" to 4" from the heat. Broil for 4 minutes, turn, then broil for 4 minutes on the other side.

In a small bowl combine the sage, lemon rind and lemon juice.

Turn the chops so the moist underside is facing up and arrange them on a platter. Add any accumulated juices from the tray to the sage mixture in the bowl. Using a pastry brush, paint the chops with the mixture. Cover loosely and let rest for 5 minutes before serving.

Per serving: 244 calories, 7 g. fat (27% of calories), 2.4 g. saturated fat, 134 mg. cholesterol, 215 mg. sodium.

Honeyed Ham Steaks

For this recipe, use low-fat ham or even turkey ham, both of which are available now at most supermarkets. If salt intake is a concern, look for a lower-sodium variety. The steaks, each about 1" thick, are first sautéed in a nonstick skillet, then coated with a sweet-hot seasoning mixture and finished under a hot broiler.

- 1 teaspoon virgin olive or canola oil
- 6 lean ham steaks (6 ounces each and ¾"–1" thick)
- ¼ cup honey
- 4 teaspoons balsamic vinegar
- ½ teaspoon ground cumin
- ¼ teaspoon ground red pepper

Preheat the broiler. Line a baking tray with aluminum foil.

Brush a large, nonstick skillet with ½ teaspoon of the oil and place it over high heat. When the oil is hot, add 3 of the ham steaks and sear them for 3 minutes on each side, until they are nicely browned. Transfer to the tray.

Brush the skillet with the remaining ½ teaspoon oil and repeat the browning process with the remaining 3 pieces of ham. Transfer these to the tray.

Combine the honey, vinegar, cumin and pepper in a small bowl. Using a spoon, coat the surface of the steaks with about half the seasoning mix.

Place the steaks under the broiler on the second rack from top, so they are 7" to 8" from the heat. Broil them for 5 to 6 minutes. Transfer the steaks to a platter and coat them with the remaining honey mixture. Pour any sauce remaining on the tray over the steaks. Serve immediately.

Per serving: 234 calories, 6.8 g. fat (26% of calories), 3.2 g. saturated fat, 90 mg. cholesterol, 1,702 mg. sodium.

Honeyed Ham Steaks (page 176) topped with Black Bean Relish (page 228) and Cauliflower with Herbed Crumb Topping (page 242)

Navarin of Lamb

Yield: 6 servings

his dish is more flavorful if it is prepared ahead. The meat can be browned and cooked with the onions, garlic, water, flour and seasonings up to a day in advance. The potatoes, carrots and peas can be added a few hours before serving. Other vegetables can be substituted for those listed here; make your choices based on the time of year and market availability.

2 large potatoes (1 pound)

2 tablespoons corn, safflower or canola oil

1½ pounds lean leg of lamb, trimmed of all visible fat and cut into 2″ pieces

1 medium onion (5 ounces), peeled and thinly sliced (1 cup)

1 tablespoon all-purpose flour

3 cups water

2–3 cloves garlic, peeled, crushed and finely chopped (1½ teaspoons)

1 teaspoon salt

½ teaspoon freshly ground black pepper

2 bay leaves

2 carrots, trimmed, peeled and cut into sticks 2″ × ½″

1 cup fresh peas or frozen petite peas, cooked in boiling water until tender

Chopped fresh parsley leaves

Peel the potatoes and cut them into 1½″ dice. Place in a bowl of cold water to prevent discoloration. Set aside.

Heat the oil in a large, heavy pot over high heat. When it is hot, add the lamb. Reduce the heat to medium and cook for about 15 minutes, turning the pieces so they brown on all sides. Using a slotted spoon, transfer the meat to a plate. Pour out and discard the fat accumulated in the pot; return the meat (and any liquid that has accumulated on the plate) to the pot.

Add the onions to the pot, stir well and sauté for 1 minute over medium heat. Then add the flour, mix well and cook again for 1 minute. Mix in the water, garlic, salt, pepper and bay leaves. Bring to a boil, cover, reduce the heat to low and boil gently for 30 minutes.

Drain the potatoes well and add them to the pot along with the carrots.

Bring the mixture to a boil, then reduce the heat to low and boil it gently for another 25 minutes. (The *navarin* doesn't have much sauce, so I prefer to cook the carrots until soft and the potatoes until a bit mushy.) Add the peas and cook for 5 minutes longer. Remove and discard the bay leaves.

Arrange the meat and vegetables on a large platter or divide it among individual plates, sprinkle with the parsley and serve immediately.

Per serving: 244 calories, 6 g. fat (22% of calories), 1.9 g. saturated fat, 57 mg. cholesterol, 413 mg. sodium.

When browning meat, be sure to use a pan large enough to hold the pieces in a single layer, preferably with a little space around them. If the meat is overcrowded, it will begin to stew rather than brown. Work in batches if you do not have a pan large enough to properly accommodate all the pieces at once.

Broiled Lamb Kabobs

Yield: 6 servings

I usually broil these kabobs under my oven broiler, but you can do them outside on a barbecue grill for about the same length of time and then transfer them to a warm oven, as indicated in the recipe. Select very lean lamb, preferably from the leg. Trim it well and cut it into thin pieces, each about 2" across. Although lemon juice is sprinkled over the meat just before it is served, I don't use it in the marinade because it tends to set the protein in the meat and turn it a whitish color.

2	tablespoons soy sauce
2	teaspoons dried thyme
4	cloves garlic, peeled, crushed and finely chopped (2 teaspoons)
1½	teaspoons virgin olive oil
1	teaspoon salt
½	teaspoon freshly ground black pepper
3	medium onions (12 ounces), peeled
1¾	pounds lean leg of lamb, trimmed of all visible fat and cut into 36 pieces about 2" × 2" × ⅜"
3	green bell peppers (12 ounces), halved, cored, seeded and cut into 6 square pieces each
12	large domestic mushrooms (8 ounces), washed and with stems removed (reserve stems for another use)
1	tablespoon lemon juice

A few hours before serving, combine the soy sauce, thyme, garlic, oil, salt and black pepper in a bowl large enough to hold the meat and vegetables.

Cut the onions into 6 wedges each, being careful to keep the layers attached as well as possible at the root and top ends. Cut each wedge in half crosswise. Place in the bowl. Add the lamb, green peppers and mushrooms. Mix well, cover and refrigerate.

At cooking time, remove the meat and vegetables from the marinade. On each of 6 metal skewers, alternately thread 6 pieces of meat, 6 pieces of onion, 3 pieces of green pepper and 2 mushroom caps, beginning and ending with onions. Don't pack the skewers too tightly. Balance the ends of the filled skewers on opposite sides of a baking pan so the meat and vegetables are suspended over the pan without touching it.

Preheat the broiler.

Place the pan under the broiler and broil the meat and vegetables on each

Broiled Lamb Kabobs (page 180) and Brown Rice with Celery and Onions (page 272)

side for 3 to 4 minutes. Transfer the pan to a warm place (such as a 200° to 250° oven) and allow the kabobs to rest for a few minutes.

Unthread the skewers and serve the contents of 1 skewer per person on individual plates, sprinkling the meat and vegetables with a little of the pan juices (but not any uncooked marinade) and the lemon juice.

Per serving: 197 calories, 6.6 g. fat (30% of calories), 2.2 g. saturated fat, 67 mg. cholesterol, 288 mg. sodium.

Roasted Leg of Lamb with Mirepoix (page 183) and Pommes Boulangère (page 262)

Roasted Leg of Lamb
with Mirepoix

Yield: 6 servings

*i*t is important here that the lamb be well trimmed; in fact, I even recommend opening the rolled leg as it comes from the market and cutting off additional visible fat and sinews. The leg is first browned on top of the stove, then roasted in the oven on a *mirepoix (finely diced carrots, onions and mushrooms)* along with whole cloves of garlic. Note that since there is little fat and sinew to hold the muscles of the well-trimmed leg together, they may tend to separate into pieces during cooking. When slicing the leg at serving time, follow the shape of the meat, cutting each piece into thin slices. The meat should be pink and tender.

  1 boneless leg of lamb (4 pounds)

  1 teaspoon dried rosemary

  2 teaspoons herbes de Provence (see page 13)

 ¼ teaspoon chili powder

 ½ teaspoon salt

 ½ teaspoon freshly ground black pepper

 ½ teaspoon virgin olive oil

  2 large onions (about 14 ounces), peeled and cut into ½″ dice (2½ cups)

  2 medium carrots (5½ ounces), trimmed, peeled and cut into ½″ dice (1 cup)

5–6 medium domestic mushrooms (about 3 ounces), washed and cut into ½″ dice (1 cup)

 12 cloves garlic, peeled

  1 cup water

 ½ cup V-8 juice

 ¼ cup dry white wine

  1 tablespoon Worcestershire sauce

  1 tablespoon soy sauce

    Trim as much visible fat as possible from the surface of the rolled lamb leg, then unroll the leg as well as you can and cut out any visible pieces of fat or sinews from the interior, not worrying if a little remains. (You should have about 3 pounds of meat.) Sprinkle the inside surface of the leg with the rosemary and 1 teaspoon of the herbes de Provence.

(continued)

In a small bowl, combine the chili powder, ¼ teaspoon of the salt and ¼ teaspoon of the pepper. Sprinkle this mixture evenly on the interior of the leg. Reroll the leg and tie it securely at intervals with string to hold it together. Sprinkle the exterior of the roast with the remaining ¼ teaspoon salt and ¼ teaspoon pepper.

Brush a very large cast-iron skillet with the oil. Place the skillet over high heat until it is hot. Add the lamb and brown it over medium to high heat for 10 minutes, turning it in the pan as it browns, until it is evenly colored on all sides.

Meanwhile, combine the onions, carrots, mushrooms and garlic in a bowl. Sprinkle them with the remaining 1 teaspoon herbes de Provence and toss well to mix.

Remove the browned lamb from the skillet and set it aside on a plate. Add the onion mixture to the drippings in the pan, tossing the vegetables to coat them with the drippings, and sauté for 1 minute over medium to high heat. Return the lamb to the skillet, placing the lamb on top of the vegetables, and add any juices that have accumulated on the plate.

Preheat the oven to 400°.

Place the skillet in the oven for 20 minutes. Turn the lamb over and roast for 15 minutes longer, or until an instant-read thermometer inserted in the center reads 115° to 120° for medium-rare meat. Remove the skillet from the oven. Transfer the lamb to a platter, cover and set aside for 20 minutes.

While the lamb is resting, combine the water, V-8 juice, wine, Worcestershire sauce and soy sauce in a bowl. Add these to the drippings and vegetables in the skillet. Bring the mixture to a strong boil. Reduce the heat to low and simmer for 5 minutes. (You should have about 2 cups.) Add any juices that have collected around the lamb to the sauce.

To serve, cut several thin, diagonal slices from the leg. Pour a little sauce on the serving platter and arrange the slices on the platter alongside the uncut portion of the leg. Finish slicing the roast at the table and serve 2 or 3 slices per person. Serve with the additional sauce.

Per serving: 315 calories, 10.7 g. fat (31% of calories), 3.6 g. saturated fat, 115 mg. cholesterol, 544 mg. sodium.

Lamb Steaks in Sweet Piquant Sauce

Yield: 6 servings

he sweet-sour sauce served with these lamb steaks is also good with Spicy Flank Steak with Lettuce Fajitas (page 204), Pepper Steak (page 199) or sautéed chicken breasts.

- 6 lamb steaks cut from the leg, trimmed of all visible fat (4 ounces each)
- ¾ teaspoon freshly ground black pepper
- 1 tablespoon corn or canola oil
- ⅓ cup white wine vinegar
- ½ teaspoon dried oregano
- ¾ cup Poultry Brown Base Sauce (page 16)
- 1 tablespoon currant jelly
- ¾ teaspoon salt

Pound the lamb steaks to ¾″ thickness and season on both sides with the pepper.

Heat the oil in a very large nonstick skillet (or 2 smaller ones) set over high heat. When it is hot, add the lamb in a single layer and cook for about 1½ minutes on each side for medium-rare meat. Transfer the lamb to a plate and set it aside near the stove while you make the sauce.

Add the vinegar and oregano to the skillet (or divide between the 2 skillets) and cook, stirring with a wooden spatula to help melt any solidified juices, until the mixture is reduced to 2 tablespoons. (If using 2 skillets, at this point combine the contents of both into 1 of the pans.)

Mix in the base sauce, jelly, salt and any juices that have accumulated around the meat on the plate. Cook for about 1 minute to reduce the mixture to about ¾ cup.

To serve, arrange the steaks, whole or cut into slices, on warm individual plates. Top each serving with 3 tablespoons of the sauce.

Per serving: 158 calories, 7.3 g. fat (43% of calories), 2.1 g. saturated fat, 57 mg. cholesterol, 337 mg. sodium.

Sautéed Veal Chops
with Vegetables

Yield: 6 servings

t is important that you use good-quality veal for this dish. Plume de veau, *pale pink with very white fat,* or provimi *veal is best. Each chop should be approximately ¾" thick and be trimmed of all surrounding fat. I don't cook the veal very long; instead, I set it aside for a short while before serving so it can continue to cook until moist and tender in its own residual heat.*

- 1 tablespoon plus 2 teaspoons virgin olive oil
- 6 bone-in veal chops (6–8 ounces each), trimmed of all visible fat
- 1 medium green bell pepper (about 5 ounces)
- 1 medium red bell pepper (about 5 ounces)
- 8 ounces radishes (about 20), each cut in half
- ½ cup water
- 12 ounces large domestic mushrooms, washed and cut into ¼" slices (about 3½ cups)
- ¾ teaspoon salt
- 1 tablespoon chopped fresh chives

Heat 1 tablespoon of the oil in a very large skillet (or 2 smaller ones). When it is hot, add the chops in a single layer and cook them over medium to high heat for 3 minutes. Then turn the chops over and cook them on the other side for 3 minutes. Remove the pan from the heat, cover with a lid and set the chops aside for at least 15 minutes before serving. (Juices will emerge from the veal and create a natural gravy.)

Peel the green and red peppers with a vegetable peeler. Halve the peppers and remove the cores and seeds; cut each half into 12 strips. Set aside.

Arrange the radishes in a single layer in a stainless steel saucepan and add the water. Bring to a boil and cook the radishes for 4 to 5 minutes, until they are softened slightly but still crunchy. Set aside.

Heat the remaining 2 teaspoons oil in a skillet. When it is hot, add the mushrooms and sauté them for about 3 minutes, or until the liquid that emerges from them evaporates. Add the pepper strips, radishes and salt. Sauté the mixture for another minute over high heat.

Sautéed Veal Chops with Vegetables

Divide the vegetables among 6 warm plates and place a veal chop in the center of each plate. Pour any natural juices that have emerged from the chops on top and sprinkle with the chives. Serve immediately.

Per serving: 180 calories, 7.3 g. fat (37% of calories), 1.5 g. saturated fat, 92 mg. cholesterol, 369 mg. sodium.

Pan-Seared Veal Chops
with Herbes de Provence

Yield: 6 servings

*V*eal chops are expensive, but it is important that you select good-quality, well-trimmed ones for this dish. The chops are flavored with herbes de Provence and sautéed in a cast-iron or heavy aluminum skillet to ensure that there will be some caramelization of the cooking juices—not a certainty when meat is cooked in nonstick pans. Although the chops are removed from the heat before they are fully cooked, they finish cooking in their own residual heat as they rest on a platter before serving. A light lemon-thyme sauce, in combination with the reserved cooking juices, complements the veal.

VEAL

2 teaspoons herbes de Provence (see page 13)

½ teaspoon freshly ground black pepper

¼ teaspoon salt

6 boneless veal chops (4 ounces each and ¾″ thick), trimmed of all surrounding fat

1 teaspoon virgin olive oil

LEMON-THYME SAUCE

2 tablespoons lemon juice

2 teaspoons chopped fresh thyme leaves

2 teaspoons soy sauce

1 scallion, washed, trimmed and finely chopped (2 tablespoons)

2 teaspoons virgin olive oil

To make the veal: Combine the herbes de Provence, pepper and salt in a small bowl. Sprinkle the veal chops with the mixture.

Heat a 10″ to 12″ cast-iron skillet over high heat. Brush the skillet with ½ teaspoon of the oil. Add 3 of the veal chops and cook them over high heat for 3 minutes on each side. Remove the chops from the heat (they are not fully cooked at this point) and place them on a platter. Cover and set aside for 4 to 5 minutes to continue cooking in their own residual heat. Pour any juices that have accumulated in the skillet into a small bowl.

Brush the skillet with the remaining ½ teaspoon oil and cook the remaining 3 chops as indicated above. Transfer them to the plate with the other chops, cover and let rest for 4 to 5 minutes. Add any accumulated juices in the skillet to the previously reserved juices.

To make the lemon-thyme sauce: While the veal rests, combine the lemon juice, thyme, soy sauce, scallions and oil in a small bowl. Add the reserved cooking juices and any juices that have accumulated around the meat on the plate.

Transfer the veal to a serving platter. Pour the sauce over them. Serve immediately.

Per serving: 129 calories, 6 g. fat (43% of calories), 1.8 g. saturated fat, 71 mg. cholesterol, 351 mg. sodium.

Veal Scallopini with Snow Peas and Asparagus (page 191)
and Basic Couscous (page 273)

Veal Scallopini
with Snow Peas and Asparagus

Yield: 6 servings

his scallopini requires very good quality veal. Select your meat from a large muscle, preferably the top round, and instruct your butcher to trim it completely. If the scallopini is cut to the ⅜" thickness called for here, cook it as instructed; if it is thinner, however, reduce the cooking time so the meat doesn't dry out. This same recipe also can be prepared with turkey breast steaks, which are less expensive than veal and are quite tasty.

6	veal scallopini from the top round (6 ounces each and ⅜" thick)
4–5	spears asparagus with tight, firm tips (6 ounces), peeled, trimmed and cut into 2" lengths (2 cups)
6	ounces snow peas, strings removed (2 cups)
⅔	cup Poultry Brown Base Sauce (page 16)
⅔	cup water
12	large cherry tomatoes (7 ounces), halved
½	teaspoon salt
½	teaspoon freshly ground black pepper

Lightly coat a large skillet with vegetable cooking spray and heat it on top of the stove. When the pan is hot, add the veal in a single layer and sauté over medium to high heat for about 1½ minutes on each side. Transfer the meat to a platter and keep it warm.

Add the asparagus, snow peas, base sauce, water, tomatoes, salt and pepper to the skillet. Cook the mixture for 3 to 4 minutes, just until the vegetables are tender.

Arrange the scallopini on a platter and pour the sauce and vegetables over it. Serve.

Per serving: 361 calories, 11.4 g. fat (28% of calories), 3.8 g. saturated fat, 200 mg. cholesterol, 359 mg. sodium.

Fricadelles of Veal in Tomato Sauce

Yield: 6 servings

B *uy veal stew meat for this dish; it is less expensive than other cuts, and you can select only the leanest pieces and then remove any remaining fat and sinews from the meat before proceeding with the recipe. Alternatively, you can use white turkey meat instead of veal.*

You'll notice that I add ice to the meat when I'm grinding it in the food processor. That adds moisture, making the patties juicier. Additional moisture comes from vegetables that extend the meat and lend color and flavor to the patties. The dish is attractively framed with red tomato sauce.

If prepared ahead, the patties will keep for 30 to 40 minutes in a 180° oven, but their cooking time should be shortened a little to compensate for this.

2–3 slices bread, processed into crumbs in a food processor (1⅓ cups)

½ cup skim milk

1½ pounds veal stew meat, trimmed of all fat and cut into 1″ cubes

½ cup crushed ice

¼ teaspoon salt

⅛ teaspoon freshly ground black pepper

½ small leek (2–3 ounces), trimmed, chopped and washed (½ cup)

1–2 medium carrots, trimmed, peeled and cut into ¼″ dice (1 cup)

2–3 ounces spinach, trimmed and washed (2 cups)

1 small zucchini (4 ounces), washed, trimmed and cut into ⅜″ dice (1 cup)

1 tablespoon unsalted butter

1 tablespoon canola or corn oil

3 cups Tomato Sauce (page 18), warmed

Place the bread crumbs in a bowl and add the milk. Let the crumbs soak in the milk.

Meanwhile, place half of the veal in the bowl of a food processor and process until it is ground. Add half of the ice and process briefly to blend. Add half of the salt, half of the pepper and half of the bread mixture; process for 5 seconds. Transfer the mixture to a large bowl. Repeat with the remaining meat, ice, salt, pepper and bread mixture. Transfer to the bowl. Set aside.

Bring about ¼″ of water to a boil in a large stainless steel saucepan. When it is boiling, add the leeks and carrots; cook them for 2 to 3 minutes. Then add the spinach and zucchini; cook for another minute, until the spinach is wilted and most of the moisture has evaporated.

Transfer the vegetables to a platter and allow them to cool to room temperature. When they are cool, drain off and discard any moisture that has collected around them. Add the vegetables to the bowl containing the meat mixture. Mix well and form into 6 equal-size patties, each about ¾″ thick.

Heat the butter and oil in a large skillet over high heat. When hot, add the patties, reduce the heat and cook over medium to low heat for 6 to 8 minutes, until nicely browned. Then turn them over and cook them for 2 to 3 minutes on the other side, just long enough to cook them through without drying them out. Serve immediately or keep warm in a 180° oven until ready to serve.

At serving time, spoon ½ cup of the tomato sauce onto each of 6 plates, top with a veal patty and serve.

Per serving: 264 calories, 13.4 g. fat (45% of calories), 3.7 g. saturated fat, 77 mg. cholesterol, 433 mg. sodium.

When dicing carrots, first cut a thin lengthwise strip from the vegetable. Place the carrot, cut side down, on your cutting board; that prevents it from rocking as you proceed with the dicing. This technique works well with any rounded vegetable.

Veal Roast
with Shiitake Mushrooms and Onions

Yield: 6 servings

this is a costly, luxurious dinner, so you must take care not to overcook the veal. I suggest you use either the top or bottom round—both are very lean. Containing little fat or sinew, these cuts don't require lengthy cooking to become tender, and a shorter cooking time means that they retain their pink interior color and don't shrink too much.

Browning the roast first on top of the stove crystallizes the meat's surface and gives it an intense flavor. After cooking, the roast can be kept in a 180° oven for up to one hour. Any juices it releases can be added to the sauce.

- 1 cup dried shiitake mushrooms (about 1½ ounces)
- 1¼ cups water
- 1 lean veal roast (2¼ pounds) from the top or bottom round, trimmed of all surrounding fat
- ½ teaspoon dried thyme
- ¼ teaspoon freshly ground black pepper
- 1 tablespoon unsalted butter
- 50–55 frozen boiling onions (about half a 16-ounce package, 1¼ cups)
- 12–15 cloves garlic, peeled
- ½ cup Poultry Brown Base Sauce (page 16)
- ½ teaspoon salt

In a small bowl, combine the mushrooms and water. Set aside to soak.

Sprinkle the roast with the thyme and pepper. Heat the butter in a large, heavy, ovenproof, nonstick skillet. When it is hot, add the roast and brown it over medium-high heat, turning it every 3 or 4 minutes, for a total of 10 minutes.

Preheat the oven to 400°.

Place a meat thermometer in the meat at its thickest part and roast for 30 minutes, until the thermometer registers 120° to 130°. Remove the meat from the skillet and set it aside in a warm place.

Remove the shiitake mushrooms from the soaking liquid, reserving the liquid; cut off and discard their stems, which are tough. Add the mushroom caps, onions and garlic to the drippings in the skillet and sauté them for 1 to 2 minutes. Add the reserved mushroom liquid, pouring it in carefully and leaving behind any sandy residue in the bottom of the soaking dish.

Stir in the base sauce and salt. Bring the mixture to a boil, cover, reduce the

Veal Roast with Shiitake Mushrooms and Onions

heat to low and boil very gently for 5 minutes. Mix in any juices that have accumulated around the roast.

Place the roast on a platter and surround it with the vegetables and the sauce. Cut the meat into slices and serve.

Per serving: 224 calories, 7.9 g. fat (32% of calories), 3.5 g. saturated fat, 112 mg. cholesterol, 286 mg. sodium.

Veal Stew Niçoise

Yield: 6 servings

For this stew, I use veal from the shoulder, chuck or shank, all lean cuts that are moist because they are gelatinous. I like my stew meat cut into large (2" to 3") cubes, making one or two pieces of meat sufficient per serving. Since most packaged stew meat from the supermarket is cut into smaller pieces, you may want to start with a whole piece of meat and either cut and trim it yourself or ask your butcher to do this for you. The stew is flavored with shiitake mushrooms and, as the word niçoise *implies, tomatoes and olives. Domestic mushrooms can be substituted for the shiitakes if you want to contain costs a little.*

1	teaspoon virgin olive oil
2¼	pounds veal stew meat from the shoulder, chuck or shank, well trimmed of fat and cut into 2″–3″ cubes
1	cup water
1	tablespoon all-purpose flour
1	cup dry, fruity white wine
½	cup White Chicken Stock (page 14) or lower-salt canned chicken broth
1	small onion (about 3 ounces), peeled and chopped (½ cup)
½	small leek (2 ounces), trimmed, chopped and washed (½ cup)
¾	teaspoon salt (adjust if canned broth is used)
½	teaspoon freshly ground black pepper
	About 24 tiny pearl onions (5 ounces), peeled
18	fresh shiitake mushrooms (4 ounces), washed and with stems removed
1	medium tomato (about 7 ounces), peeled, seeded and cut into ½″ pieces (1 cup)
12	kalamata olives, drained and pitted

Brush a 12″ nonstick skillet with ½ teaspoon of the oil. Heat the oil until it is hot and add half the meat in a single layer. Cook the meat over high heat, turning it as it browns, for 5 minutes, until it is browned on all sides.

Using tongs, transfer the meat to a Dutch oven or cocotte (an earthenware casserole with a tight-fitting lid). Add ½ cup of the water to the drippings in the pan. Swirl the water in the skillet and pour it into a small bowl.

Brush the skillet with the remaining ½ teaspoon oil, brown the remainder of the meat and add it to the Dutch oven or cocotte. Swirl the remaining ½ cup of water in the skillet to deglaze it and add the liquid to the bowl.

Sprinkle the flour over the meat and mix well. Add the wine, stock or broth, chopped onions, leeks, salt and pepper. Stir in the reserved liquid from the bowl and mix well. Bring the mixture to a boil, reduce the heat to low, cover and boil gently for 30 minutes.

Add the pearl onions and mushrooms and continue cooking the stew, covered, over low heat for 15 minutes.

Add the tomatoes and olives, bring the mixture to a boil and set the stew aside, covered, for 5 to 10 minutes. Serve, dividing the meat and vegetables among 6 plates.

Per serving: 245 calories, 8 g. fat (29% of calories), 2.5 g. saturated fat, 106 mg. cholesterol, 402 mg. sodium.

When cooking with wine, it is not necessary to buy an expensive bottle. But it should be wine that you would want to drink. Do not use wine labeled "cooking wine." It often has added salt and is not of high quality.

Pepper Steak (page 199) and Boiled Potatoes (page 261)

Pepper Steak

*P*epper steak is excellent when prepared with freshly crushed black pepper-corns, and the Tellicherry and Java varieties give the best results. You can vary the amount of pepper used according to your own taste preferences. A shell steak—sometimes called New York strip or strip loin steak—is the best choice for this dish, although any other lean steak that is tender enough to be sautéed will be fine.

 2 tablespoons whole black peppercorns, preferably Tellicherry or Java
 6 shell steaks (5 ounces each and ½" thick), trimmed of all surrounding fat
 1 tablespoon corn, canola or safflower oil
 1 cup dry, fruity red wine
 5–6 cloves garlic, peeled, crushed and finely chopped (1 tablespoon)
 1 cup Onion Sauce (page 19) or Poultry Brown Base Sauce (page 16)
 ¾ teaspoon salt

Arrange the peppercorns together on a cutting board and crush them by pressing on them in a forward rolling movement with the base of a heavy skillet. Spread the crushed pepper evenly on the board and press the steaks into the pepper, coating them on both sides.

Divide the oil between 2 large nonstick skillets and place over medium-high heat. When it is very hot, place 3 steaks in each skillet and sauté them for 1½ minutes on each side for medium-rare. Transfer to a platter and set aside.

Add the wine and garlic to 1 of the skillets. Bring the wine to a boil, stirring constantly with a wooden spoon to loosen any solidified juices clinging to the bottom of the skillet, then pour the contents of that skillet into the other skillet. Again, bring the mixture to a boil, stirring to loosen and incorporate solidified juices in the second skillet; cook the mixture over high heat until the liquid is reduced to about 1 tablespoon. Stir in the onion sauce or base sauce and the salt. Bring the mixture to a boil.

Arrange the steaks on individual plates and pour some of the sauce over each steak. Serve immediately.

Per serving: 319 calories, 15.1 g. fat (43% of calories), 5.5 g. saturated fat, 95 mg. cholesterol, 364 mg. sodium.

Clockwise from top: Beef Stew with Red Wine Sauce (page 201);
Veal Stew Niçoise (page 196) and Navarin of Lamb (page 178)

Beef Stew with Red Wine Sauce

Yield: 6 servings

*i*t is important to use meat from the shoulder blade or shank for this stew, as it is moist even when most of the fat has been removed. I prefer my stew meat cut into 1½" to 2" pieces, larger than what is available packaged at the supermarket. You may want to buy a larger piece and either have the butcher cut it up for you or cut it yourself.

The meat is stewed gently in chicken stock and red wine flavored with a bouquet garni, which is a mixture of fresh herbs tied securely together into a package that can be easily removed from the stew before serving.

1	tablespoon virgin olive oil
2½	pounds beef stew meat from the shoulder blade or shank, cut into 1½"–2" cubes
1	cup White Chicken Stock (page 14) or lower-salt canned chicken broth
1½	cups dry, fruity red wine
1	medium onion (about 7 ounces), peeled and chopped (1 cup)
5–6	cloves garlic, peeled, crushed and finely chopped (1 tablespoon)
¾	teaspoon salt (adjust if canned broth is used)
¼	teaspoon freshly ground black pepper
1	bouquet garni (see page 202)
18	medium domestic mushrooms (12 ounces), washed
3–4	medium carrots (10–12 ounces), trimmed, peeled, halved lengthwise and cut into 1" pieces (2 cups)
	About 24 tiny pearl onions (4–5 ounces), peeled
1	tablespoon cornstarch
2	tablespoons soy sauce
2	tablespoons water
½	cup shelled fresh peas or thawed petite frozen peas
2	tablespoons chopped fresh parsley leaves

Brush a large nonstick pan with ½ tablespoon of the oil and place it over high heat. When the oil is hot, add about half the meat and brown it on all sides for 5 minutes. Remove the pieces of meat with tongs and place them in a

(continued)

Dutch oven. Add ½ cup of the stock or broth to the pan, swirl the liquid in the pan to release any cooking juices and pour this deglazing liquid into a small bowl.

Repeat this procedure with the remaining oil, meat and stock or broth. Add the meat to the Dutch oven and the deglazing liquid to the bowl.

To the meat in the Dutch oven add the wine, chopped onions, garlic, salt, pepper, bouquet garni and the reserved deglazing liquid. Mix well. Bring the mixture to a strong boil over high heat, reduce the heat to low, cover and boil very gently for 1¼ hours.

Add the mushrooms, carrots and pearl onions to the Dutch oven, moving the meat in the pan with tongs to make room for the vegetables. Bring the mixture back to a boil. Reduce the heat to low, cover and boil very gently for 15 minutes. Remove and discard the bouquet garni.

In a small bowl, dissolve the cornstarch in the soy sauce and water. Stir into the stew. Add the peas. Bring the stew back to a boil.

To serve, divide the meat and vegetables among 6 plates. Garnish each serving with a little of the parsley.

Per serving: 493 calories, 23 g. fat (42% of calories), 8.6 g. saturated fat, 140 mg. cholesterol, 386 mg. sodium.

To make a bouquet garni, use string to securely tie together a bundle consisting of 4 or 5 sprigs fresh thyme, 3 bay leaves, a small bunch of fresh parsley, half a stalk of celery plus a few sprigs of other fresh herbs, such as rosemary or oregano.

It's easy to remove a bouquet garni from a stew or sauce if you use a long string to tie up the herbs. Attach the loose end to the handle of your pot (making sure it's not so long that it will come in contact with the burner). When the food is finished cooking, simply untie the string and pull out the bouquet garni.

Carbonnade of Beef

Yield: 6 servings

*C*arbonnade of beef, a specialty of northern France and Belgium, is one of those earthy stews that develops more flavor if made a few hours ahead. If diet restrictions dictate, you can replace the beer with water, chicken stock or canned chicken broth. This stew is best served with baked potatoes.

 2 tablespoons corn, canola or safflower oil
1½ pounds beef chuck, cut into 1″ pieces
 3 tablespoons all-purpose flour
 2 medium onions (8 ounces), peeled and thickly sliced (2 cups)
 2 tablespoons water
 1 teaspoon salt (adjust if canned broth is used)
 1 teaspoon freshly ground black pepper
 ½ teaspoon dried thyme
 2 bay leaves
 2 cans beer (12 ounces each) or 3 cups White Chicken Stock (page 14) or lower-salt chicken broth

Heat 1 tablespoon of the oil in a large, heavy skillet. When it is hot, add half of the meat and brown it lightly on all sides. Stir in 1½ tablespoons of the flour and toss the meat in the flour to coat it lightly. Transfer the meat to a platter.

Repeat the cooking process with the remaining oil, meat and flour. Transfer the second batch of meat to the platter.

Add the onions to the meat drippings in the skillet and cook them for about 2 minutes over medium heat. Add the water and stir with a wooden spoon to loosen and melt any solidified juices in the skillet and to incorporate them into the mixture. Add the salt and pepper.

Arrange a layer of the meat in a heavy pot, preferably cast iron; cover with a layer of the onions. Repeat this layering procedure.

Place the thyme and bay leaves on top and pour in the beer, stock or broth. (The meat should be completely immersed.) Bring the mixture to a boil, cover tightly, reduce the heat to low and boil very gently for 1½ hours. Remove and discard bay leaves before serving.

Per serving: 298 calories, 12.4 g. fat (38% of calories), 3.4 g. saturated fat, 77 mg. cholesterol, 404 mg. sodium.

Spicy Flank Steak with Lettuce Fajitas

Yield: 6 servings

his marinated flank steak can be served on its own but is even more satisfying when combined with the onion-pepper mixture. In standard fajitas, the onions, green peppers and steak would be rolled up in a flour tortilla. Instead, I roll the meat and vegetables in large, crisp leaves of iceberg lettuce.

STEAK
1 medium onion (6 ounces), peeled and coarsely chopped (about 1 cup)
2 tablespoons honey
2 tablespoons dark soy sauce
1 tablespoon white or red wine vinegar
2 cloves garlic, peeled and lightly crushed
½ small jalapeño pepper, seeded if desired (to remove some of its hotness), and chopped (about 2 teaspoons)
1 flank steak (about 1½ pounds), trimmed of all surrounding fat

ONION-PEPPER MIXTURE
2 large onions (1 pound), peeled and thinly sliced (3½ cups)
1 green bell pepper (8 ounces), halved, cored, seeded and thinly sliced (2 cups)
¼ teaspoon salt

ASSEMBLY
24 large iceberg lettuce leaves
3 cups Salsa Cruda (page 21), pureed in a food processor

To make the steak: Place the onions, honey, soy sauce, vinegar, garlic and peppers in the bowl of a food processor or blender and process well.

Place the steak in a plastic bag and pour in the marinade. Seal the bag and refrigerate the steak for at least 2 hours (preferably overnight), turning it in the marinade occasionally.

Preheat a grill or the broiler until very hot.

Remove the steak from the bag (reserving the marinade) and grill or broil it about 5″ from the heat for approximately 2½ minutes a side for medium-rare. Transfer the steak to a platter.

Bring the reserved marinade to a boil in a small saucepan and pour it over the steak. Then set the steak aside in a warm oven or on top of the stove or bar-

Spicy Flank Steak with Lettuce Fajitas

becue grill; allow to rest, uncovered, for at least 15 minutes while you make the onion-pepper mixture.

To make the onion-pepper mixture: Lightly coat a large nonstick skillet with vegetable cooking spray and set the skillet over high heat. When it is hot, add the onions, peppers and salt; sauté over high heat for 5 minutes.

To assemble the fajitas: Cut the steak diagonally against the grain into thin slices. Spread the lettuce leaves out on a flat work surface and spoon about 2 tablespoons of the onion-pepper mixture into the center of each leaf. Top with slices of steak, dividing it equally among the leaves. Roll the stuffing in the leaves to make 24 packages. Serve 4 packages per person with ½ cup of the salsa.

Per serving: 304 calories, 11.1 g. fat (33% of calories), 4.6 g. saturated fat, 56 mg. cholesterol, 722 mg. sodium.

Beef Chili with Navy Beans

Beef Chili with Navy Beans

*i*t is important that you buy lean beef for this dish. One of the best ways to assure leanness is to use stewing beef; you can look the pieces over, select those that are most lean and then trim off any remaining fat or sinew. Start with one 1 pound of trimmed meat for this dish and cut it into ¼" pieces.

This dish is best prepared one or two days ahead, as it develops more taste if it stands. It can also be frozen for future use. You can easily reheat it in a microwave or in a saucepan (add a little water to keep it from sticking to the pan).

1	pound dry navy beans
1	pound lean stew beef, trimmed of all fat and cut into ¼" pieces
2	medium onions (about 8 ounces), peeled and cut into ½" dice (about 1½ cups)
1	large tomato (about 8 ounces), cut into ½" dice (about 1½ cups)
2	tablespoons tomato paste
5–6	cloves garlic, peeled, crushed and finely chopped (1 tablespoon)
1	tablespoon chili powder
1	teaspoon salt
6	cups cold water
	Tabasco hot-pepper sauce (optional)
2–3	cups shredded iceberg lettuce

Sort the beans, discarding any stones or damaged beans. Wash the beans in a sieve under cold water.

Place the beans in a pot and add the beef, onions, tomatoes, tomato paste, garlic, chili powder, salt and water. Bring the mixture to a boil, cover, reduce the heat to low and boil very gently for 2 to 2½ hours.

The mixture should be soupy but not too watery. If there is too much liquid, uncover the chili and boil it to reduce it; if the chili is too dry, add a little water.

Taste the chili and add the hot-pepper sauce, if desired. Serve in bowls or on soup plates with shredded lettuce sprinkled on top as a garnish.

Per serving: 401 calories, 6.7 g. fat (15% of calories), 2.1 g. saturated fat, 51 mg. cholesterol, 447 mg. sodium.

Pasta Primavera

Pasta Primavera

Primavera means "springtime" in Italian, and this dish should be made with an array of the first spring vegetables. The selection of vegetables here is especially appealing, but you can make substitutions based on market availability. The vegetable mixture can be prepared ahead, but the pasta should be cooked at the last moment and tossed with the vegetables just before serving.

2	tablespoons pine nuts
¾	cup loosely packed fresh parsley leaves
4	cloves garlic, peeled and lightly crushed
½	cup cold water
1½	cups broccoli florets, washed
3–4	spears asparagus with tight, firm heads (3 ounces), peeled, trimmed and cut into ½″ dice (1 cup)
3–4	medium domestic mushrooms (2 ounces), washed and cut into ½″ dice (1 cup)
1	small zucchini, washed, trimmed and cut into ½″ dice (1 cup)
½	green bell pepper, halved, cored, seeded and cut into ½″ dice (½ cup)
½	red bell pepper, halved, cored, seeded and cut into ½″ dice (½ cup)
1	small stalk celery (2 ounces), washed, trimmed and cut into ¼″ dice (⅓ cup)
1–2	scallions, washed, trimmed and thinly sliced (⅓ cup)
⅓	cup Poultry Brown Base Sauce (page 16) or lower-salt canned beef broth
12	ounces angel hair pasta
1½	tablespoons virgin olive oil
½	teaspoon salt (adjust if canned broth is used)

Preheat the oven to 400°. Place the pine nuts on a small baking tray. Bake for 5 minutes, or until lightly toasted. Set aside.

Bring about 3 quarts of water to a boil in a pot.

Meanwhile, place the parsley, garlic and ¼ cup of the water in the bowl of a food processor and process to a puree. Transfer to a small bowl and set aside.

Heat a large skillet and add the broccoli, asparagus, mushrooms, zucchini, green peppers, red peppers, celery, scallions and the remaining ¼ cup water.

(continued)

Penne in Clam Sauce

Bring the mixture to a boil, cover, reduce the heat and cook over medium to high heat for 2 minutes. Then remove the lid and cook until all the liquid has evaporated.

Combine the base sauce or broth with the parsley mixture and add it to the vegetables in the skillet. Mix well.

Just before serving, add the pasta to the boiling water and cook it according to the package instructions until it is al dente, still slightly firm to the bite. Drain well.

Transfer the contents of the skillet to a large serving bowl and add the pasta, oil and salt. Toss well.

Divide the mixture among 6 warm plates and garnish with the pine nuts.

Per serving: 267 calories, 6.8 g. fat (22% of calories), 0.7 g. saturated fat, 49 mg. cholesterol, 220 mg. sodium.

Penne in Clam Sauce

Yield: 6 servings

When I prepared this recipe, the fresh clams I used yielded about three cups of juice. If your fresh clams yield less juice or if you elect to use canned clams, add enough bottled clam juice to bring the liquid to three cups.

- 36 littleneck clams (7½ pounds unshelled)
- 1 large onion (about 7 ounces), peeled and chopped (1½ cups)
- 1 cup dry white wine, preferably a Chardonnay
- 3 scallions (2 ounces), washed, trimmed and thinly sliced (½ cup)
- 5–6 cloves garlic, peeled, crushed and finely chopped (1 tablespoon)
- 1 tablespoon dried oregano
- ½ teaspoon dried thyme
- ¼ teaspoon crushed red pepper flakes
- 7 medium domestic mushrooms (4 ounces), washed and cut into ½″ dice (1½ cups)
- 1 pound penne pasta
- 1 cup coarsely chopped fresh parsley leaves
- 3 tablespoons virgin olive oil
- Grated Parmesan cheese (optional)

Bring about 3 quarts of water to a boil in a pot.

Meanwhile, wash the clams in several changes of cold water, rubbing them together under the water to dislodge as much sand and dirt from the shells as possible. Lift the clams from the water and use a clam knife to open them; work over a bowl to catch the clam juice. (You should have 1⅓ cups of shelled clams and 3 cups of juice.) Discard the shells.

Lift the clams from the juice and place them in another bowl. Let the juice settle for 5 minutes, then carefully pour it into a large saucepan, leaving behind any sand and dirt that has settled in the bottom of the bowl.

Add the onions, wine, scallions, garlic, oregano, thyme and pepper flakes to the saucepan and mix well. Bring the mixture to a full boil, then reduce the heat to low, cover and boil gently for 5 minutes. Add the mushrooms, cover and continue boiling gently for 5 additional minutes.

Add the penne to the pot of boiling water and cook it for 12 minutes, or until it is al dente, still slightly firm to the bite.

(continued)

While the penne is cooking, add the clams to the vegetables in the saucepan, return the mixture to a boil, cover and set aside off the heat until ready to serve.

Before draining the pasta, remove ¾ cup of the cooking liquid from the pot and place it in the bowl you will use to serve the pasta. Stir in the parsley, oil and, if desired, Parmesan. Drain the penne, add it to the bowl and toss well. Cover the bowl and set aside for 4 to 5 minutes before serving.

To serve, divide the pasta among 6 plates. Using a slotted spoon, transfer the clam mixture to the plates, placing it in the center of each serving. Pour the clam sauce over and around the pasta. If desired, sprinkle on more Parmesan.

Per serving: 522 calories, 11.1 g. fat (19% of calories), 1.5 g. saturated fat, 132 mg. cholesterol, 132 mg. sodium.

Provence Pizza

hese pizzas are particularly good when prepared just before serving. Depending on your oven, you may have to cook them longer than indicated here to get them crisp on the bottom. If you use a pizza stone (a flat ceramic stone that you place on one of the wire racks in your oven), the pizzas will get browner and crustier on the bottom than if you use oiled cookie sheets. For added crispness, make the dough as thin as possible when shaping it into circles.

CRUST

⅔ cup warm water (110°–115°)

1 package active dry yeast (about 2 teaspoons)

¼ teaspoon sugar

2 cups all-purpose flour

¼ teaspoon salt

TOPPINGS

4 large onions (2 pounds), peeled and thinly sliced (about 6 cups)

1 cup water

1 tablespoon virgin olive oil

1 teaspoon salt

1 teaspoon freshly ground black pepper

4 cloves garlic, peeled, crushed and finely chopped (2 teaspoons)

2 ripe medium tomatoes (14 ounces), seeded and coarsely chopped

1 small zucchini (6 ounces), washed, trimmed and cut crosswise into ¼″ slices (1 cup)

8 ounces domestic mushrooms, washed and cut into ¼″ slices

1 medium red bell pepper (4 ounces), cored, seeded and cut crosswise into thin rings (about ¾ cup)

1 medium green bell pepper (4 ounces), cored, seeded and cut crosswise into thin rings (about ¾ cup)

4 ounces part-skim mozzarella cheese, shredded

To make the crust: Place the water, yeast and sugar in a mixing bowl. Stir well and let rest for 5 minutes. Add the flour and salt; mix with the dough hook of an electric mixer at low speed for 3 minutes.

Place the dough in a large bowl, cover the bowl with plastic wrap and set it aside in a warm place (75° to 80°) for about 2 hours, or until the dough has doubled in volume. (When the dough is ready, touching it firmly will leave an indentation.)

While the dough is rising, spray 2 aluminum cookie sheets or pizza pans lightly with vegetable cooking spray and set them aside.

To make the toppings: Place the onions, water, oil, salt and pepper in a large skillet or saucepan. Bring the mixture to a boil over high heat, cover and reduce the heat to medium. Boil for about 12 minutes, or until most of the water has evaporated. Uncover and continue to cook, stirring often, until the onions begin to brown. Add the garlic, mix well and set the pan aside off the heat.

After the dough has doubled in volume, punch it down gently and divide it in half. Place half the dough on 1 of the prepared sheets or pans and shape it into a 10″ round, with the edges slightly thicker than the center. (The dough will have a tendency to spring back; you will need to push and press on it firmly to extend it.) Repeat this procedure with the remaining dough, spreading it out on the other prepared sheet or pan.

Arrange the tomatoes evenly over the dough and layer on the zucchini, mushrooms, red peppers and green peppers. Divide the onion mixture between the pizzas and top with the mozzarella.

Preheat the oven to 425°.

Bake the pizzas for 25 to 30 minutes, or until the crust on each is brown throughout. Let the pizzas cool for 3 to 4 minutes, cut them into wedges and serve.

Per serving: 321 calories, 6.4 g. fat (19% of calories), 2.5 g. saturated fat, 11 mg. cholesterol, 548 mg. sodium.

Provence Pizza (page 213)

Tomatoes Stuffed with White Beans

Yield: 6 servings

*T*his dish can be made up to one day ahead and reheated or eaten at room temperature. For best results, complete the recipe up to the point of stuffing the tomatoes and then assemble and bake the dish within a few hours of serving.

   6 medium tomatoes (about 2½ pounds)
   6 ounces dry white beans (navy, pea or great Northern)
   3 cups cold water
   ⅓ cup uncooked white rice
   ⅔ cup White Chicken Stock (page 14) or lower-salt canned chicken broth
   1 small piece fresh ginger, peeled and chopped (1 tablespoon)
   2 cloves garlic, peeled, crushed and finely chopped (1 teaspoon)
   1 teaspoon seeded and chopped jalapeño peppers
   2 tablespoons corn, canola or virgin olive oil
   4 ounces spinach, trimmed and washed (about 3 cups)
   1 teaspoon ground cumin
   1 teaspoon curry powder
   1 teaspoon salt (adjust if canned broth is used)

Core the tomatoes. Cut off the smooth end of each tomato about ¼ of the way down and reserve the pieces you remove to use as lids. Scoop out the insides of the tomatoes, using a metal measuring spoon (because these spoons have sharp edges) and leaving a wall about ¼″ thick. Chop and reserve the flesh from the insides.

Sort the beans, discarding any stones or damaged beans. Wash the beans in a sieve. Place the beans in a pot with the water. Bring the mixture to a boil, reduce the heat to low, cover and boil the beans gently for about 1½ hours, or until they are tender. Drain off any remaining water and place the beans in a large bowl.

Meanwhile, combine the rice and stock or broth in a medium saucepan, bring to a boil, reduce the heat, cover and boil gently for 20 to 25 minutes, until the rice is tender. Add the rice to the bowl containing the beans.

In a small bowl, mix together the ginger, garlic and peppers.

Heat the oil in a large skillet until hot. Add the garlic mixture and sauté it over high heat for about 10 seconds. Then add the spinach, still wet from washing, and toss it briefly to incorporate the garlic (and prevent it from

Tomatoes Stuffed with White Beans

burning in the bottom of the skillet). Cover the skillet and cook the mixture for 2 minutes, until the spinach is soft and tender.

Transfer the spinach mixture to the bowl containing the beans and rice. Stir in the cumin, curry powder, salt and the reserved tomato flesh. Mix well.

Preheat the oven to 400°.

Stuff the tomatoes with the spinach mixture and top each with a reserved tomato lid. Arrange the tomatoes in an ovenproof dish and bake them for 30 to 40 minutes. Serve immediately or cool to room temperature before serving.

Per serving: 218 calories, 5.8 g. fat (23% of calories), 0.8 g. saturated fat, 0 mg. cholesterol, 392 mg. sodium.

Vegetable Ragout with Bulgur

Yield: 6 servings

his is the ideal vegetarian dish. Containing several vegetables and bulgur wheat, it has a lot of fiber. Bulgur is wheat that has been cracked into pieces, then steamed and dried before you buy it. It can be reconstituted in cold water for use in salads, but for this recipe, I cook it briefly in boiling water and flavor it with onion and olive oil. If some of the vegetables I use in this colorful and satisfying stew are not available, substitute others. If you want to serve the bulgur as a side dish, half of the recipe is sufficient.

VEGETABLES

6	plum tomatoes (12 ounces), cut into ¾" thick slices
2	medium onions (8 ounces), peeled and chopped (2 cups)
2	cups cold water
12–15	cloves garlic, peeled and thinly sliced (⅓ cup)
1	tablespoon virgin olive oil
1	teaspoon salt
1	teaspoon dried thyme
½	teaspoon caraway seeds
¼	teaspoon freshly ground black pepper
¼	teaspoon Tabasco hot-pepper sauce
1	pound green cabbage, cut lengthwise and then across into 1" squares (5–6 cups)
4–5	carrots (12 ounces), trimmed, peeled and cut into 1" lengths (2½ cups)
3–4	small turnips (12 ounces), peeled and cut in half (2½ cups)
1	red bell pepper (6 ounces), halved, cored, seeded and cut into 12 strips (1½ cups)
1	pound broccoli, florets separated from the stalks and stalks peeled and cut into strips 2" × ½" (5 cups)
3	zucchini (1 pound), washed, trimmed and cut into ¾" rounds (4 cups)

BULGUR

1 tablespoon virgin olive oil

1 medium onion (6 ounces), peeled and coarsely chopped (1 cup)

½ teaspoon salt

¼ teaspoon freshly ground black pepper

1½ cups bulgur wheat

3½ cups boiling water

To make the vegetables: Place the tomatoes, onions and water in the bowl of a food processor. Process the mixture until it is pureed, then transfer it to a large pot. Add the garlic, oil, salt, thyme, caraway seeds, black pepper and hot-pepper sauce. Bring the mixture to a boil over high heat and cook it for 5 minutes.

Then add the cabbage, carrots, turnips and red peppers, cover the pan and cook the mixture for 20 minutes. Add the broccoli and zucchini; bring the mixture back to a boil. Cover and cook an additional 10 minutes.

To make the bulgur: Heat the oil in a saucepan. Add the onions and cook over high heat for 2 to 3 minutes. Add the salt and pepper. Stir in the bulgur. Continue stirring the mixture for 1 minute. Add the water. Mix well, cover the pan, reduce the heat to low and boil the mixture gently for 10 minutes. Remove from the heat and let the bulgur sit, covered, for an additional 20 minutes.

To serve, arrange the vegetables on a serving platter. Make a well in the center and fill it with bulgur. Bring the platter to the table and serve guests from it. (Alternatively, mound the bulgur on individual plates in the kitchen and spoon the vegetables and juices on top.)

Per serving: 299 calories, 6 g. fat (16% of calories), 0.9 g. saturated fat, 0 mg. cholesterol, 632 mg. sodium.

Accompaniments

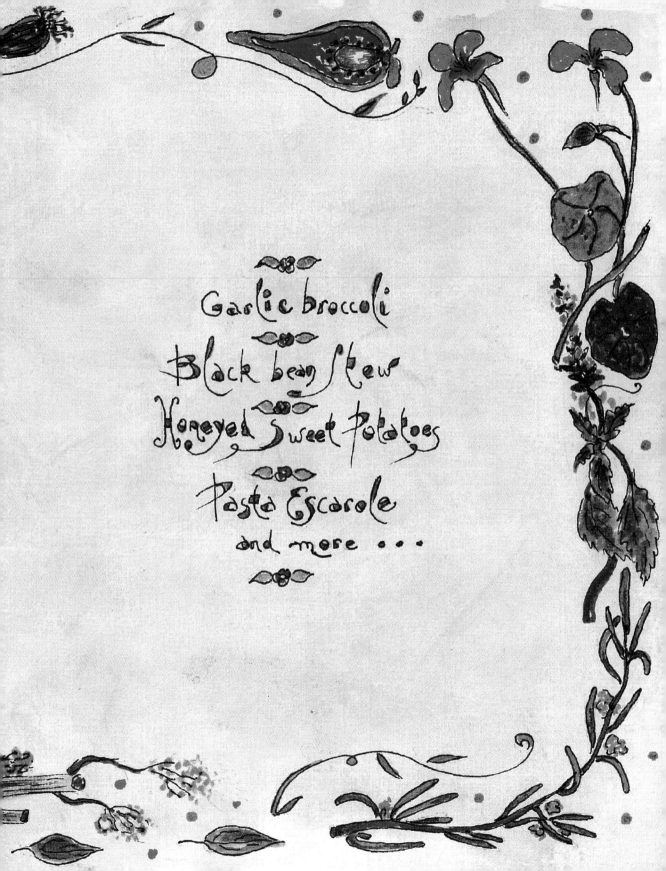

Garlic broccoli

Black bean stew

Honeyed Sweet Potatoes

Pasta Escarole

and more ...

Green Beans and Red Onions

Yield: 6 servings

his is a variation on a classic French dish featuring very thin French green beans—haricots verts—and shallots. I substitute conventional green beans here and cook them with red onions, but if you can find the thinner haricots verts, *use them instead, taking particular care not to overcook them. They are a little costlier but well worth the additional expense. Note that the beans are cooked in a minimum of water, so that by the time they are tender the liquid has essentially evaporated. Prepared this way, the beans retain nutrients that other- wise would be thrown away with excess cooking liquid.*

2	cups water
1½	pounds green beans, trimmed
1½	tablespoons virgin olive oil
1	medium red onion (5 ounces), peeled and coarsely chopped (1 cup)
¼	teaspoon salt
¼	teaspoon freshly ground black pepper
½	cup coarsely chopped fresh parsley leaves

Bring the water to a boil in a large stainless steel saucepan. Add the beans, bring the water back to a boil, cover and cook over high heat for 8 minutes. (All the water should be gone at this point.) Transfer the beans to a platter and set them aside.

Heat the oil in the same saucepan. When it is hot, add the onions and sauté them over high heat for 1 minute. Return the beans to the pan and add the salt and pepper. Toss the mixture well, then add the parsley and toss again to combine the ingredients. Serve immediately.

Per serving: 79 calories, 3.8 g. fat (43% of calories), 0.7 g. saturated fat, 0 mg. cholesterol, 95 mg. sodium.

Green Beans and Red Onions

Clockwise from top: Lentil and Carrot Stew (page 227); Hominy, Cilantro and Cumin Stew (page 232) and Black Bean Stew (page 225)

Black Bean Stew

Yield: 6 servings

*C*ontaining only a small amount of oil and salt, this spicy bean stew is
nonetheless flavorful and satisfying. Black beans, sometimes called black
turtle beans, are widely used in Mexican cooking as well as in the cooking of the
Southwest. If you don't find them appealing, you can substitute red, white or
cranberry beans. Often recipes indicate that dry beans should be soaked before
cooking; I do not find this step essential and usually cook them as I do here.

1	pound dry black beans
6	cups cold water
¾	teaspoon salt
1½	tablespoons corn, safflower or canola oil
3	medium onions (1 pound), peeled and cut into 1″ cubes
5–6	cloves garlic, peeled, crushed and finely chopped (1 tablespoon)
3	tablespoons chili powder
1	teaspoon ground cumin
½	teaspoon Tabasco hot-pepper sauce
1	large tomato (8–10 ounces), coarsely chopped (1½ cups)
6	scallions, washed, trimmed and thinly sliced (1 cup)
½	cup coarsely chopped fresh cilantro leaves
¼	cup white wine vinegar

Sort the beans, discarding any stones or damaged beans. Wash the beans in
a sieve under cold water. Drain.

Place the beans in a large pot with the water and salt. Bring to a boil,
reduce the heat to low, cover and boil the beans gently for about 1½ hours, or
until they are tender but not broken down into a puree.

Heat the oil in a nonstick skillet. When it is hot, add the onions and sauté
them for 10 minutes, stirring occasionally, until they are lightly browned. Add
the garlic, stir well and add the mixture to the beans in the pot. Stir in the chili
powder, cumin and hot-pepper sauce. Cover the pot and boil the mixture gently
for 10 minutes. Then add the tomatoes, scallions, cilantro and vinegar. Return
the mixture to a boil. Serve immediately.

*Per serving: 287 calories, 5.1 g. fat (16% of calories), 0.3 g. saturated fat, 0 mg.
cholesterol, 317 mg. sodium.*

Puree of Lima Beans

Yield: 6 servings

i often elect to prepare dried lima beans at home instead of great Northern, pea or navy beans because the limas cook faster. Small dried limas cook in as little as 20 to 25 minutes, for example, with the larger ones taking about 45 minutes. Either size can be used for this creamy puree, which is great with meat, poultry or fish. The puree will keep, refrigerated, for several days. For best results, reheat it in a microwave oven before serving.

  8 ounces large dry lima beans
  3 cups water
  ½ teaspoon salt
  ⅛ teaspoon herbes de Provence (see page 13)

Sort the beans, discarding any stones or damaged beans. Wash the beans in a sieve under cold water. Drain.

Place the beans in a large saucepan or small pot. Add the water, salt and herbes de Provence. Bring the mixture to a boil. Cover, reduce the heat to low and boil gently for 45 minutes, until the beans are very tender.

Transfer the mixture (there should be about 3 cups, including the liquid) to the bowl of a food processor and process for 20 to 30 seconds, until very smooth. Serve about ⅓ cup per person.

Per serving: 104 calories, 0.3 g. fat (3% of calories), 0.1 g. saturated fat, 0 mg. cholesterol, 179 mg. sodium.

Lentil and Carrot Stew

Yield: 6 servings

*C*ilantro is often sold with the roots attached. I follow my wife's practice of using the chopped roots and stems as a flavoring in soups and stews and add them to this stew of lentils and carrots. I also garnish the finished dish with cilantro leaves.

6 ounces dry lentils (1 cup)

3 cups water

5 medium carrots (12 ounces), trimmed, peeled, quartered lengthwise and cut into 1″ pieces (2½ cups)

1 large or 2 medium onions (8 ounces), peeled and thinly sliced (2 cups)

1 small stalk celery (about 2 ounces), washed, trimmed and chopped (¼ cup)

3 bay leaves

1 teaspoon salt

1 bunch fresh cilantro, washed

Sort the lentils, discarding any stones or damaged lentils. Wash in a sieve under cold water. Drain.

Place the lentils in a large pot. Add the water, carrots, onions, celery, bay leaves and salt.

Cut the leaves from the cilantro and reserve as a garnish. Chop the stems and roots; add to the pot. Bring the mixture to a boil over high heat. Reduce the heat to low, cover and cook at a very gentle boil for 45 minutes. Then remove the lid and continue to cook for a few additional minutes to evaporate most of the remaining liquid in the pot. Remove and discard the bay leaves.

Serve in bowls, garnishing each serving with several of the cilantro leaves.

Per serving: 137 calories, 0.5 g. fat (3% of calories), 0.1 g. saturated fat, 0 mg. cholesterol, 580 mg. sodium.

Black Bean Relish

Yield: 5 cups

good complementary dish for poultry or roasted meat, this can also be served on its own as a kind of hors d'oeuvre. There is no need to soak the beans before cooking them; just wash and sort them, then start them in cold water. Although it took the beans I used 1½ hours to cook, yours may need more or less cooking time. Add water as needed during the cooking period so that there is still a little water surrounding the beans when they are tender. Covered and set aside off the heat at this point, they will absorb this excess moisture. The relish will keep for at least a week under refrigeration.

- 8 ounces dry black beans (about 1½ cups)
- 3 cups cold water
- ¾ teaspoon salt
- 1 small yellow onion (about 2 ounces), peeled and finely chopped (⅓ cup)
- 2 small jalapeño peppers
- 1 ear sweet corn (12 ounces), husked with kernels cut off the cob (1 cup)
- 1 small red onion (4 ounces), peeled and cut into ¼″ dice (⅔ cup)
- 3 tablespoons red wine vinegar
- 3–4 cloves garlic, peeled, crushed and finely chopped (1½ teaspoons)
- 1 teaspoon chili powder
- ½ teaspoon Tabasco hot-pepper sauce
- 1 medium tomato (about 6 ounces), peeled, seeded and coarsely chopped (1 cup)
- ¾ cup loosely packed fresh cilantro leaves, coarsely chopped (⅓ cup)

Sort the beans, discarding any stones or damaged beans. Wash the beans in a sieve under cold water. Drain.

Place the beans in a large saucepan with the water, salt and yellow onions. Bring the mixture to a boil over high heat, then reduce the heat to low, cover and cook for 1½ hours, or until the beans are tender (but not mushy) and only about ½ cup of water remains. Do not drain.

Set the beans aside, covered, off the heat for about 10 minutes; they will absorb the excess liquid as they sit.

If desired, remove the seeds and ribs from the peppers to eliminate some of their hotness. Chop the peppers.

Black Bean Relish

After 10 minutes (while the beans are still hot), add the peppers, corn, red onions, vinegar, garlic, chili powder and hot-pepper sauce. Mix well. Set aside until cooled to room temperature. Mix in the tomatoes and cilantro. Serve.

Per ½ cup: 130 calories, 0.6 g. fat (4% of calories), 0.1 g. saturated fat, 0 mg. cholesterol, 193 mg. sodium.

White Bean Fricassée with Curry

White Bean Fricassée with Curry

Yield: 6 servings

i cook dried great Northern or navy beans for this dish, but you can shorten the preparation time by substituting canned white beans instead. The beans are cooked simply with onions, leeks, garlic, tomatoes and a little curry, which gives the fricassée a special zest.

10	ounces dry great Northern or navy beans (1½ cups)
3	cups White Chicken Stock (page 14) or lower-salt canned chicken broth
2	cups water
½	teaspoon salt (adjust if canned broth is used)
1	medium tomato (about 7 ounces), peeled, seeded and cut into ½″ dice (1 cup)
1	small onion (about 3 ounces), peeled and chopped (½ cup)
1	small piece leek (about 2 ounces), trimmed, thinly sliced and washed (½ cup)
4–5	cloves garlic, peeled, crushed and finely chopped (2 teaspoons)
2	teaspoons curry powder

Sort the beans, discarding any stones or damaged beans. Wash the beans in a sieve under cold water. Drain.

Place the beans in a large saucepan with the stock or broth, water and salt. Bring the mixture to a boil over high heat, then reduce the heat to low, cover and cook at a very gentle boil for 1½ hours, or until the beans are tender but not mushy.

Meanwhile, combine the tomatoes, onions, leeks, garlic and curry powder in a medium bowl.

When the beans are tender, add the tomato mixture to the saucepan and cook for 15 minutes. Serve.

Per serving: 178 calories, 0.9 g. fat (4% of calories), 0.2 g. saturated fat, 0 mg. cholesterol, 186 mg. sodium.

Hominy, Cilantro and Cumin Stew

Yield: 6 servings

I use canned white and yellow hominy in this stew. A staple of the American Indians that was adopted from them by the pioneers, hominy is made through a process that treats whole corn kernels with ashes. The kernels puff up as a result, becoming large and chewy with a distinctive taste that I find addictive.

2	tablespoons canola oil
1	medium onion (about 5 ounces), peeled and chopped (1 cup)
6–8	scallions (about 5 ounces), washed, trimmed and chopped (1 cup)
2	small zucchini (8 ounces), washed, trimmed and cut into ½″ dice (about 1½ cups)
5–6	medium domestic mushrooms (about 3 ounces), washed and chopped (1½ cups)
5–6	cloves garlic, peeled, crushed and finely chopped (1 tablespoon)
1½	teaspoons ground cumin
¼	teaspoon crushed red pepper flakes
1	can (15½ ounces) white hominy
1	can (15½ ounces) yellow hominy
1	medium tomato (7 ounces), peeled, seeded and cut into ½″ pieces (1 cup)
1	cup loosely packed fresh cilantro leaves, chopped (½ cup)

Heat the oil in a large saucepan or pot. When it is hot, add the onions and scallions and cook for 1 minute. Then add the zucchini, mushrooms, garlic, cumin and pepper flakes; cook for 3 to 4 minutes.

Add the white and yellow hominy (with liquid) to the saucepan and bring the mixture to a full boil. Then reduce the heat to low, cover and cook for 10 minutes. The consistency of the mixture should be moist but not fluid. If there is too much liquid, reduce it by boiling the mixture, uncovered, over high heat; if there is too little moisture, add a few tablespoons of water.

Stir in the tomatoes and cilantro, bring the stew back to a boil and boil for 1 minute.

Per serving: 182 calories, 6.3 g. fat (30% of calories), 0.6 g. saturated fat, 0 mg. cholesterol, 315 mg. sodium.

Roasted Beets

Yield: 6 servings

I like the flavor of beets that have been roasted in the oven; this cooking method tends to concentrate their taste and make them sweeter than other faster modes of cooking. Although the beets are peeled and cut into slices in this recipe, they can be served whole—peeled or not—as a vegetable garnish for roast meat or poultry. When peeling beets, be certain to place them on a piece of plastic wrap and to cover your hands with plastic gloves to avoid discoloring your work surface or fingers.

6	medium to large beets (about 2½ pounds)
2	teaspoons virgin olive oil
1½	teaspoons red wine vinegar
¼	teaspoon salt
¼	teaspoon freshly ground black pepper

Preheat the oven to 400°.

Remove the tops from the beets with a sharp knife and trim them at the root ends. Rinse the beets in cold water and wrap them together in a large piece of aluminum foil.

Place the foil package on a baking tray and place the tray on the upper rack of the oven. Bake for 1½ to 2 hours, or until the beets are tender but still somewhat firm.

Remove the beets from the foil and set them aside until they are cool enough to handle. Then peel off and discard the outer skin and cut them into ¼″ slices. Place the sliced beets in a bowl and, while they are warm, add the oil, vinegar, salt and pepper; toss well.

Serve warm or at room temperature.

Per serving: 55 calories, 1.6 g. fat (25% of calories), 0.2 g. saturated fat, 0 mg. cholesterol, 154 mg. sodium.

Garlic Broccoli

his is an excellent dish if the broccoli remains bright green and is slightly crunchy after steaming. Notice that the broccoli is steamed very quickly in a small amount of water, so that by the time the vegetable is cooked, most of the water has evaporated. This concentrates the flavor of the broccoli and safeguards nutrients. When broccoli is cooked in a lot of water, as it often is conventionally, nutrients are discarded along with the cooking water.

- 2 **bunches broccoli with very tight heads (about 3 pounds)**
- 1 **cup water**
- 1 **tablespoon virgin olive oil**
- 3–4 **cloves garlic, peeled, crushed and finely chopped (2 teaspoons)**
- ¼ **teaspoon freshly ground black pepper**
- ¼ **teaspoon salt**

Separate the broccoli into stalks. Using a vegetable peeler, remove the fibrous outer layer from the stems. Cut the stalks (including the florets) into 1″ to 2″ lengths.

Bring the water to a boil in a large, shallow, stainless steel saucepan. Add the broccoli, cover and boil over high heat for 3 to 4 minutes. Most of the water should have evaporated at this point; drain off any that remains.

Heat the oil in a large skillet. When it is hot, add the garlic and cook it for about 10 seconds. Then add the broccoli, pepper and salt and toss the mixture well. Arrange the broccoli in a serving dish and serve immediately.

Per serving: 86 calories, 3.1 g. fat (27% of calories), 0.4 g. saturated fat, 0 mg. cholesterol, 148 mg. sodium.

Puree of Broccoli with Garlic

Yield: 6 servings

he combined flavors of broccoli and garlic make this appealing puree a perfect accompaniment for plain roast meat and poultry. Potato serves as thickening agent here, and a little butter and oil are added at the end as a flavor enhancer.

1 **bunch broccoli with very tight heads (1¾ pounds)**
1 **cup water**
1 **medium potato (about 9 ounces), peeled and cut into 1″ pieces**
2 **cloves garlic, peeled**
1 **teaspoon salt**
1 **teaspoon unsalted butter**
1 **teaspoon virgin olive oil**

Separate the broccoli into stalks. Using a vegetable peeler, remove the fibrous outer layer from the stems. Cut the stalks (including the florets) into 2″ lengths.

Place the broccoli in a large saucepan with the water, potatoes, garlic and salt. Bring to a boil, cover, reduce the heat to low and boil gently for 15 minutes, or until the vegetables are tender. (You should have about ½ cup of liquid remaining.)

Place the contents of the saucepan in the bowl of a food processor and add the butter and oil. Process the mixture for about 45 seconds, until it is very smooth. Transfer the puree to a serving bowl and serve immediately.

Per serving: 87 calories, 1.9 g. fat (18% of calories), 0.6 g. saturated fat, 2 mg. cholesterol, 392 mg. sodium.

Sweet and Sour Cabbage

R ed cabbage is combined with apples, onions, apple juice, cider vinegar and raisins here to create an appealing sweet-sour mixture that goes particularly well with game.

  1 tablespoon canola oil

  ½ medium onion (2 ounces), peeled and thinly sliced (½ cup)

  1 small red cabbage (2 pounds), cored and cut into 1½″ pieces (8 cups)

  3 Granny Smith apples (1¼ pounds), unpeeled but halved, cored and cut into 1″ pieces (4½ cups)

  2 cups apple juice

  ¼ cup cider vinegar

  ¼ cup balsamic vinegar

  ¼ cup dark raisins

 12 juniper berries, crushed

  1 teaspoon salt

Heat the oil in a large saucepan. When it is hot, add the onions and sauté them for 1 minute. Then add the cabbage, apples, apple juice, cider vinegar, balsamic vinegar, raisins, juniper berries and salt; mix well. Bring the mixture to a full boil, reduce the heat to low, cover and cook for 45 minutes. Remove the lid and boil the mixture, uncovered, over high heat until only enough liquid remains to keep the cabbage moist. Serve.

Per serving: 187 calories, 3.1 g. fat (14% of calories), 0.3 g. saturated fat, 0 mg. cholesterol, 378 mg. sodium.

Look for juniper berries in the spice section of your supermarket. They're sold dried and should be crushed before being used. You can crush them using a mortar and pestle or by spreading the berries on a cutting board and pressing down on them with the bottom of a heavy skillet.

Wilted Cabbage Salad

Yield: 6 servings

he cabbage for this salad is blanched, which softens and tenderizes it so that it can absorb the dressing better. A paste of anchovies and garlic forms the base for the salad dressing. Even though there are a lot of anchovies in this dressing, the salad is a favorite with friends who insist they don't like anchovies.

1 small white cabbage or part of a larger one (1½ pounds), cored, halved and cut into ⅛″ slices (10 cups loosely packed)

1 can (2 ounces) flat anchovies in oil

¼ cup Dijon mustard

5–6 cloves garlic, peeled

2 tablespoons cider vinegar

3 tablespoons apple juice

2 tablespoons extra-virgin olive oil

¼ teaspoon freshly ground black pepper

¼ teaspoon salt

1 tablespoon poppy seeds

2 large tomatoes (about 1 pound), cut into ⅜″ slices

Bring about 2 quarts of water to a boil in a pot. Add the cabbage and cook it for 1½ minutes. (The water will not return to a boil.) Drain.

Place the anchovies (with their oil), mustard and garlic in the bowl of a food processor and process the mixture until it is smooth. Add the vinegar, apple juice, oil, pepper and salt and process until they are incorporated.

Place the lukewarm cabbage in a bowl, add the anchovy dressing and poppy seeds. Toss the mixture well. Let it marinate for at least 15 minutes.

To serve, arrange the tomato slices around the periphery of a platter and mound the cabbage in the center.

Per serving: 115 calories, 7.2 g. fat (52% of calories), 1 g. saturated fat, 8 mg. cholesterol, 654 mg. sodium.

Carottes Vichy

*t*his quick dish is always better done at the last minute so the carrots are at their nuttiest and sweetest. Persillade, *a mixture of chopped parsley and garlic, is added at the end to give the carrots that special taste of Provence. A minimal amount of water is used; by the time the carrots are cooked, the water is gone, leaving most of the vegetable's valuable nutrients intact.*

- 5–6 medium carrots (about 1 pound), trimmed, peeled and very thinly sliced (2½ cups)
- ⅓ cup water
- 1 tablespoon corn, safflower or canola oil
- 1 tablespoon honey
- ½ teaspoon freshly ground black pepper
- 3 tablespoons chopped fresh parsley leaves
- 2 cloves garlic, peeled, crushed and finely chopped (1 teaspoon)

Place the carrots, water, oil, honey and pepper in a small stainless steel saucepan. Cover, bring the mixture to a strong boil and boil for 5 minutes. Remove the cover, add the parsley and garlic and continue boiling over high heat for 3 to 4 minutes, or until most of the liquid has evaporated and the carrots start to sizzle in the small amount of remaining sauce. Serve immediately.

Per serving: 65 calories, 2.4 g. fat (32% of calories), 0.3 g. saturated fat, 0 mg. cholesterol, 47 mg. sodium.

Carottes Provençale

Baby carrots that come already peeled in packages at most supermarkets are really convenient for this recipe. Here, the carrots are cooked whole in just enough water so that by the time they're tender, the liquid has evaporated. This eliminates the need to drain off excess cooking liquid—and throw away valuable nutrients in the process. Added at the last minute, garlic and parsley lend a wonderfully fresh taste to the dish.

1 pound baby carrots, trimmed and peeled (about 3½ cups)
½ cup water
1 teaspoon sugar
¼ teaspoon salt
2 tablespoons chopped fresh parsley leaves
2 cloves garlic, peeled, crushed and finely chopped (1 teaspoon)
⅛ teaspoon freshly ground black pepper

Place the carrots, water, sugar and salt in a medium stainless steel saucepan. Bring to a boil over high heat, cover, reduce the heat to low and boil gently for 5 to 6 minutes, until the carrots are tender when pierced with the point of a sharp knife and most of the liquid has evaporated.

Add the parsley, garlic and pepper and stir well. Cook for 30 seconds and serve immediately.

Per serving: 37 calories, 0.2 g. fat (4% of calories), 0 g. saturated fat, 0 mg. cholesterol, 116 mg. sodium.

Corn Tortillas
with Peppers, Onions and Cheese

Yield: 6 servings

I use corn tortillas in this attractive, flavorful and simple dish, but if you object to their assertive taste and dry texture, use flour tortillas instead. The onion-pepper mixture can be altered to accommodate taste preferences; if you don't like green peppers, add some garlic or additional onions or tomatoes to replace them. Use the amount of mozzarella called for, however, and make certain that you buy part-skim milk mozzarella.

3–4 medium onions (about 1 pound), peeled and thinly sliced
(3½ cups)

2 medium green bell peppers (8 ounces), halved, cored, seeded
and thinly sliced (2 cups)

¼ teaspoon salt

5 corn tortillas

2 ounces part-skim mozzarella cheese, shredded

Lightly coat a large nonstick skillet with vegetable cooking spray and heat the pan until it is hot. Add the onions, peppers and salt; sauté the mixture over high heat for 4 to 5 minutes, stirring occasionally. Set aside.

Preheat the broiler.

Dampen the tortillas lightly with water and place them on a cookie sheet. Top each tortilla with a generous ½ cup of the onion mixture. Sprinkle with the mozzarella. Broil 2″ to 3″ from the heat for 4 minutes, or until the cheese is lightly browned.

Cut each tortilla into 6 wedges and serve 5 wedges per person.

Per serving: 126 calories, 2.7 g. fat (18% of calories), 1 g. saturated fat, 5 mg. cholesterol, 181 mg. sodium.

Corn Tortillas with Peppers, Onions and Cheese

Cauliflower with Herbed Crumb Topping

Yield: 6 servings

*C*hoose cauliflower that is firm and creamy white; cut off and discard any brownish spots from the top of the florets. For this recipe, I cook the florets in boiling water, then cover them with flavored crumbs and finish the dish in the oven. If the cauliflower is still hot, 10 minutes in the oven and a couple of minutes under the broiler are sufficient. If, however, the cauliflower has been cooked ahead and allowed to cool, increase the baking time to about 20 minutes.

1	head cauliflower (2 pounds)
1½	cups water
2	scallions, washed, trimmed and chopped (about 3 tablespoons)
1	tablespoon chopped fresh parsley leaves
2	teaspoons virgin olive oil
2	cloves garlic, peeled, crushed and finely chopped (1 teaspoon)
½	teaspoon salt
¼	teaspoon freshly ground black pepper
1½	slices bread, processed into crumbs in a food processor (¾ cup)

Remove and discard the base and green leaves from the cauliflower head and separate the head into florets. Cut the florets into halves or thirds. (You should have about 24 pieces of approximately equal size.)

Bring the water to a boil in a large stainless steel saucepan. Add the cauliflower, cover and cook over medium to high heat for 8 to 10 minutes, until just tender. Most of the liquid should have evaporated; drain off any that remains. Spread the cauliflower in a 9″ × 13″ gratin dish.

In a large bowl, mix together the scallions, parsley, oil, garlic, salt and pepper. Add the bread crumbs and toss just until the crumbs are moistened with the oil mixture. (Do not overmix or the mixture will become gooey.)

Preheat the oven to 425°.

Sprinkle the bread crumbs over the cauliflower and bake for 10 minutes. If additional browning is desired, turn on the broiler and place the dish under it for a few minutes. Serve.

Per serving: 64 calories, 2 g. fat (26% of calories), 0.3 g. saturated fat, 0 mg. cholesterol, 215 mg. sodium.

Braised Endive

Yield: 6 servings

i love Belgian endive braised with a dash of sugar and a little water. Endive should have a nutty taste with just a hint of bitterness, although it tends to be more bitter at some times of the year than others. Placing an inverted plate on top of the endive as it cooks helps to keep it submerged in the cooking liquid, which produces a vegetable that is moist and uniform in color. It is best served directly after cooking, although you can prepare it a day ahead, store it in the refrigerator and reheat it in its cooking liquid just before serving.

       6 **Belgian endives (2½–3 ounces each), trimmed**
    1½ **teaspoons canola oil**
       1 **teaspoon sugar**
      ½ **teaspoon salt**
      ½ **cup water**

Wash the endives and, if they are very large, cut them in half lengthwise. Arrange in a single layer in a large stainless steel saucepan. Sprinkle with the oil, sugar and salt; add the water. Place an inverted plate (smaller than the saucepan) over the endives and bring the liquid to a boil over high heat. Reduce the heat to low, cover the pan with a lid and boil the mixture very gently for 20 minutes. Then lift off the lid and the plate. Boil over high heat until the liquid is reduced to 2 or 3 tablespoons.

To serve, arrange the endives in a star pattern on a serving plate and pour the cooking juices over them. Serve.

Per serving: 25 calories, 1.3 g. fat (42% of calories), 0.1 g. saturated fat, 0 mg. cholesterol, 193 mg. sodium.

Sautéed Mushrooms with Cilantro and Lemon Juice

Yield: 6 servings

i buy medium-size mushrooms for this dish and cook them whole. Most of the mushrooms I use in my recipes come from the discount rack at the back of my neighborhood supermarket. The packaged mushrooms I find there usually have open gills and are dark underneath, but those are indicators of ripeness, and riper mushrooms tend to be more flavorful.

Any concerns about mushrooms discoloring as a result of washing can be put to rest. It is not a question of whether to wash mushrooms but rather when to wash them. Discoloration occurs only if the mushrooms are washed ahead. Croutons, added here at the end, provide a crunchy contrast in texture.

1¼ pounds medium domestic mushrooms
2 teaspoons virgin olive oil
½ teaspoon salt
2 slices bread (about 2 ounces)
¼ cup coarsely chopped fresh cilantro leaves
1 tablespoon lemon juice
2–3 cloves garlic, peeled, crushed and finely chopped
(1½ teaspoons)
¼ teaspoon freshly ground black pepper

Just before cooking, wash the mushrooms and drain them well. Place the whole mushrooms in a large skillet with the oil and salt. Set the skillet over medium heat, cover and cook for about 15 minutes, or until all the liquid that emerges from the mushrooms as they cook disappears.

Meanwhile, toast the bread and cut the slices into ½″ cubes. (You should have about 1 cup of croutons.)

Uncover the mushrooms and continue cooking them until they are nicely browned on all sides. Then add the cilantro, lemon juice, garlic and pepper. Sauté the mixture for 20 seconds. Add the croutons, toss for a few seconds and serve immediately.

Per serving: 62 calories, 2.3 g. fat (30% of calories), 0.3 g. saturated fat, 0 mg. cholesterol, 226 mg. sodium.

Onion Papillote

his versatile vegetable dish is also used elsewhere in the book as the base for Onion Sauce (page 19). Cooking the peeled onions in the oven caramelizes them, making them intensely rich in flavor. Onions like Vidalia and Maui give especially good results.

6   large white onions (8 ounces each), peeled
1   tablespoon canola, virgin olive or corn oil

Preheat the oven to 450°.

Brush each onion with ½ teaspoon of the oil and arrange, stem side up, side by side on a large sheet of aluminum foil. Gather the foil to enclose them completely and place the package on a cookie sheet.

Place the cookie sheet in the upper third of the oven and bake for 1 to 1½ hours, or until the onions are soft throughout when pierced with the point of a sharp knife; the base of each should be brown and caramelized. Serve immediately.

Per serving: 106 calories, 2.6 g. fat (21% of calories), 0.2 g. saturated fat, 0 mg. cholesterol, 7 mg. sodium.

Onion papillote is a great accompaniment for barbecued foods. You can cook the onions, in their foil packages, right on the grill; turn them often during the process. Or you can prepare the onions ahead and simply reheat them on the grill. When the big sweet onions, such as Vidalias, Mauis or Walla Wallas are in season, use them instead of regular white onions. For variety, sprinkle the onions with herbs before wrapping them in the foil.

Fettuccine in Bitter Salad

Yield: 6 generous servings

itter salad greens—escarole, radicchio and Belgian endive—are sautéed here with garlic and crushed red pepper and served over fettuccine. Although included in the accompaniments chapter, this dish would also make a good first course or light entrée. When cooking pasta for this and other recipes in the book, remember to reserve a little of the cooking liquid. Mix it into the pasta along with the sauce or topping at serving time to give added moisture and flavor to the dish. You can also serve these cooked greens without the pasta as a meat or poultry accompaniment.

4	tablespoons virgin olive oil
5–6	cloves garlic, peeled, crushed and finely chopped (1 tablespoon)
½	teaspoon crushed red pepper flakes
1	small head escarole (4 ounces), leaves separated, washed, dried and cut into 1″ pieces (5 cups)
1	small head radicchio (4 ounces), cut crosswise into ½″ slices, washed and dried (4 cups)
3	Belgian endives (4 ounces), cut in half lengthwise, then into long ¼″-thick strips, washed and dried (2½ cups)
¾	teapoon salt
1	pound fettuccine
3	tablespoons chopped fresh parsley leaves
1	tablespoon grated Parmesan cheese (optional)

Bring about 3 quarts of water to a boil in a large pot.

Meanwhile, heat 2 tablespoons of the oil in a large saucepan. When the oil is hot, add the garlic and pepper flakes; cook for 10 to 15 seconds. Then add a handful of the escarole, first pressing it down into the pan and then turning the mixture over so the garlic is mixed in with the greens and doesn't burn in the bottom of the pan. Add the remainder of the escarole plus the radicchio, endives and ½ teaspoon of the salt. Cover and cook the mixture over medium to low heat for 5 minutes, stirring occasionally.

Add the fettucine to the boiling water and return the water to a boil. Boil the pasta for about 10 minutes, or until firm to the bite (al dente).

Remove ½ cup of the pasta cooking liquid and place it in a bowl with the parsley, the remaining 2 tablespoons oil and the remaining ¼ teaspoon salt. Drain the pasta well and add it to the bowl.

Fettuccine in Bitter Salad

Add the cooked greens (with any liquid). Toss well. To serve, divide among 6 plates. If desired, sprinkle with the Parmesan.

Per serving: 354 calories, 11.3 g. fat (29% of calories), 1.6 g. saturated fat, 65 mg. cholesterol, 289 mg. sodium.

Pasta and Escarole

Yield: 6 servings

*E*scarole is best—nutty tasting and mildly bitter—when it has a white or pale green center. Take care not to let the garlic and crushed red pepper burn in the bottom of the skillet after you add the escarole. Enough moisture should emerge from the escarole as it cooks to prevent this, but if there isn't enough add a tablespoon or two of water and toss the mixture well.

I use penne pasta here because it is short, easy to eat and mixes well with the escarole. You could, however, substitute ziti or any other small shell or elbow macaroni. This recipe makes enough to serve six as a first course or side dish. If you want to serve it as a vegetarian main dish, double it.

4½	ounces penne pasta
5–6	cloves garlic, peeled, crushed and finely chopped (1 tablespoon)
⅛	teaspoon crushed red pepper flakes
1	head escarole (about 12 ounces) with the whitest possible inside, trimmed, washed and cut into 2″–3″ pieces (about 12 cups loosely packed)
1	tablespoon virgin olive oil
½	teaspoon salt

Bring about 5 cups of water to a boil in a medium pot. Add the penne and cook for 15 to 20 minutes, or until tender but still somewhat firm to the bite (al dente).

Meanwhile, lightly coat a large skillet or saucepan with vegetable cooking spray and set it over high heat. When the pan is hot, add the garlic and pepper flakes; cook, stirring, for 1 minute. Then add about half the escarole; stir well to mix in the garlic and keep it from burning in the bottom of the pan. Add the remainder of the escarole and cook it for 6 to 8 minutes, until most of the surrounding liquid has evaporated.

Drain the pasta well and add it to the escarole along with the oil and salt. Toss well to mix. Serve.

Per serving: 112 calories, 2.7 g. fat (22% of calories), 0.4 g. saturated fat, 0 mg. cholesterol, 192 mg. sodium.

Pea, Mushroom and Corn Medley

Yield: 6 servings

he most important thing to remember when preparing this quick recipe is not to overcook the vegetables. The peas and corn require only two to three minutes of cooking to achieve maximum flavor.

1 tablespoon corn oil

1 tablespoon unsalted butter

2 medium shallots (about 2 ounces), peeled, trimmed and finely chopped (⅓ cup)

8 ounces domestic mushrooms, washed and cut into ½″ dice (3 cups)

3 ears sweet corn (about 1½ pounds), husked with kernels cut off the cobs (2¾ cups)

8 ounces shelled fresh peas or equivalent amount of frozen petite peas, thawed

½ teaspoon sugar

½ teaspoon salt

¼ teaspoon freshly ground black pepper

Heat the oil and butter in a large saucepan. When they are hot, add the shallots and sauté them for 30 seconds. Add the mushrooms, cover and cook over high heat for 1 minute. Then add the corn, peas, sugar, salt and pepper; mix well, cover and cook for 2 to 3 minutes longer. Toss the mixture well and serve.

Per serving: 147 calories, 4.6 g. fat (26% of calories), 1.6 g. saturated fat, 6 mg. cholesterol, 185 mg. sodium.

Lime Peas in Tomato Cups

Yield: 6 servings

his side dish is a great accompaniment for most poultry, meat and fish main courses. The tomatoes are warmed rather than cooked, so they retain their raw taste. The peas, too, are cooked at the last moment. I advise using baby peas—sometimes referred to as petite, tender or tiny—because they have thinner skins and are more tender than large peas.

3 ripe medium tomatoes (about 1¼ pounds)
2 teaspoons unsalted butter
1 package (10 ounces) frozen tiny or petite peas, thawed
¼ teaspoon sugar
¼ teaspoon salt
⅛ teaspoon freshly ground black pepper
1 teaspoon grated lime rind

Cut the tomatoes in half crosswise and, using a metal measuring spoon (because these spoons have sharp edges), hollow them out, leaving a wall about ¼″ thick. (Reserve the scooped-out seeds, juice and ribs for use in stock, if desired.) Arrange the tomatoes on a baking tray, hollow side up, and place them in a 180° oven for 10 to 15 minutes, just long enough to warm them through.

Heat the butter in a medium saucepan. When it is hot, add the peas, sugar, salt and pepper. Cook for about 2 minutes, then add the lime rind, toss to mix well and spoon the peas into the tomato cups. Serve immediately.

Per serving: 72 calories, 1.8 g. fat (21% of calories), 0.9 g. saturated fat, 4 mg. cholesterol, 99 mg. sodium.

This recipe is designed for ripe, flavorful tomatoes, preferably those sold in season. If you buy tomatoes that are not fully ripe, store them at room temperature. Putting them in the refrigerator will inhibit further ripening.

Stuffed Red Peppers

Yield: 6 servings

*H*alved red bell peppers are first cooked briefly in water, then filled with a mixture that includes onions, celery, spinach and—for body and texture—great Northern beans.

3	medium red bell peppers (1¼ pounds), halved, cored and seeded
2	tablespoons virgin olive oil
1	medium onion (5–6 ounces), peeled and chopped (1 cup)
1	stalk celery (about 2 ounces), washed, trimmed and chopped (½ cup)
5	cloves garlic, peeled and thinly sliced (2 tablespoons)
10	ounces spinach, trimmed and washed (about 8 cups)
1	can (16 ounces) great Northern beans
¼	teaspoon freshly ground black pepper
¼	teaspoon salt
1½	tablespoons grated Parmesan cheese

Bring about 2 quarts of water to a boil in a large, deep saucepan or pot. Add the red peppers and bring the water back to a boil over high heat. Reduce the heat to low, cover and cook at a gentle boil for 10 minutes. Drain well.

Preheat the oven to 400°.

Heat the oil in a large nonstick skillet. When it is hot, add the onions and celery; sauté over medium to high heat for 1 to 2 minutes. Add the garlic and sauté the mixture for 30 seconds longer. Then add the spinach and move it around in the pan for about 1 minute, until it has wilted.

Add the beans (with liquid) and black pepper to the skillet; mix well.

Sprinkle the salt on the cut side of the red peppers and arrange them side by side in a large gratin dish. Fill the peppers with the spinach mixture, dividing it evenly among them and spooning any excess around the peppers. Sprinkle with the Parmesan. Bake the peppers for 10 minutes.

Turn on the broiler and place the peppers about 6″ from the heat for 3 to 4 minutes, until nicely browned on top. Serve immediately.

Per serving: 182 calories, 5.6 g. fat (26% of calories), 1.1 g. saturated fat, 1 mg. cholesterol, 162 mg. sodium.

Roasted Red Peppers in Rice Wine Vinegar

Yield: 6 servings

*F*or this recipe, I first broil red bell peppers until their skin is charred, then wrap them in foil and let them stand until the skin loosens and can be slid off. I think this procedure, although somewhat time consuming, is well worth the effort, as the peppers are very good when prepared this way. If, however, you don't have time for this initial step, you can substitute a can of peeled pimentos for the roasted peppers. When fresh rosemary is available, use 1 teaspoon of it in place of the dried herb. These peppers keep in the refrigerator for at least two weeks.

4–6   red bell peppers (2 pounds)
¼   cup rice wine vinegar
¼   cup toasted sunflower seeds
½   teaspoon salt
½   teaspoon sugar
½   teaspoon paprika
½   teaspoon dried rosemary
¼   teaspoon freshly ground black pepper
6   strips lemon rind removed with a vegetable peeler

Preheat the broiler.

Line the rack of an oven broiler pan with aluminum foil and arrange the red peppers on the rack with as much space between them as possible. Place them under the broiler so the tops are about 4″ from the heat. Broil for about 6 minutes, until the skin on top is charred. Giving the peppers a quarter turn at a time with tongs, continue broiling them for a total of 15 minutes, or until the skin is charred on all sides. Transfer the peppers to a large sheet of aluminum foil, wrap the foil around them and set them aside to steam for 10 minutes.

Meanwhile, in a bowl large enough to hold the peppers, combine the vinegar, sunflower seeds, salt, sugar, paprika, rosemary, black pepper and lemon rind.

Peel the black skin from the peppers, halve them and remove the cores and seeds. Cut the peppers lengthwise into ½″ strips. Add the pepper strips to the bowl and mix well. Cover and refrigerate; allow the peppers to marinate for a few hours before serving.

Per serving: 79 calories, 3.3 g. fat (33% of calories), 0.4 g. saturated fat, 0 mg. cholesterol, 181 mg. sodium.

Roasted Red Peppers in Rice Wine Vinegar

Rice wine vinegar is a light vinegar with a slightly sweet flavor. It is available in many grocery stores in the Asian-foods section.

Some books tell you to peel roasted peppers by holding them under running water. But rinsing may remove some of the peppers' intense flavor. It's just as easy to use a knife or your fingers to peel off the skin.

Spinach and Crouton Mélange

F or this quickly prepared dish, I cook spinach in a little olive oil flavored with garlic and crushed red pepper. Homemade croutons serve as a delightful garnish.

1	piece French-style baguette bread loaf (3 ounces), cut into 1″ cubes (1½ cups, loosely packed)
2	tablespoons virgin olive oil
2–3	cloves garlic, peeled and thinly sliced (1 tablespoon)
1	teaspoon crushed red pepper flakes
2½	pounds spinach, trimmed and washed
⅓–½	cup water
¾	teaspoon salt

Preheat the oven to 400°.

To make the croutons, arrange the bread cubes in a single layer on a cookie sheet and bake them for 12 minutes, or until they are browned on all sides.

Heat the oil in a very large saucepan. When it is hot, add the garlic, pepper flakes and 2 handfuls (about half) of the spinach, still wet from washing. Add ⅓ to ½ cup water (depending on how wet the spinach is). Turn the mixture in the pan to bring the garlic from underneath and prevent it from burning.

Add the remainder of the spinach, pressing it into the pan. Cover and cook the spinach over high heat for 5 minutes, removing the lid and stirring it occasionally.

Season the spinach with the salt, then transfer it to a serving dish, garnish with the croutons and serve immediately.

Per serving: 114 calories, 5.5 g. fat (40% of calories), 0.8 g. saturated fat, 0 mg. cholesterol, 441 mg. sodium.

Glazed Turnips

Yield: 6 servings

hese turnips develop an intensely nutty flavor during baking. I start by cooking them in a lot of water—something I don't recommend for other vegetables. I do this because turnips have a very assertive taste, and I find that this makes them milder and more flavorful.

     4 medium white turnips (about 1 pound), peeled
     4 cups boiling water
     2 teaspoons canola, corn or virgin olive oil
     2 tablespoons white wine vinegar
     1 teaspoon sugar
    ⅛ teaspoon freshly ground black pepper

Cut the turnips into ½″ slices and arrange them in a large skillet. Add the water, bring the water back to a boil and cook the turnips for 2 minutes. Drain.

Brush a gratin dish with the oil. Arrange the turnips in the dish, turning them once in the oil so they are coated on both sides. Sprinkle with the vinegar, sugar and pepper.

Preheat the oven to 400°.

Bake the turnips for 30 minutes, or until they are soft. Turn on the broiler and brown the turnips for 1 to 2 minutes. Serve as soon as possible.

Per serving: 30 calories, 1.6 g. fat (42% of calories), 0.1 g. saturated fat, 0 mg. cholesterol, 36 mg. sodium.

Let turnips give plain mashed potatoes an interesting flavor. Simply boil some cut turnips with the potatoes and mash everything together.

Seared Tomatoes with Bread Topping

*B*est made with ripe, full-season tomatoes, this delightful dish is good company fare, since it can be partially prepared ahead. You can halve the tomatoes, sear them and sprinkle them with the seasoned bread crumbs up to an hour beforehand. Then you can finish them under a hot broiler just before serving.

6 medium tomatoes (2½ pounds)
1 tablespoon plus ½ teaspoon virgin olive oil
2 slices bread
3 scallions (about 2 ounces), washed, trimmed and chopped (⅓ cup)
1 tablespoon chopped fresh thyme
2 cloves garlic, peeled, crushed and finely chopped (1 teaspoon)
½ teaspoon salt
¼ teaspoon freshly ground black pepper

Cut the tomatoes in half crosswise. Brush a very large nonstick skillet with ½ teaspoon of the oil and place it over high heat. When the oil is hot, add the tomato halves, cut side down, and sear for 5 minutes, or until they are nicely browned. Transfer the tomatoes to a large gratin dish, placing them seared side up and side by side in the dish.

Preheat the oven to 400°.

Break the bread into the bowl of a food processor and process it until crumbed. Add the scallions, thyme, garlic, salt and pepper and pulse until the mixture is combined. Then transfer the crumb mixture to a small bowl and toss it lightly with the remaining 1 tablespoon oil. (Do not overmix or it will become gooey.)

Sprinkle the bread crumb mixture on top of the tomatoes, taking care not to press on the crumbs or pack them. Bake in the center of the oven for 10 minutes. Then turn on the broiler, move the dish to the top shelf of the oven and broil for a few minutes, watching closely, until the crumbs are brown.

Per serving: 90 calories, 3.6 g. fat (33% of calories), 0.5 g. saturated fat, 0 mg. cholesterol, 238 mg. sodium.

Seared Tomatoes with Bread Topping

Cold Stuffed Tomatoes with Bulgur and Raw Tomato Sauce

Cold Stuffed Tomatoes
with Bulgur and Raw Tomato Sauce

Yield: 6 servings

his makes a great side dish but can also be served as a vegetarian main dish for a light summer dinner. Bulgur—made from wheat kernels that have been steamed, dried and crushed—must be reconstituted before use. I soak it in hot stock here, which softens it more quickly than letting it stand in cold water.

5½ ounces bulgur wheat (1 cup)

1½ cups Clear Vegetable Stock (page 15) or canned
    vegetable broth

  6 medium tomatoes (about 6 ounces each)

  2 tablespoons virgin olive oil

 ¼ teaspoon freshly ground black pepper

1¼ teaspoons salt (adjust if canned broth is used)

  1 medium cucumber (11 ounces), trimmed, peeled, seeded
    and cut into ¼″ dice (1½ cups)

  1 red bell pepper (4 ounces), halved, cored, seeded and
    cut into ¼″ dice (1 cup)

 ½ cup cooked fresh peas or frozen peas blanched for 1 minute

  1 cup loosely packed fresh parsley leaves, chopped (½ cup)

 ½ cup loosely packed fresh mint leaves, minced (¼ cup)

 ¼ cup dark raisins

 ¼ cup lemon juice

 ½ teaspoon Tabasco hot-pepper sauce

Place the bulgur and stock or broth in a large saucepan and bring the mixture to a strong boil. Remove the pan from the heat, cover and set aside for 45 minutes.

Core the tomatoes. Cut off the smooth end of each tomato about ¼ of the way down and reserve the pieces you remove to use as lids. Scoop out the insides of the tomatoes, using a metal measuring spoon (because these spoons have sharp edges) and leaving a wall about ¼″ thick. Set the tomatoes aside.

Place the tomato flesh and seeds in the bowl of a food processor and puree. Strain the mixture into a bowl, at first shaking the strainer while tapping firmly on its edge with a dull knife (so as not to clog the mesh initially and thus

(continued)

restrict the flow of the liquids) and then, finally, pressing on the solids to extract any remaining juice. Mix in the oil, black pepper and ¼ teaspoon of the salt. Set aside.

Fluff the bulgur with a fork and add the cucumbers, red peppers, peas, parsley, mint, raisins, lemon juice, hot-pepper sauce and the remaining 1 teaspoon salt. Toss to mix well.

Stuff the tomatoes with the bulgur mixture, lightly packing it into the shells and mounding it on top. Pour about ½ cup of the reserved tomato sauce on a platter and arrange the tomatoes on top. Lean a tomato lid alongside each tomato and serve, passing any extra stuffing and tomato sauce.

Per serving: 212 calories, 5.6 g. fat (22% of calories), 0.8 g. saturated fat, 0 mg. cholesterol, 474 mg. sodium.

This is a wonderful buffet dish. If you are serving many items, make smaller versions of these tomatoes by using plum tomatoes instead of the larger ones specified here. Cut them in half lengthwise and proceed as directed.

Successful dishes often have contrasts in flavors, textures and colors. Here the assertive flavors of mint, raisins, lemon and hot-pepper sauce give pizzazz to the bland bulgur. The brilliant reds and greens of the vegetables and herbs make this dish visually stimulating. And the contrasting textures of the soft bulgur and the crunchy cucumbers and peppers make it extra appealing.

Boiled Potatoes

y family likes plain boiled potatoes so much that we sometimes eat them as a light supper main dish with only a green salad accompaniment. Usually, of course, we enjoy them—sometimes peeled, sometimes not—with dishes like roast chicken or poached fish. For best results when preparing this simple dish, drain the potatoes immediately after they are cooked. The result is creamier and richer than if the potatoes are left standing in the cooking liquid until serving time.

16–20	**small red potatoes (2 pounds), scrubbed**
¼	**teaspoon salt**

Peel the potatoes (or leave them unpeeled, removing only the eyes and blemishes). Wash the potatoes and place them in a large saucepan with enough cold water to cover them by ½″. Add the salt.

Bring the water to a boil over high heat. Then reduce the heat to low, cover and boil the potatoes gently for 25 to 30 minutes, or until they are tender when pierced with the point of a sharp knife.

Drain off the water; most of the remaining moisture in the potatoes will emerge as steam. Cover the pan and set the potatoes aside briefly. They will absorb any additional moisture, becoming creamy smooth, densely textured and rich in taste. Serve.

Per serving: 129 calories, 0.2 g. fat (1% of calories), 0 g. saturated fat, 0 mg. cholesterol, 96 mg. sodium.

Pommes Boulangère

his dish develops even more flavor if made a few hours ahead and reheated in a regular or microwave oven just before serving. Named boulangère *after the baker's wife, the dish used to be prepared in a crock and cooked slowly in the baker's oven, which gave it a wonderfully concentrated flavor.*

4–6	medium boiling potatoes (2 pounds), scrubbed
1	tablespoon virgin olive oil
2	medium onions (12 ounces), peeled and thinly sliced (3 cups)
3	cups White Chicken Stock (page 14) or lower-salt canned chicken broth
6–7	large cloves garlic, peeled and thinly sliced (3 tablespoons)
2	bay leaves
1	teaspoon dried thyme
¼	teaspoon salt (adjust if canned broth is used)
¼	teaspoon freshly ground black pepper
2	tablespoons chopped fresh parsley leaves

Remove any eyes or damaged areas from the potatoes with a paring knife. Peel the potatoes, then wash them under cool tap water and cut them crosswise into ⅛″ slices. Without rinsing them after slicing, layer the potatoes in a large gratin dish. The potato layer should be about 1″ thick.

Preheat the oven to 400°.

Heat the oil in a large skillet. When it is hot, add the onions and sauté them for 4 to 5 minutes. Add the stock or broth, garlic, bay leaves, thyme, salt and pepper. Bring the mixture to a strong boil, pour it over the potatoes and mix the ingredients together to distribute the onion mixture evenly throughout.

Bake for 1 to 1½ hours, until the potatoes are soft when pierced with the point of a sharp knife and the dish is well browned on top. Set aside for 20 minutes, then remove and discard the bay leaves. Sprinkle with the parsley and serve.

Per serving: 178 calories, 2.6 g. fat (13% of calories), 0.4 g. saturated fat, 0 mg. cholesterol, 101 mg. sodium.

Baked Stuffed Potatoes

Yield: 6 servings

i don't recommend baking potatoes wrapped in foil; they tend to steam rather than bake, and the skin is not nearly as appealing.

The stuffing used here contains yogurt cheese. Mixed with fresh chives and scallions, it imitates very well the flavor of a traditional sour cream topping, without all the fat and calories.

6	baking potatoes (10 ounces each), scrubbed
1½	cups nonfat yogurt cheese (see below)
3	scallions (about 2 ounces), washed, trimmed and finely chopped (6 tablespoons)
3	tablespoons chopped fresh chives
¾	teaspoon salt
½	teaspoon freshly ground black pepper
6	sprigs fresh dill, chopped

Preheat the oven to 400°.

Remove any eyes or damaged areas from the potatoes with a paring knife. Place the potatoes on a baking tray and bake for about 1 hour and 10 minutes, or until they are tender when pierced with the point of a sharp knife.

Mix the yogurt cheese, scallions, chives, salt and pepper in a bowl.

To serve, make intersecting slits, one lengthwise and one crosswise, through the skin of each potato; squeeze the potatoes lightly, pushing toward the center to open the slits and lightly loosen the flesh. Mound about ¼ cup of the stuffing mixture in the opening of each potato, sprinkle with the dill and serve.

Per serving: 325 calories, 0.4 g. fat (1% of calories), 0.2 g. saturated fat, 1 mg. cholesterol, 338 mg. sodium.

To make yogurt cheese, pour about 3 cups of plain nonfat yogurt into a strainer lined with dampened paper towels. Use yogurt that has not been thickened with gelatin, or it won't drain. Set the strainer over a large bowl. Cover and refrigerate for 4 to 6 hours to drain. Discard the whey that drains into the bowl. To store, cover tightly and refrigerate.

Roasted New Potatoes

Yield: 6 servings

I particularly like the taste of potatoes and garlic together. Here, I roast unpeeled red potatoes with unpeeled garlic. To extract the mild, tender garlic flesh from the surrounding skin, either press lightly on the cloves with the tines of a fork until the flesh slides out or use your fingers to squeeze the garlic out of its skin and directly into your mouth.

12	small red potatoes (2 pounds), scrubbed
1	tablespoon virgin olive oil
1	head garlic, unpeeled but divided into cloves (12–14)
4–5	sprigs fresh rosemary
¼	teaspoon salt

Preheat the oven to 400°.

Remove any eyes or damaged areas from the potatoes with a paring knife.

Place the oil in a large ovenproof skillet. Add the potatoes and mix well to coat them with oil. Add the garlic, rosemary and salt. Bake for 30 minutes, then turn the potatoes over and return the skillet to the oven for 30 minutes longer. Serve, dividing the potatoes and garlic among 6 plates.

Per serving: 148 calories, 2.4 g. fat (15% of calories), 1.8 g. saturated fat, 0 mg. cholesterol, 96 mg. sodium.

Roasted garlic can be used in many ways. You can serve it as a vegetable with roast chicken, roast beef or other simply prepared meats. You can add it to all manner of pasta dishes. Or you can squeeze the softened garlic from its skin and spread it on bread as a low-fat substitute for butter.

Mashed Potatoes and Carrots

Yield: 6 servings

i *prepare this attractive and delicious combination often at home. The cloves of garlic cooked with the potatoes and carrots give the dish a wonderful taste. Instead of using milk to soften the puree, I use the cooking liquid from the vegetables. Take care not to overprocess the vegetables; small pieces of carrot should be visible in the mixture. I add a tablespoon of butter (which amounts to only ½ teaspoon per person) at the end, when it will most enhance the flavor. For the tastiest result, use only good-quality, unsalted butter.*

- 3 medium potatoes (about 1 pound), scrubbed
- 3 medium carrots (about 8 ounces), trimmed, peeled and cut into 2″ chunks
- 2 cloves garlic, peeled
- 1 tablespoon unsalted butter
- ½ teaspoon salt
- ¼ teaspoon freshly ground black pepper

Remove any eyes or damaged areas from the potatoes with a paring knife. Peel the potatoes and cut them into 2″ chunks.

Place the potatoes, carrots and garlic in a large saucepan and add enough water to just cover the vegetables by ½″. Bring the water to a boil over high heat, then reduce the heat to low, cover and cook until the vegetables are soft. Drain, retaining the liquid. (You should have ½ cup of liquid; if you have more, return the liquid to the saucepan and boil it until it is reduced to ½ cup.)

Place the vegetables and the cooking liquid in the bowl of a food processor with the butter, salt and pepper. Process briefly, just until combined. (Small carrot chunks—about ¼″—should still be visible.) Serve.

Per serving: 100 calories, 2.2 g. fat (19% of calories), 1.3 g. saturated fat, 6 mg. cholesterol, 195 mg. sodium.

Garden-Style Potato Salad

Yield: 6 servings

otato salad is a must for any type of picnic or outside dining, and this leaner version of the classic dish—without mayonnaise—is a staple at our house, especially during hot-weather months. The addition of garlic, scallions and leeks gives the dish a wonderful garden-fresh flavor. Although I prefer to leave the potatoes unpeeled, you can peel them after cooking if you object to the taste and texture of potato skin.

6 medium new potatoes (2 pounds), scrubbed

1 tablespoon canola oil

1 small leek (3–4 ounces), trimmed, finely chopped and washed (¾ cup)

6 scallions (about 4 ounces), washed, trimmed and thinly sliced (1 cup)

4 cloves garlic, peeled, crushed and finely chopped (2 teaspoons)

⅓ cup dry white wine

2 tablespoons chopped fresh tarragon leaves

1 tablespoon Dijon mustard

½ teaspoon salt

½ teaspoon freshly ground black pepper

2 tablespoons virgin olive oil

2 tablespoons sherry vinegar

Remove any eyes or damaged areas from the potatoes with a paring knife. Place the potatoes in a large saucepan and add enough cold water to cover them by ½″.

Bring the water to a boil, reduce the heat to medium or low and cook the potatoes gently (adding water to the pan as needed to keep them covered) for about 35 minutes, or until the potatoes are tender when pierced with the point of a sharp knife. Drain immediately and let cool to lukewarm.

Cut the potatoes crosswise into ½″ slices and put them in a large serving bowl.

Heat the canola oil in a large skillet. When it is hot, add the leeks and sauté them for 1 minute. Then add the scallions and garlic and sauté them for 30 seconds. Add the wine, bring the mixture to a boil and pour it over the potatoes.

Add the tarragon, mustard, salt and pepper; mix well. Then add the olive oil and vinegar and toss the salad ingredients together gently but thoroughly.

Serve warm or cool.

Per serving: 222 calories, 7.3 g. fat (29% of calories), 0.8 g. saturated fat, 0 mg. cholesterol, 225 mg. sodium.

Honeyed Sweet Potatoes

Yield: 6 servings

great garnish for turkey, duck or game, this dish is ideal for Thanksgiving or the Christmas holiday season. You can prepare it up to one day ahead and reheat it just before serving. Although I don't peel the potatoes for this recipe, you can do so if you object to the taste or texture of the peel.

    5 sweet potatoes (about 3 pounds), scrubbed
    2 tablespoons canola, corn or safflower oil
    ¼ teaspoon freshly ground black pepper
    3 tablespoons honey

Remove any eyes or damaged areas from the potatoes with a paring knife. Cut the potatoes on a crosswise slant into 1½" slices.

Place the slices in a large saucepan with enough water to cover them by ½". Bring the water to a boil, reduce the heat to medium or low and boil the potatoes gently for 5 minutes. Drain.

Heat the oil in a very large skillet (or 2 smaller ones). When it is hot, add the potato slices in a single layer, sprinkle them with the pepper and sauté them over medium to high heat for 2 minutes on each side. Add the honey. Reduce the heat to low, cover and cook the potatoes for 2½ minutes longer on each side. Serve.

Per serving: 255 calories, 4.7 g. fat (16% of calories), 0.4 g. saturated fat, 0 mg. cholesterol, 18 mg. sodium.

Orecchiette Pasta with Red Onion

Yield: 6 generous servings

For this dish, I like to use ear-shaped orecchiette. If you can't find it in your store, use bow-tie pasta. Both are easy to eat, and, because they're unevenly shaped, tend to hold sauce well. This dish could also be served as a first course or light entrée.

3	tablespoons virgin olive oil
3	medium or 2 large red onions (1 pound), peeled and thinly sliced (4 cups)
1	cup water
1	pound orecchiette pasta
1	can (2 ounces) flat anchovies in oil, cut into ¼″ pieces
4–5	cloves garlic, peeled, crushed and finely chopped (2 teaspoons)
¼	cup chopped fresh oregano
½	teaspoon salt
½	teaspoon freshly ground black pepper
	Grated or thinly sliced Parmesan cheese

Bring about 3 quarts of water to a boil in a pot.

Meanwhile, heat the oil in a large saucepan. When it is hot, add the onions and 1 cup water; mix well and bring the mixture to a boil. Then reduce the heat to low, cover and cook for 10 minutes, until the water evaporates. Remove the lid and cook the onions for 5 minutes over high heat, stirring occasionally, until lightly browned.

Add the pasta to the boiling water and return the water to a boil, stirring the pasta occasionally at first so it doesn't stick together or to the pot. Cook the pasta for 12 minutes, or until firm to the bite (al dente).

Remove ¾ cup of the pasta cooking liquid from the pot and reserve it.

Add the anchovies, garlic and oregano to the onions in the saucepan, mix well and stir in the salt, pepper and the reserved pasta cooking liquid.

Drain the pasta well and add it to the onion mixture. Toss to mix, then divide among 6 plates. Serve topped with the Parmesan.

Per serving: 374 calories, 10 g. fat (24% of calories), 1.5 g. saturated fat, 73 mg. cholesterol, 540 mg. sodium.

Orecchiette Pasta with Red Onion

Basic Rice

Yield: 6 servings

We often serve this basic boiled rice at home as an accompaniment for stews, chili and other dishes that have a lot of liquid, but we even enjoy it with fish and other entrées. Using the ingredients listed below in the proportions indicated, my wife often prepares rice in a rice cooker, which does a great job. Cooking the rice in a saucepan, as suggested in the recipe, produces good results, too. I used standard long-grain rice here, but other varieties—short-grain white or Thai, for example—can be substituted.

2 cups water

¼ teaspoon salt

1 cup uncooked long-grain white rice

Place the water and salt in a medium saucepan, preferably stainless steel or nonstick. Bring the water to a boil, then add the rice, stir well and return the water to a boil. Immediately reduce the heat to very low, cover the pan with a lid and cook the rice for 20 minutes, or until it is tender but not mushy. Fluff the rice with a fork and serve about ½ cup per person.

Per serving: 113 calories, 0.2 g. fat (2% of calories), 0.1 g. saturated fat, 0 mg. cholesterol, 90 mg. sodium.

Many supermarkets and health food stores sell rice in bulk. That enables you to buy rice at lower prices and in smaller quantities. It also gives you a chance to sample the many different varieties available.

Spicy Rice

his spicy side dish goes with a myriad of main courses—anything from fish to poultry to meat. Cut back on the jalapeño pepper if you prefer your food less hot.

1	small jalapeño pepper
2	tablespoons corn, safflower or canola oil
1	large onion (about 7 ounces), peeled and coarsely chopped (about 1½ cups)
5–6	cloves garlic, peeled, crushed and finely chopped (1 tablespoon)
1	teaspoon ground coriander
1	teaspoon ground cumin
½	teaspoon ground turmeric
1½	cups uncooked long-grain white rice
3	cups water
½	teaspoon salt

If desired, remove the seeds and ribs from the pepper to eliminate some of its hotness. Chop the pepper.

Place the peppers in a large, heavy saucepan. Add the oil, onions, garlic, coriander, cumin and turmeric. Cook the mixture gently over medium heat for 5 minutes, until the onions are soft.

Add the rice and mix well. Then add the water and salt; bring the mixture to a boil, stirring occasionally. Reduce the heat to very low, cover and cook gently for 20 minutes without stirring. Serve, if possible, within the next hour. If reheating is required, do so in a microwave oven for best results.

Per serving: 228 calories, 5 g. fat (20% of calories), 0.7 g. saturated fat, 0 mg. cholesterol, 196 mg. sodium.

Brown Rice with Celery and Onions

*B*rown rice can be a little tricky to prepare properly. Depending on the rice itself, the amount of water required and the length of time the rice must cook to be tender can vary dramatically. The 1¼ cups of brown basmati rice I prepared for this recipe absorbed 3 cups of water and took an hour to cook; the rice you use may absorb more or less liquid and require a longer or shorter cooking time.

1 tablespoon canola or corn oil

1 medium stalk celery (about 2 ounces), washed, trimmed and chopped (½ cup)

1 small onion (about 3 ounces), peeled and chopped (½ cup)

1¼ cups uncooked brown basmati rice

2 bay leaves

¼ teaspoon salt (adjust if canned broth is used)

¼ teaspoon freshly ground black pepper

3 cups White Chicken Stock (page 14) or lower-salt canned chicken broth

Heat the oil in a large saucepan. When it is hot, add the celery and onions and sauté for 1 minute. Then add the rice, bay leaves, salt and pepper and mix well. Add the stock or broth and bring the mixture to a boil over high heat, stirring occasionally to keep the rice from sticking to the bottom of the pan.

Reduce the heat to very low, cover and cook at a very gentle boil for 1 hour. At this point, the liquid should have been absorbed and the rice should be tender, moist and a little sticky. Remove and discard the bay leaves. Serve, dividing the rice among 6 plates.

Per serving: 173 calories, 3.5 g. fat (18% of calories), 0.4 g. saturated fat, 0 mg. cholesterol, 102 mg. sodium.

Basic Couscous

*C*ouscous, consisting of fine grains made from semolina flour, is a staple in North Africa. Although conventional couscous takes hours to cook, the instant variety available in most supermarkets is ready in about ten minutes.

1½ cups fast-cooking couscous
¼ teaspoon salt
1¼ cups boiling water

Place the couscous and salt in a heat-resistant bowl. Pour in the water. Mix well, cover the bowl with a lid and let stand for a minimum of 10 minutes.

Fluff the couscous with a fork to separate the grains and serve about ⅓ cup per person.

Per serving: 173 calories, 0.3 g. fat (2% of calories), 0 g. saturated fat, 0 mg. cholesterol, 93 mg. sodium.

The best way to reheat leftover couscous is in a microwave. It won't dry out or become soggy that way.

Served at room temperature, couscous is a delicious base for a salad. You can add any type of leftover cooked meats and vegetables. Season the mixture with lemon juice, your choice of herbs or spices and a small amount of oil.

Basil Couscous
with Red Pepper and Sunflower Seeds

Yield: 6 servings

*S*unflower seeds are available toasted at most supermarkets. If you aren't able to find them, however, spread untoasted seeds out on a cookie sheet and bake them at 400° for seven to eight minutes, until lightly browned. To season the couscous, I toss it with an herb paste featuring basil and parsley. You can serve the couscous warm as a vegetable, at room temperature as a first course or cold as a salad.

- 2 cups fast-cooking couscous
- 2 cups boiling water
- 2 cups lightly packed fresh basil leaves
- 1½ cups lightly packed fresh parsley leaves
- ¼ cup White Chicken Stock (page 14) or lower-salt canned chicken broth
- 8 cloves garlic, peeled
- 3 tablespoons virgin olive oil
- 1 teaspoon salt (adjust if canned broth is used)
- ¼ teaspoon freshly ground black pepper
- 1 medium red bell pepper (5 ounces), halved, cored, seeded and chopped (about 1 cup)
- ⅓ cup toasted sunflower seeds

Place the couscous in a heat-resistant bowl and pour the 2 cups water over it. Mix well, cover the bowl with a lid and let stand for a minimum of 10 minutes.

Meanwhile, bring about 4 cups of water to a boil in a medium saucepan. Blanch the basil and parsley by dropping them into the pan of boiling water for 10 to 15 seconds. Drain the herbs well and place them in the bowl of a food processor. Add the stock or broth and garlic; process until smooth. Add the oil, salt and black pepper; process just until incorporated.

Fluff the couscous with a fork to separate the grains. Transfer to a large serving bowl. Add the herb mixture and combine it well with the couscous. Sprinkle on the red peppers and sunflower seeds. Toss well.

Per serving: 358 calories, 11.6 g. fat (29% of calories), 1.4 g. saturated fat, 0 mg. cholesterol, 371 mg. sodium.

Basil Couscous with Red Pepper and Sunflower Seeds

The easiest way to separate the cloves from a head of garlic is to peel off the loose outer skin and then hit the head with the heel of your hand or a sturdy object, such as a saucepan or rolling pin. To peel individual cloves, cut off the root end of each and then use a wide-bladed knife to press down on the clove hard enough to crack the clove open. The skin will come off easily.

Whole-Wheat Couscous
with Vegetables

Yield: 6 servings

hole-wheat couscous is widely available. It takes only ten minutes to reconstitute in boiling water. I use the couscous essentially as a flavorful binder in this stew, which contains the contents of the vegetable drawer of my refrigerator on the day I made it—butternut squash, zucchini, red bell pepper, mushrooms, cauliflower, green beans and leeks. Make substitutions at will, using a total of about 8½ cups of vegetables, and stir in the couscous at the end. A delicious accompaniment for meat and poultry, this also makes a delightful vegetarian main dish. If you can't find whole-wheat couscous, use the regular variety.

    1   cup fast-cooking whole-wheat couscous
  1¼   teaspoons salt
    1   cup boiling water
    2   tablespoons virgin olive oil
    ½   small leek, both white and green parts (about 2 ounces),
        trimmed, chopped and washed (½ cup)
    3   tablespoons pumpkin seeds
  4–5   cloves garlic, peeled, crushed and finely chopped (2 teaspoons)
  1½   cups water
    1   piece butternut squash (1 pound), peeled, seeded and cut
        into ½″ cubes (2½ cups)
    8   ounces cauliflower, divided into small florets (2 cups)
    1   small zucchini (about 3 ounces), washed, trimmed and cut
        into ½″ cubes (1¼ cups)
    1   small red bell pepper (4 ounces), halved, cored, seeded
        and cut into ½″ pieces (1 cup)
  3–4   medium domestic mushrooms (about 2 ounces), washed and
        cut into ½″ slices (1 cup)
    4   ounces green beans, trimmed and cut into ½″ pieces (¾ cup)

Place the couscous and ¼ teaspoon of the salt in a heat-resistant bowl and pour the boiling water over it. Mix well, cover the bowl with a lid and let stand for a minimum of 10 minutes.

Meanwhile, heat the oil in a large saucepan. When it is hot, add the leeks and cook them for 1 minute over high heat. Then add the pumpkin seeds and garlic; cook, stirring, for 30 seconds longer. Add the 1½ cups water, squash, cauliflower, zucchini, peppers, mushrooms, beans and the remaining 1 teaspoon salt.

Bring the mixture to a full boil over high heat, cover, reduce the heat to low and cook for 10 minutes. Most of the liquid should be gone at this point; lift the lid and cook the vegetables over high heat to eliminate any remaining liquid.

Fluff the couscous with a fork to separate the grains. Add the couscous to the vegetables in the pan. Mix well. Heat the mixture through, if needed, and serve.

Per serving: 228 calories, 6.9 g. fat (26% of calories), 1.1 g. saturated fat, 0 mg. cholesterol, 457 mg. sodium.

A kitchen scale is the most accurate way to measure. If you prefer to use cup measurements, here is a way to measure irregularly shaped ingredients. If you want 2 cups of cauliflower, for instance, take a very large glass measure and put 4 cups of water in it. Add enough pieces of cauliflower to bring the water to the 6-cup mark. Drain and use.

Couscous with Raisins

this is a slightly fancier version of couscous. Like Basic Couscous (page 273), it goes beautifully with different types of stews, especially those featuring lamb.

1½ teaspoons corn or canola oil

1½ cups fast-cooking couscous

⅓ cup dark raisins

¼ teaspoon salt

1¼ cups boiling water

Heat the oil in a medium saucepan. When it is hot, add the couscous, raisins and salt; mix well to coat the couscous with the oil. Pour the water into the pan, cover and let stand off the heat for a minimum of 10 minutes.

Fluff the couscous with a fork to separate the grains. Serve about ⅓ cup per person.

Per serving: 207 calories, 1.5 g. fat (6% of calories), 0.2 g. saturated fat, 0 mg. cholesterol, 94 mg. sodium.

There are many interesting dried fruits available that can substitute for raisins in recipes. Dried currants and cherries are especially good and are always appropriate. Other fruits, such as dried cranberries and blueberries, are also tasty. Be aware, though, that sometimes they have sugar added for sweetness. Check the label to be sure.

Plum Compote

Yield: 6 servings

his compote is strongly accented with vinegar, sugar, mustard seeds, garlic and hot pepper. It works particularly well as a condiment with simple poultry dishes, like poached chicken, and will keep for weeks under refrigeration.

1	cup light brown sugar
½	cup cider vinegar
½	cup dark raisins
1	small onion (about 2 ounces), peeled and thinly sliced (½ cup)
1	small piece fresh ginger, peeled and cut into thin slivers (¼ cup)
1	teaspoon mustard seeds
2	cloves garlic, peeled, crushed and finely chopped (1 teaspoon)
1	teaspoon crushed red pepper flakes
10–12	purple plums, preferably Santa Rosa (1 pound), halved and pitted

Combine the sugar and vinegar in a large saucepan and bring the mixture to a boil over high heat. Add the raisins, onions, ginger, mustard seeds, garlic and pepper flakes. Return the mixture to a boil and boil for 1 minute.

Add the plums, cover and cook over medium heat for 8 to 10 minutes, or until the plums are soft and the cooking liquid has thickened into a syrup. Let cool to room temperature, cover and refrigerate until ready to serve.

Per serving: 226 calories, 0.8 g. fat (3% of calories), 0.1 g. saturated fat, 0 mg. cholesterol, 14 mg. sodium.

Orzo à la Puttanesca

Yield: 6 generous servings

*O*rzo is a pasta that looks like rice. I've featured it here in a type of risotto. (You could also use rizo, another rice-shaped pasta.) The dish, containing anchovies, capers, garlic, onions and scallions, has a wonderfully intense flavor. No salt is needed; the anchovy fillets supply enough to season the dish, which also makes a good first course or light entrée.

2	cans (2 ounces each) flat anchovies in oil, coarsely chopped
2	tablespoons small drained capers
1	pound orzo pasta
2	tablespoons virgin olive oil
1	small onion (3 ounces), peeled and chopped (½ cup)
2–3	scallions (about 2 ounces), washed, trimmed and chopped (⅓ cup)
5	cloves garlic, peeled and thinly sliced (2 tablespoons)
1	teaspoon dried summer savory
½	teaspoon freshly ground black pepper
2	medium tomatoes (about 14 ounces), seeded and cut into ½″ dice (2 cups)
3	tablespoons finely shredded fresh oregano
6	tablespoons grated Parmesan cheese (optional)

In a small bowl, combine the anchovies and capers. Set aside.

Bring about 3 quarts of water to a boil in a large pot. Add the orzo and boil it for 10 to 12 minutes, or until it is as tender as you like.

Meanwhile, heat the oil in a large saucepan. When it is hot, mix in the onions, scallions, garlic, savory and pepper and cook for 1 minute. Then add the tomatoes and the anchovy-caper mixture; toss to combine well. Cover and set aside off the heat.

Before draining the pasta, remove ½ cup of the pasta cooking liquid from the pot and add it to the anchovy mixture in the saucepan. Drain the pasta well and add it to the saucepan. Sprinkle on the oregano and toss the mixture to combine the ingredients well.

Divide among 6 soup plates. If desired, sprinkle with the Parmesan.

Per serving: 374 calories, 8.8 g. fat (21% of calories), 1.4 g. saturated fat, 81 mg. cholesterol, 755 mg. sodium.

Orzo à la Puttanesca

Desserts

Aangel cake.

Raspberry Soufflé in raspberry Sauce

Orange délice

Apricot Whip

and more .....

Angel Cake

Yield: 12 slices

his light, airy cake is a classic American dessert. It is best prepared in a standard angel food cake pan.

- ¾ cup sifted confectioners' sugar
- 1 cup sifted cake flour
- 10 egg whites (1½ cups)
- 1 teaspoon almond extract
- 1¼ cups granulated sugar

Preheat the oven to 350°.

Combine the confectioners' sugar and flour in a small mixing bowl.

Place the egg whites in a large copper or stainless steel mixing bowl and add the almond extract. Beat the mixture by hand with a large balloon whisk or with an electric mixer (fitted with a whisk attachment) at medium to high speed. When the whites hold a firm peak, gradually beat in the granulated sugar, then continue beating the mixture for 10 seconds. The whites should be stiff and shiny.

Sift the flour mixture directly on top of the egg whites and fold it in with a rubber spatula just until it is incorporated. Do not overmix! Pour the batter into a 10″ tube pan.

Bake in the center of the oven for 35 minutes, or until the cake springs back when lightly touched. Immediately invert the pan onto an overturned metal funnel or a cake rack and cool it completely.

To remove the cake from the pan, run a sharp, thin-bladed knife around the edges of the cake with a steady stroke to loosen it from the pan. Invert the cake onto a serving plate, cut (or pull apart with forks) and serve.

Per slice: 147 calories, 0 g. fat (0% of calories), 0 g. saturated fat, 0 mg. cholesterol, 46 mg. sodium.

Angel Cake (page 284) with Chocolate Sauce (page 340)

Yogurt Cake

Yogurt Cake

Yield: 10 slices

oist and flavorful, this is an excellent basic cake that freezes well. Defrost the cake under refrigeration for serving. I like to serve the cake with blueberries, as suggested below. (If you don't have fresh blueberries, use unsweetened frozen ones that you've thawed slightly.) This cake is also good topped with Citrus-Raisin Compote (page 310), Strawberries in Strawberry Sauce (page 335) or Apricot Sauce with Dried Fruits (page 341).

- ½ cup sugar
- 3 tablespoons corn or canola oil
- 1 teaspoon vanilla extract
- ¼ cup skim milk
- ¼ cup plain nonfat yogurt
- 1 cup sifted cake flour
- ½ teaspoon baking soda
- 2 egg whites
- 5 cups fresh blueberries, washed, drained and patted dry

Preheat the oven to 350°. Lightly coat an 8″ round cake pan with vegetable cooking spray and set the pan aside.

Place the sugar, oil and vanilla in a large mixing bowl. Combine with a whisk until well blended. Add the milk and yogurt; mix well. Then add the flour and baking soda and mix gently until they are incorporated.

Place the egg whites in a copper or stainless steel mixing bowl. Beat by hand with a large balloon whisk or with an electric mixer (fitted with a whisk attachment) at medium to high speed until the whites form stiff peaks when the beaters are lifted. Fold them into the batter. Pour the batter into the prepared pan.

Bake for 30 to 35 minutes.

Cool the cake in the pan on a cake rack until it is lukewarm, then invert it onto the rack and cool it completely.

To serve, cut the cake into 10 pieces. Top each piece with ½ cup blueberries.

Per slice: 162 calories, 4.5 g. fat (24% of calories), 0.6 g. saturated fat, 0 mg. cholesterol, 64 mg. sodium.

Applesauce Cake

here is a minimum of oil and only two eggs in this easily prepared cake. So to lend moisture to the batter, I use both applesauce and pieces of apple. The result is a dense, flavorful cake that will keep, wrapped and refrigerated, for a few days.

  2 cups all-purpose flour
  ½ cup sugar
  1 tablespoon baking powder
  1 teaspoon ground cinnamon
  ¼ teaspoon ground nutmeg
  1 cup applesauce
  ¼ cup canola oil
  2 large eggs
  1 tablespoon vanilla extract
  1 Granny Smith apple (about 8 ounces), unpeeled but halved, cored and cut into ½″ pieces (2 cups)

Preheat the oven to 350°. Lightly coat a 9″ × 5″ loaf pan with vegetable cooking spray.

Combine the flour, sugar, baking powder, cinnamon and nutmeg in a large mixing bowl. Add the applesauce, oil, eggs and vanilla. Mix well with a whisk. Stir in the apple pieces. Pour the batter into the prepared pan.

Bake for 65 to 70 minutes, until a toothpick inserted in the center comes out clean. Cool thoroughly on a rack before unmolding and slicing.

Per slice: 184 calories, 5.7 g. fat (28% of calories), 0.6 g. saturated fat, 36 mg. cholesterol, 94 mg. sodium.

Apricot Whip

his is a good light dessert to serve after a rich meal. Although it can be served while puffed and hot directly from the oven as a kind of soufflé, it is better to let it cool to lukewarm or room temperature; the apricot flavor will be more intense if the dessert isn't too hot.

- ½ teaspoon canola, corn or safflower oil
- 6 tablespoons sugar
- 5 ounces dried California apricots
- ½ cup coarsely chopped walnuts
- 1 teaspoon vanilla extract
- 5 egg whites

Brush a 6- to 8-cup gratin dish with the oil and coat the bottom and sides of the dish with 2 tablespoons of the sugar (shake the dish to distribute the sugar evenly). Set aside.

Place the apricots in a medium saucepan and add enough water to cover them. Bring the water to a boil, reduce the heat to low and cook the apricots at a gentle boil for about 10 minutes, until they are tender when pierced with the point of a sharp knife.

Drain the apricots and chop them coarsely. (There should be about 1 generous cup of apricot pieces.) In a small bowl, mix together the apricots, walnuts and vanilla. Set aside.

Preheat the oven to 375°.

Place the egg whites in a large copper or stainless steel mixing bowl. Beat by hand with a large balloon whisk or with an electric mixer (fitted with a whisk attachment) at medium to high speed. When the whites hold a firm peak, gradually add the remaining 4 tablespoons sugar, then keep beating the mixture for 10 seconds. The whites should be stiff and shiny.

Gently fold the reserved apricot mixture into the egg whites.

Pour the mixture into the prepared dish and bake for 20 to 25 minutes, until the dessert is puffy and lightly browned on top.

Cool and serve lukewarm or at room temperature.

Per serving: 184 calories, 6.4 g. fat (29% of calories), 0.4 g. saturated fat, 0 mg. cholesterol, 48 mg. sodium.

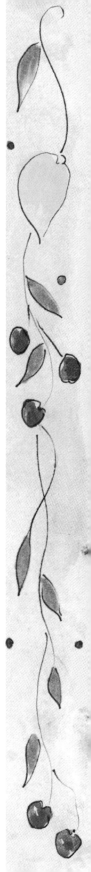

Oat Bran and Butter Wafers

Yield: 18 wafers

hese cookies can be made quickly and are especially good when very thin. To ensure that they are that way, spread the batter for the cookies very thinly on a cookie sheet, ignoring small holes throughout. Use a good-quality nonstick cookie sheet so the cookies can be easily removed after baking. I leave the cookies flat here, but you could roll them into a cornucopia shape while they are still hot from the oven. You could also form them into a cup shape by molding them around an inverted cup. Be sure to use pure oat bran, not oat flakes or rolled oats.

⅓ cup sugar

2 tablespoons unsalted butter, melted

½ teaspoon vanilla extract

2 egg whites

½ cup all-purpose flour

½ cup oat bran

Preheat the oven to 400°. Lightly coat 1 large cookie sheet (or 2 smaller ones) with vegetable cooking spray and set aside.

In a large bowl, mix together the sugar, butter and vanilla. Add the egg whites, flour and oat bran and stir just until they are incorporated. The mixture will still be slightly liquid.

Spoon the batter onto the cookie sheet, dividing it into 18 equal portions. Spread each portion out to form a 3¾″ to 4″ round. (Rotating the cookie sheet helps in the spreading process and tapping the sheet afterward on a solid surface helps to smooth out the batter.)

Bake for 10 to 12 minutes, until the wafers are brown. Remove the wafers from the sheets while they are still warm and cool them on a rack. Serve about 3 wafers per person.

Per wafer: 47 calories, 1.6 g. fat (28% of calories), 0.9 g. saturated fat, 4 mg. cholesterol, 6 mg. sodium.

Clockwise from top: Snowball Cookies (page 293); Oatmeal and Currant Cookies (page 292) and Oat Bran and Butter Wafers (page 290)

Oatmeal and Currant Cookies

Yield: 18 cookies

These crunchy cookies contain dried currants, which are tiny raisins; if currants are not available, substitute regular raisins—whole or cut up. The cookies can be prepared ahead and stored in an airtight container.

- ⅔ **cup all-purpose flour**
- ¼ **cup sugar**
- ¼ **cup apple juice**
- 2⅔ **tablespoons unsalted butter**
- 1 **teaspoon baking powder**
- 1 **cup old-fashioned rolled oats**
- ¼ **cup dried currants or regular raisins**

Preheat the oven to 400°.

Place the flour, sugar, apple juice, butter and baking powder in the bowl of a food processor and process for 5 to 10 seconds, just until the mixture forms into a ball. Transfer the dough to a cutting board and gently knead the oats and currants or raisins into it.

Divide the dough into 18 equal pieces. Wet your hands and roll the pieces into balls. Divide the balls between 2 ungreased nonstick cookie sheets, placing the balls as far apart as possible.

Using a piece of plastic wrap to prevent the dough from sticking to your hands, press the dough to form cookies that are about ¼" thick and 2½" in diameter.

Bake for 15 to 18 minutes.

Remove the hot cookies from the cookie sheets with a spatula and place them on a rack until cooled to room temperature. Keep the cookies in an airtight container to prevent them from softening. Serve 2 or 3 cookies per person.

Per cookie: 98 calories, 4.1 g. fat (36% of calories), 2.2 g. saturated fat, 9 mg. cholesterol, 19 mg. sodium.

Snowball Cookies

Yield: 12 cookies

S tore these rich cookies in an airtight container. They freeze well and can be eaten while still frozen as well as thawed.

- ½ **cup sifted confectioners' sugar**
- ½ **cup coarsely chopped pecans**
- 1 **small egg white (2 tablespoons)**
- ¼ **teaspoon vanilla extract**

Preheat the oven to 350°.

Place the sugar and pecans in the bowl of a food processor and process them for about 30 seconds, or until the nuts are ground. Transfer to a mixing bowl and add the egg white and vanilla. Stir with a spatula to form a soft paste.

Drop the mixture by teaspoonfuls into 12 mounds on an ungreased nonstick cookie sheet, leaving space between the mounds for expansion. Bake for 10 minutes; the batter will spread immediately to form 2″ disks, and the finished cookies will measure about 3″ across.

Let the cookies cool and become hard before removing them from the cookie sheets. Serve 2 cookies per person.

Per cookie: 48 calories, 3 g. fat (55% of calories), 0.2 g. saturated fat, 0 mg. cholesterol, 5 mg. sodium.

Crêpes with Caramelized Apples and Pecans

Yield: 6 servings

illed with caramelized apples and pecans, these crêpes should be served lukewarm. The intense flavor resulting from the combination of the caramelized sugar and the other ingredients makes this a particularly satisfying dessert. You will note that I do not peel the apples here; I like the chewy texture of the skin.

¼ cup sugar

6 tablespoons water

3–4 Red or Golden Delicious apples (1½ pounds), unpeeled but cored and cut into ½" pieces (5 cups)

8 strips lemon rind removed with a vegetable peeler

3 tablespoons lemon juice

2 tablespoon honey

¼ cup pecan pieces

12 crêpes (page 338)

Place a large nonstick skillet over medium-high heat and add the sugar and 2 tablespoons of the water. Cook the mixture until the sugar is brown and caramelized (but not burned), about 2 minutes. Add the apples and sauté them for about 1 minute.

Meanwhile, stack the pieces of lemon rind and cut them lengthwise into thin julienne strips. Place in a small bowl and add the lemon juice, honey and the remaining 4 tablespoons water; mix well. Add this mixture to the skillet, cover and cook for 5 minutes over medium heat. Remove the cover, add the pecans and cook for 2 to 3 minutes, until most of the liquid has boiled away and the sugar caramelizes again.

Lay the crêpes out on a flat surface and spoon 2 to 3 tablespoons of the apple mixture into the center of each. Fold in the sides of the crêpes to partially cover the filling. Serve 2 crêpes per person.

Per serving: 234 calories, 5.9 g. fat (21% of calories), 0.5 g. saturated fat, 1 mg. cholesterol, 36 mg. sodium.

Crêpes with Caramelized Apples and Pecans

Sweet Wonton Crisps
with Strawberries and Frozen Yogurt

Yield: 6 servings

his is a stunning dessert for a special party. I use strawberries, but any berries in season—blueberries, raspberries, blackberries—can be substituted. For each dessert, about ½ cup of frozen nonfat yogurt is sandwiched between wonton wraps that have been blanched, then baked until crisp. A dusting of confectioners' sugar and cut berries complete the beautiful picture.

18 wonton wrappers, each 3″ square (4½ ounces)
24 ounces nonfat frozen vanilla or strawberry yogurt
    About 2 tablespoons confectioners' sugar
24 ripe strawberries (about 2 pints), washed, hulled and quartered lengthwise

Preheat the oven to 375°.

Bring about 2 quarts of water to a boil in a large pot. Add 9 of the wonton wrappers, dropping them into the water 1 at a time. Cook for 1½ minutes, then remove them from the water carefully with a skimmer and transfer them to a large bowl of cold water.

Lightly coat a 16″ × 14″ cookie sheet with vegetable cooking spray. Place your hands in the bowl containing the wrappers and carefully unfold them 1 at a time under the water. Transfer them, still wet, to the cookie sheet, arranging them side by side. Lightly spray the surface with more cooking spray.

Bake for 16 to 18 minutes, or until dry and brown. Transfer the crisped wrappers to a cake rack to cool.

Repeat with the remaining wonton wrappers.

Using 3 crisps for each serving, assemble each dessert as follows: Place a wonton crisp on a dessert plate and top it with a flattened 2-ounce scoop of the yogurt. Place another wonton crisp on top of the yogurt, positioning it at about a 45° angle in relation to the first crisp. Add a second flattened 2-ounce scoop of the yogurt. Cap with a third wonton crisp.

Sprinkle the top crisp with 1 teaspoon of powdered sugar and decorate the dessert with the equivalent of 4 berries.

Per serving: 195 calories, 0.3 g. fat (1% of calories), 0 g. saturated fat, 0 mg. cholesterol, 128 mg. sodium.

Sweet Wonton Crisps with Strawberries and Frozen Yogurt

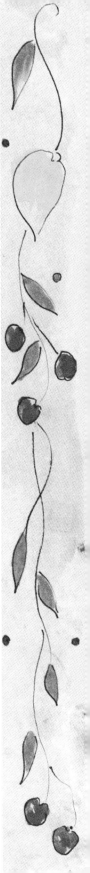

Creamy Rice Pudding with Dried Fruit

DESSERTS

Creamy Rice Pudding with Dried Fruit

Yield: 6 servings

i use only 1 cup of rice with a great amount of milk—5 cups—to produce a baked pudding that's somewhat soupy. Then I stir dried fruit and honey into the hot pudding. Although the pudding thickens as it cools, it remains moist enough so that no additional milk need be added at serving time. I prefer to flavor this pudding with ¼ cup amaretto (almond-flavored liqueur), but you can also use the mixture of vanilla and almond extract listed in the ingredients.

- 5 cups skim milk
- 1 cup uncooked long-grain white rice (6 ounces)
- 6 ounces dried fruit (peaches, apples and pears), cut into ¼" dice (1 cup)
- ¼ cup dark raisins
- ½ cup honey
- 1 teaspoon vanilla extract
- ½ teaspoon almond extract
- ¼ cup crushed pistachio nuts

Preheat the oven to 350°.

Combine the milk and rice in a large ovenproof saucepan. Bring the mixture to a full boil (watching carefully so it doesn't boil over), remove it from the heat and cover the pan. Place the pan in the oven.

Bake for 1 hour.

Combine the fruit, raisins, honey, vanilla and almond extract in a bowl.

Remove the rice from the oven (the mixture will be soupy) and stir in the fruit mixture. Cool.

To serve, spoon the pudding into dessert dishes and serve it at room temperature or cool (not cold), with a sprinkling of pistachios on top.

Per serving: 413 calories, 3.3 g. fat (7% of calories), 0.6 g. saturated fat, 3 mg. cholesterol, 119 mg. sodium.

Sautéed Apple Rings
in Honey and Maple Sauce

Yield: 6 servings

he combination of a few flavorful ingredients makes this simple dessert very tasty. Use large Golden Delicious apples or, for a more tart result, Granny Smiths. The dish can be prepared ahead and will keep, covered with plastic wrap, for a couple of days in the refrigerator.

4 Golden Delicious or Granny Smith apples (1¾ pounds)
1 tablespoon lemon juice
3 tablespoons honey
3 tablespoons maple syrup
1 tablespoon unsalted butter

Peel off a little skin from the top and bottom of the apples and cut each apple crosswise into 3 slices, each about ¾″ thick. Remove the center core from each slice with a small, round cookie cutter or knife. Place the apple slices in a baking dish large enough to accommodate the 12 slices in a single layer. Add the lemon juice and toss the slices with the juice until they are coated.

Heat a large nonstick skillet and coat it lightly with vegetable cooking spray. Working in batches if necessary, add the apple slices to the pan in a single layer and sauté them over medium heat for 3 to 4 minutes, or until lightly browned. Then turn the slices over and sauté them for 3 minutes on the other side. As you finish sautéing the slices, return them to the baking dish.

Preheat the oven to 400°.

In a small bowl, mix together the honey and maple syrup and drizzle the mixture over the apples. Break the butter into small pieces and dot the apples with the butter.

Bake for 10 minutes.

To serve, turn the apples over in the cooking liquid and serve, warm or cool. Allow 2 slices and some of the cooking liquid per person.

Per serving: 154 calories, 2.5 g. fat (14% of calories), 1.3 g. saturated fat, 6 mg. cholesterol, 3 mg. sodium.

Sweet Apple Flake Confections

Yield: 6 servings

hese oven-dried apple slices make a delicious, healthful snack on their own and also can be served in place of cookies for dessert. I dry the apples in a convection oven, but you can also do it in a regular oven: Spread the slices on a nonstick cookie sheet and bake in a preheated 225° oven for 1½ hours, or until they're dry and lightly browned. Here, for a light but luscious finish to a meal, I press the slices into scoops of nonfat frozen yogurt.

> 2 **firm apples (1 pound), preferably Golden Delicious, Russet or Rome Beauty**
>
> **Juice of 1 lemon (1½ tablespoons)**
>
> 3 **cups nonfat frozen vanilla or coffee yogurt**

Preheat a convection oven to 250°.

Core the apples but do not peel them. Using a mandoline or potato slicer, slice the apples crosswise into very thin (1⁄16″) slices. You should have about 40 slices.

Pour the lemon juice on a plate. Rub the apple slices in the lemon juice, moistening them lightly on both sides. Arrange them, side by side, on a large wire rack set on a cookie sheet.

Place the cookie sheet in the oven; allow them to bake for about 50 minutes, until they are fairly dry and lightly browned.

Remove from the oven. Immediately lift the slices from the rack and reposition them (to prevent them from sticking). Allow to cool (they'll dry further). When thoroughly cooled, the slices should be dry and crunchy. Place in a metal or plastic storage container with a tight-fitting lid and store at room temperature until ready to use.

Shortly before serving time, transfer the frozen yogurt from the freezer to the refrigerator to soften.

At serving time, place a scoop (about ½ cup) of frozen yogurt in the center of each of 6 dessert plates. Press 6 or 7 of the apple slices around the sides and across the top of each scoop, encasing the scoop with the slices. (Alternatively, arrange the apple slices on or around the yogurt scoops in another design to your liking.) Serve immediately.

Per serving: 117 calories, 0.3 g. fat (2% of calories), 0 g. saturated fat, 0 mg. cholesterol, 53 mg. sodium.

Banana Strips
with Apricot Sauce and Blueberries

Yield: 6 servings

i f you have all the ingredients on hand, this is a five-minute dessert, perfect for unexpected guests. Canned apricots in unsweetened juice are transformed into a sauce in a food processor, flavored and poured over banana strips. Blueberries, sprinkled on top, provide a color and flavor contrast that complements this easy dish.

1 can (17 ounces) apricots packed in unsweetened juice
2 tablespoons dark rum (optional)
1 tablespoon lemon juice
6 ripe medium bananas (1¾ pounds)
½ cup fresh blueberries, washed, drained and patted dry

Pour the apricots with their juice into the bowl of a food processor and process them into a puree. Add the rum, if using, and process briefly to incorporate. (You should have 2 cups.)

Pour the lemon juice onto the platter you will use for serving the bananas. Peel the bananas and quarter them lengthwise. Arrange the banana pieces on the platter and roll them in the lemon juice (to prevent discoloration). Pour the apricot sauce over the bananas and sprinkle the blueberries on top. Carry the platter to the table and serve the equivalent of 1 banana per person with some of the sauce and berries.

Per serving: 162 calories, 0.6 g. fat (3% of calories), 0.2 g. saturated fat, 0 mg. cholesterol, 5 mg. sodium.

Banana Strips with Apricot Sauce and Blueberries

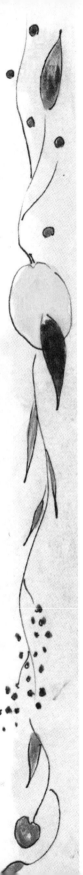

Banana Ricotta Cream with Fresh Fruits

Yield: 6 servings

*i f preparing this creamy dessert ahead, cover it with plastic wrap, making
certain that the wrap touches the surface of the cream to prevent a skin from
forming on top. Although the lemon juice retards discoloration of the bananas,
the cream on top may discolor slightly; any surface discoloration can be stirred
into the remainder of the cream before serving. For best results, combine the
assembled ingredients just before serving or, at most, not more than two hours
ahead.*

- 3 very ripe bananas (about 1 pound)
- 1 container (15 ounces) light ricotta cheese
- 1 tablespoon honey
- 1 tablespoon lemon juice
- 12 ripe strawberries (about 1 pint), washed, hulled and quartered lengthwise
- 1 honeydew melon (1 pound), halved, seeded and cut into 12 thin wedges

Cut the bananas into chunks and place them in the bowl of a food
processor with the ricotta. Process about 10 seconds. Add the honey and lemon
juice; process again, just until blended. Transfer the mixture to a bowl.

At serving time, spoon ½ cup of the ricotta mixture onto each plate and top
each serving with the equivalent of 2 strawberries. Surround each dessert with
2 wedges of the melon. Serve.

*Per serving: 152 calories, 2.5 g. fat (14% of calories), 0.1 g. saturated fat, 10 mg.
cholesterol, 6 mg. sodium.*

Banana Ricotta Cream with Fresh Fruits

Gratin of Bananas

Yield: 6 servings

*H*igh in potassium, bananas are available year-round. I like them best
when little black specks begin to form on their skin, indicating that the
flesh is ripe and flavorful. For this recipe, I bake lightly sweetened banana rounds
with a topping of granola and serve them with a garnish of plain yogurt.

    Grated rind and juice of 1 lemon (about 1½ teaspoons
    rind and 3 tablespoons juice)

6 medium bananas (1¾ pounds)

¼ cup firmly packed light brown sugar

3 ounces low-fat granola (1 generous cup)

½ cup plain nonfat yogurt (optional)

Preheat the oven to 400°.

Place the lemon rind and lemon juice in a bowl large enough to hold the
bananas. Peel the bananas and cut them crosswise into ¼″ slices. Place in the
bowl. Add the sugar and mix well.

Distribute the mixture evenly in a 6-cup gratin dish. Sprinkle with the
granola.

Bake for 12 to 15 minutes.

Serve at room temperature, plain or garnished with yogurt.

*Per serving: 204 calories, 3 g. fat (12% of calories), 1.8 g. saturated fat, 0 mg.
cholesterol, 33 mg. sodium.*

Banana-Strawberry Sherbet

Yield: 6 servings

*I*t is absolutely essential that the strawberries and bananas used in this dessert be very ripe; if they are not, the sherbet will be too tart. The bananas should have skin that's speckled with black dots, and the berries should be a deep purple-red throughout. Since it is not always possible to get perfectly ripened fruits, it is a good idea to buy them when you see them, cut them up and freeze them for later. Pack the fruit in plastic bags and store it for up to a month. Let the frozen fruit soften slightly (but not thaw) in the refrigerator for 1½ to 2 hours before proceeding with the recipe. (Or let it stand at room temperature for at least 30 minutes.)

1	pound very ripe fresh strawberries or unsweetened frozen strawberries
4–5	very ripe medium bananas (1½ pounds)
½	cup plain nonfat yogurt
1	tablespoon honey (optional)

If using fresh strawberries, wash them and remove their hulls. Peel the bananas. Cut both fruits into 1″ pieces and arrange the pieces in a single layer on a cookie sheet. Freeze until firm but not solid, about 2 hours. (If the fruit is left for a longer period in the freezer, allow it to soften slightly in the refrigerator before proceeding with the recipe.)

Meanwhile, chill the bowl of a food processor.

Place the firm berries and bananas in the cold processor bowl, add the yogurt and, if desired, the honey. Process until smooth, about 30 seconds.

Serve the sherbet immediately in glass dessert dishes or keep it in the freezer until serving time.

Per serving: 138 calories, 0.9 g. fat (5% of calories), 0.2 g. saturated fat, 0 mg. cholesterol, 16 mg. sodium.

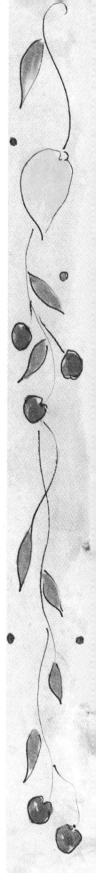

Fruit Sorbets

*S*orbets are excellent do-ahead desserts. This assortment features fresh fruit. The fruit is pureed, then combined with a sugar syrup before being frozen in a commercial ice cream maker. Strawberries, watermelon, pineapple, kiwi and grapefruit—the fruits used here—all make delicious sorbets.

Since the addition of too much sugar will prevent a sorbet from freezing properly, most professional kitchens use a Baumé hydrometer, which measures the density of sugar syrup. Syrup is added to a fruit puree until the hydrometer registers the proper level. I have tried to approximate this technique by suggesting the amount of syrup that should be added to each of the fruit purees.

SUGAR SYRUP

- 1 cup water
- 1 cup sugar

STRAWBERRY SORBET

- 2½ cups pureed strawberries
- ¾ cup sugar syrup
- 2 tablespoons lemon juice

WATERMELON SORBET

- 3 cups pureed watermelon
- ¾ cup sugar syrup
- 1 tablespoon lemon juice

PINEAPPLE SORBET

- 2 cups pureed pineapple
- ¾ cup sugar syrup
- 1 tablespoon lemon juice

KIWI SORBET

- 2 cups pureed kiwi
- 1 cup sugar syrup
- 1 tablespoon lemon juice

GRAPEFRUIT SORBET

- 2 cups grapefruit juice
- 1 cup sugar syrup

To make the sugar syrup: Place the water and sugar in a small saucepan and warm the mixture over low heat, stirring, until the sugar is dissolved. Cool the syrup to room temperature and store it in a jar, covered, in the refrigerator. This makes about 1½ cups of syrup.

To make the sorbet: In a bowl, combine the amount of puree, syrup and lemon juice (if called for) specified for the type of sorbet you're preparing. Transfer the mixture to an ice cream maker and freeze according to the manufacturer's instructions.

Per serving
Strawberry Sorbet: 120 calories, 0.3 g. fat (2% of calories), 0 g. saturated fat, 0 mg. cholesterol, 1 mg. sodium.

Kiwi Sorbet

Watermelon Sorbet: 127 calories, 0.5 g. fat (2% of calories), 0 g. saturated fat, 0 mg. cholesterol, 3 mg. sodium.

Pineapple Sorbet: 128 calories, 0.3 g. fat (2% of calories), 0 g. saturated fat, 0 mg. cholesterol, 1 mg. sodium.

Kiwi Sorbet: 167 calories, 0.3 g. fat (1% of calories), 0 g. saturated fat, 0 mg. cholesterol, 4 mg. sodium.

Grapefruit Sorbet: 151 calories, 0 g. fat (0% of calories), 0 g. saturated fat, 0 mg. cholesterol, 0 mg. sodium.

Citrus-Raisin Compote

his can be served as a side dish or condiment with meat or poultry, but it also makes a delicious dessert with Angel Cake (page 284) or Yogurt Cake (page 287). Cooked citrus fruit slices give the compote a very assertive flavor, so a little goes a long way. It will keep for several weeks in a covered jar in the refrigerator. Serve the compote very cold.

- ½ medium grapefruit with skin on, seeded and cut into ¼″ slices (about 1 cup)
- 2 medium navel oranges with skin on, halved and cut into ¼″ slices (about 2½ cups)
- 1 large lime with skin on, halved, seeded and cut into ¼″ slices (about ¾ cup)
- ¾ cup sugar
- 4 cups water
- ½ cup dark raisins
- 1 tablespoon cognac or rum (optional)
  Fresh mint leaves, for garnish

Place the grapefruit slices, orange slices and lime slices in a large stainless steel saucepan and cover them with enough cold water to extend 1″ above the fruit. Bring the water to a boil and boil the fruit for 10 to 15 seconds over high heat to eliminate some of its bitterness. Drain the fruit in a colander and rinse it under cold tap water. Rinse out the saucepan.

Return the fruit to the saucepan with the sugar and 4 cups water. Bring the water to a boil and boil the mixture gently, uncovered, for 50 minutes. Add the raisins and continue cooking the compote for 10 minutes. (There should be only enough liquid left to moisten the fruit.)

Let the mixture cool to room temperature, cover and refrigerate until ready to use. If desired, just before serving, add the cognac or rum. Serve, garnishing each serving with a few mint leaves.

Per serving: 187 calories, 0.2 g. fat (1% of calories), 0 g. saturated fat, 0 mg. cholesterol, 2 mg. sodium.

Citrus-Raisin Compote

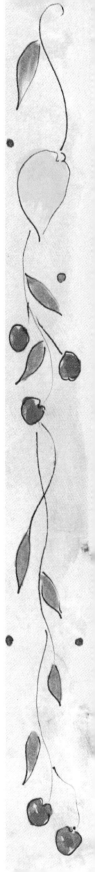

Melon with Lime Sauce

Melon with Lime Sauce

Yield: 6 servings

*B*e sure to choose a ripe, flavorful, sweet melon for this quick dessert. Although this dish can be served right after it is made, it is at its best if made at least a few hours before serving and can be prepared up to a day ahead. For an interesting color and flavor combination, use half honeydew and half cantaloupe.

- 1 large honeydew melon or 2 small cantaloupe
- 1 large lime
- 1 tablespoon sugar
- 1 tablespoon rum (optional)
   Mint leaves or lime wedges, for garnish

Cut the honeydew or cantaloupe in half and remove the seeds. Using a melon baller, remove balls of the melon flesh and place them in a large bowl. (You should have 4 cups.)

With a vegetable peeler, remove the lime rind in thin strips. Then stack the strips together and cut them into fine julienne pieces. Add the strips to the melon.

Squeeze the lime over a small bowl and mix the juice (approximately ⅓ cup) with the sugar and rum, if using. Stir the mixture into the melon balls and set them aside for 1 to 2 hours.

At serving time, divide the melon balls among 6 dessert dishes, garnish with mint leaves or lime wedges and serve.

Per serving: 57 calories, 0.1 g. fat (2% of calories), 0 g. saturated fat, 0 mg. cholesterol, 12 mg. sodium.

Cold Fruit Compote

this is a good do-ahead dish, since it will keep for at least a week in the refrigerator. It makes an appealing dessert and can also be served at breakfast instead of the more traditional grapefruit halves or fruit juice. A rich concoction, the compote consists of a mixture of dried and fresh fruits that are lightly sweetened with honey and cooked with the juice and rind of an orange and a lime.

 3 Granny Smith apples (1–1¼ pounds), peeled, halved, cored and cut into ½″ wedges

 3 Bartlett pears (1–1¼ pounds), peeled, halved, cored and cut into 1″ pieces

 18 dried apricot halves (4 ounces)

 1 cup water

 ⅓ cup dried cranberries or dried cherries

 ⅓ cup honey

 1 tablespoon grated orange rind

 1 teaspoon grated lime rind

 Juice of 1 orange (½ cup)

 Juice of 1 lime (1½ tablespoons)

Place the apples, pears, apricots, water, cranberries or cherries, honey, orange rind, lime rind, orange juice and lime juice in a large stainless steel saucepan. Mix well to dissolve the honey. Bring the mixture to a boil over high heat. Reduce the heat to low, cover and boil very gently for 10 minutes. Set the compote aside to cool to room temperature, then cover and refrigerate overnight. Serve cold in dessert dishes.

Per serving: 208 calories, 0.7 g. fat (3% of calories), 0 g. saturated fat, 0 mg. cholesterol, 4 mg. sodium.

Hot Orange Soufflés with Orange Segments

Yield: 6 servings

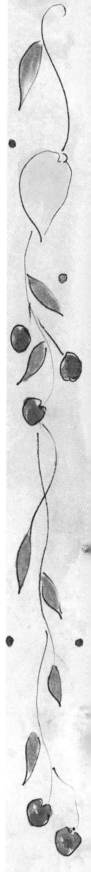

*S*everal steps in the preparation of this elegant party dessert can be done ahead: The orange skin can be grated and mixed with the sugar; the oranges can be sectioned; and the mint garnish can be readied. For best results, however, be certain that you don't beat the egg whites more than 45 minutes before the soufflé is to be baked.

I usually bake this soufflé mixture in individual molds, but you could do it in a single 4-cup soufflé mold. Increase the baking time to 18 to 20 minutes.

2 navel oranges (10–12 ounces each)
⅓ cup sugar
4 egg whites (⅔ cup)

Grate the rind from 1 of the oranges. Place in a small bowl and add the sugar. Set aside.

Peel the oranges with a sharp knife, removing all the skin and the underlying white pith so the flesh of the fruit is totally exposed. Then cut down the side of each membrane to release clean sections of orange flesh in wedgelike pieces. Reserve the segments in a small bowl in the refrigerator.

Preheat the oven to 400°. Lightly coat 6 individual soufflé molds (½ to 1 cup each) with vegetable cooking spray. Set aside.

Place the egg whites in a large copper or stainless steel mixing bowl. Beat by hand with a large balloon whisk or with an electric mixer (fitted with a whisk attachment) at medium to high speed. When the whites hold a firm peak, gradually beat in the sugar mixture, then continue beating the mixture for 10 seconds. The whites should be stiff and shiny.

Fill the prepared molds with the soufflé mixture, dividing it evenly among them. Place the molds on a baking tray and bake them for 8 to 10 minutes, until the tops are browned and the soufflés are well inflated and firm to the touch.

To serve, run a sharp knife around the edge of the soufflés and invert each onto a dessert plate. Surround the soufflés with the reserved orange sections, dividing them equally among the plates. Serve immediately.

Per serving: 96 calories, 0.1 g. fat (1% of calories), 0 g. saturated fat, 0 mg. cholesterol, 37 mg. sodium.

Oranges in Yogurt Cream

Yield: 8 servings

create yogurt cheese by straining nonfat yogurt over a bowl in the refrigerator for several hours. With the moisture drained off, the yogurt has the consistency of sour cream but has only a fraction of its calories. Here, the yogurt cheese is mounded on top of a flavorful apricot sauce and surrounded with halved orange slices. I use dried cranberries as a decoration for this dessert, but you can use dried cherries or raisins if you prefer.

- 32 ounces plain nonfat yogurt
- 3 navel oranges (10–12 ounces each)
- 1 cup apricot preserves
- 3 tablespoons orange juice or Grand Marnier liqueur (orange brandy)
- ¼ cup dried cranberries

Line a large strainer with dampened paper towels. Pour in the yogurt. Set the strainer over a large bowl. Refrigerate and allow to drain for 4 to 6 hours. Discard the whey that's drained from the yogurt (or drink it); cover the yogurt cheese and refrigerate until needed.

With a vegetable peeler, remove 6 long strips from the skin of the oranges and set them aside for use as a decoration. Then peel the oranges with a sharp knife, removing all the skin and the underlying white pith so the flesh of the fruit is totally exposed. Cut the oranges crosswise into ½" slices, then halve each of the slices.

Combine the preserves and orange juice or liqueur in a small bowl to create a sauce.

To serve, divide the sauce among 6 dessert plates, spreading it over the base of the plates so it coats the center of the plates lightly and is thicker around the edges. Mound ⅓ to ½ cup of the yogurt cream in the center of each plate and arrange the halved orange slices attractively around the periphery to create a border surrounding the sauce.

Sprinkle the cranberries on top. Cut a 1" lengthwise slit in the center of each of the reserved orange peels and pull one end of the peel through the slit to create a loose loop. Place a peel in the center of each plate as a decoration.

Per serving: 238 calories, 0.2 g. fat (1% of calories), 0 g. saturated fat, 1 mg. cholesterol, 75 mg. sodium.

Oranges in Yogurt Cream

Orange Floating Islands with Orange-Yogurt Sauce

Yield: 6 servings

*I*f you prepare orange soufflés and allow them to cool overnight before unmolding them, you'll end up with this delightful cold dessert. I serve the deflated soufflés with a creamy orange-yogurt sauce.

- 2 navel oranges (10–12 ounces each)
- ⅓ cup sugar
- 1 cup plain nonfat yogurt
- ¼ cup frozen unsweetened orange juice concentrate, thawed
- 2 tablespoons fresh orange juice
- 4 egg whites (⅔ cup)
  Fresh mint leaves, for garnish

Grate the rind from 1 of the oranges. Place in a small bowl and add the sugar. Set aside.

Peel the oranges with a sharp knife, removing all the skin and the underlying white pith so the flesh of the fruit is totally exposed. Then cut down the side of each membrane to release clean sections of orange flesh in wedgelike pieces. Reserve the segments in a small bowl; cover and refrigerate until needed.

Place the yogurt, orange juice concentrate and fresh orange juice in the bowl of a food processor. Process for 10 seconds, just until the mixture is emulsified. Transfer the mixture to a bowl, cover and refrigerate until needed.

Preheat the oven to 400°. Lightly coat 6 individual soufflé molds (½ to 1 cup each) with vegetable cooking spray. Set aside.

Place the egg whites in a large copper or stainless steel mixing bowl. Beat by hand with a large balloon whisk or with an electric mixer (fitted with a whisk attachment) at medium to high speed. When the whites hold a firm peak, gradually add the reserved sugar mixture and keep beating for 10 seconds. The whites should be stiff and shiny.

Fill the prepared molds with the soufflé mixture, dividing it evenly among them. Place the molds on a baking tray and bake them for 8 to 10 minutes, until the tops are browned and the soufflés are well inflated and firm to the touch. Remove from the oven and allow the cooked soufflés to deflate and cool to room temperature, at least 1 hour. Cover the soufflés with plastic wrap and refrigerate overnight.

At serving time, run a sharp knife around the soufflés to loosen them from the molds. Invert and unmold them on individual serving plates. Pour some of the yogurt mixture on top of and around the soufflés and decorate with the reserved orange slices and mint. Serve.

Per serving: 161 calories, 0.2 g. fat (1% of calories), 0 g. saturated fat, 1 mg. cholesterol, 66 mg. sodium.

Orange Délice

Yield: 6 servings

his colorful dessert is excellent at the end of the summer, when fresh raspberries are available. At other times of the year, you may substitute unsweetened frozen raspberries.

6 navel oranges (10–12 ounces each)
12 ounces fresh or thawed unsweetened frozen raspberries
¼ cup sugar
1 tablespoon *eau de vie de framboise* or other raspberry brandy (optional)
Fresh mint sprigs, for garnish

Peel the oranges with a sharp knife, removing all the skin and the underlying white pith so the flesh of the fruit is totally exposed. Then cut down the side of each membrane to release clean sections of orange flesh in wedgelike pieces. Reserve the segments in a small bowl.

Place the raspberries in the bowl of a food processor and process them until they are pureed. Strain the puree through a fine strainer into a mixing bowl. Stir in the sugar and the brandy, if using.

At serving time, place 2 to 3 tablespoons of the raspberry sauce on each of 6 plates and arrange the orange wedges in a circle on top. Decorate each dessert with a sprig of mint, arranging it attractively in the center.

Per serving: 120 calories, 0.5 g. fat (3% of calories), 0 g. saturated fat, 0 mg. cholesterol, 0 mg. sodium.

Poached Oranges

Poached Oranges

*P*oached oranges make a good, fast, refreshing dessert. Although oranges are available year-round, they are better at some times than others; try to get juicy, seedless navel oranges with thin skin.

- **6 navel oranges (10–12 ounces each)**
- **⅓ cup sugar**
- **⅓ cup water**
- **2 tablespoons Grand Marnier liqueur (orange brandy) (optional)**

Peel the oranges with a sharp knife, removing all the skin and the underlying white pith so the flesh of the fruit is totally exposed. Cut the oranges crosswise into slices ½" to ¾" thick.

Place the orange slices in a large saucepan with the sugar and water. Cover and bring the mixture to a boil. Then reduce the heat to low and boil the oranges gently, still covered, for 2 minutes.

Using a slotted spoon, carefully remove the orange slices from the pan and place them in a serving dish. Boil the cooking liquid in the pan over low to medium heat until it is reduced to about ⅓ cup. Pour this syrup over the oranges and set them aside to cool to room temperature. If desired, just before serving, sprinkle the orange slices with the liqueur.

Per serving: 102 calories, 0.2 g. fat (1% of calories), 0 g. saturated fat, 0 mg. cholesterol, 0 mg. sodium.

You can make this recipe ahead and refrigerate it until needed. For best flavor, let the oranges come to room temperature before serving.

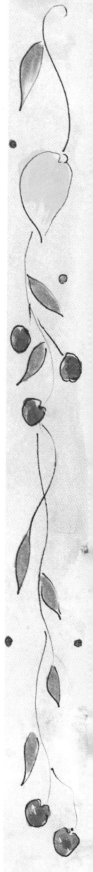

Pears in Red Wine

Yield: 6 servings

Pears poached in red wine are delicious, especially when they are served with the reduced cooking liquid, which has a concentrated wine taste and a beautiful mahogany color. This dessert is particularly good if made with ripe, flavorful, full-season pears, which may cook in as little as five minutes. If, on the other hand, the Bartlett pears you use are unripe or you substitute a Seckel or Bosc variety, the pears may have to cook for as long as an hour to become tender.

  5 medium to large Bartlett pears (about 1½ pounds),
     peeled, quartered and cored
1½ cups hearty red wine
  ⅓ cup sugar
     Grated rind of 1 lemon
  ¼ cup lemon juice

Place the pears, wine, sugar, lemon rind and lemon juice in a large saucepan. Bring the mixture to a boil, reduce the heat to low, cover and boil the mixture gently for about 25 minutes (less if the pears are very ripe, more if they are unripe or if a harder variety is used). Pierce the pears with the point of a sharp knife to determine tenderness.

Using a slotted spoon, transfer the pears to a serving bowl.

You should have about 1¼ cups of liquid (more if the pears have rendered a lot of juice). Bring it to a boil and boil it until it is reduced to about ⅔ cup. Add it to the pears and cool to room temperature. (The liquid should become syrupy.)

Divide the pear quarters among 6 small, deep dessert dishes. Spoon on some of the syrup and serve.

Per serving: 152 calories, 0.5 g. fat (3% of calories), 0 g. saturated fat, 0 mg. cholesterol, 3 mg. sodium.

Pears in Red Wine

Pineapple in Maple Syrup

Pineapple in Maple Syrup

Yield: 6 servings

*i*t is important to use a ripe pineapple for this dessert. One good indicator of ripeness is that the juice will be somewhat sticky. The pineapple is halved, peeled and sliced, then layered with strawberries in a gratin dish and flavored with maple syrup and cherry brandy. (You can omit the brandy if you want the dessert to be nonalcoholic.) The pineapple will be more flavorful if you set the dessert aside in the refrigerator for a few hours or overnight before serving, but it can be eaten immediately.

> 1 **ripe pineapple (3 pounds), top removed and base trimmed**
> ⅓ **cup maple syrup**
> 2 **tablespoons lemon juice**
> 2 **tablespoons kirschwasser (cherry brandy) (optional)**
> 6–7 **ripe strawberries (about 4 ounces), washed, hulled and cut lengthwise into thin slices (1 cup)**

Halve the pineapple lengthwise, cut off the skin (removing all brown areas) with a sharp knife and cut out and discard the core. Place the prepared halves, cut side down, on a cutting board and cut them crosswise into ½″ slices. Arrange half the slices in a 6-cup gratin dish.

Combine the maple syrup, lemon juice and kirschwasser, if using, in a small bowl. Mix in the strawberries and spoon half the mixture evenly over the pineapple slices. Arrange the remaining pineapple slices on top and spoon on the rest of the berry mixture. Cover and let marinate for a few hours or overnight in the refrigerator. Serve in deep dessert dishes.

Per serving: 125 calories, 0.6 g. fat (4% of calories), 0 g. saturated fat, 0 mg. cholesterol, 3 mg. sodium.

Plum Stew with Pecans

Yield: 6 servings

o make this dessert, I cook fleshy Santa Rosa plums until tender in a wine sauce sweetened with preserves and flavored with cinnamon. Pecans add a little crunch to this flavorful dessert. This dish also makes a wonderful accompaniment to a brunch.

About 8 large Santa Rosa plums (2 pounds)
- ¾ **cup plum preserves**
- 1 **teaspoon cornstarch**
- 1 **cup fruity red wine**
- 1 **cinnamon stick**
- ⅓ **cup pecan halves, broken into pieces**

Halve the plums and remove and discard the pits. Cut each plum into 6 wedges. Place the plums in a large saucepan with the preserves.

In a small bowl, dissolve the cornstarch in the wine. Add this mixture to the saucepan with the cinnamon stick. Bring the mixture to a full boil, then reduce the heat to low, cover and cook at a very gentle boil for 20 to 25 minutes, or until the plums are very soft and tender. Cool and remove the cinnamon stick. Serve, sprinkled with the pecan pieces, in dessert dishes.

Per serving: 263 calories, 5 g. fat (17% of calories), 0.4 g. saturated fat, 0 mg. cholesterol, 7 mg. sodium.

To make sure you always have nuts on hand, buy unsalted varieties and store them in the freezer. They'll remain loose so you can easily scoop out the quantity you need.

Plum Stew with Pecans

Poached Pears in Lemon-Apricot Sauce

Yield: 6 servings

It is best to use ripe fruit for poaching, partly because it cooks more quickly and partly because it's sweeter. Here, I use Bosc pears, a firm variety that takes a long time to cook even when ripe. If you want, you can substitute Bartlett or Anjou pears, which will cook faster than Boscs. Fruit that's not quite ripe may need more jam for sweetening than is called for here. This dessert can be made several days ahead and stored in the refrigerator.

6 ripe Bosc pears (about 2½ pounds)

1 lemon

6 cups water

⅓ cup apricot jam

Leave the stems in place but peel the pears. Using a melon baller, remove most of the core from the base of the pears. Set aside.

Remove 12 thin strips of rind from the lemon with a vegetable peeler; set aside. Squeeze the juice from the lemon. (You should have ⅓ cup.)

In a stainless steel saucepan large enough to hold the pears in a single layer, combine the water, jam, lemon juice and lemon rind. Add the pears and weigh them down by placing an inverted plate (smaller than the saucepan) on top. (The object is to keep the pears submerged; any part of the fruit that rises above the surface is likely to discolor. After the pears are poached, they will automatically sink below the surface of the poaching liquid and will not discolor further.)

Bring the mixture to a boil, cover, reduce the heat and cook the pears at a gentle boil over low heat for about 10 minutes, or until they are tender when pierced with the point of a sharp knife. Set the mixture aside and let it cool, uncovered, in the cooking liquid for 30 minutes.

Remove the pears from the pan with a slotted spoon and stand them upright in a gratin dish.

There should be about 4 cups of liquid in the pan. Bring it to a boil and cook it for 30 to 35 minutes, or until it is reduced to ¾ cup. Pour the liquid over the pears, then cool, cover and refrigerate them until serving time.

Serve 1 pear per person with some of the cooking juices and a few pieces of lemon rind.

Per serving: 165 calories, 0.7 g. fat (4% of calories), 0 g. saturated fat, 0 mg. cholesterol, 3 mg. sodium.

Stewed Prunes in Red Wine

Yield: 6 servings

I flavor these prunes with nutmeg and cinnamon, but if other spices are more to your liking, substitute them. The cooking liquid is thickened lightly with a little cornstarch to give it some viscosity. Best consumed cool, this dish will keep for at least a week under refrigeration.

About 36 unpitted prunes (1 pound)
1¼ **cups red wine**
½ **cup water**
⅛ **teaspoon ground nutmeg**
¼ **teaspoon ground cinnamon**
½ **teaspoon cornstarch dissolved in 1 tablespoon water**
Pound cake or cookies (optional)

Place the prunes, wine, water, nutmeg and cinnamon in a large stainless steel saucepan. Bring the mixture to a boil, then reduce the heat to low, cover and boil gently for 10 minutes.

Add the dissolved cornstarch to the pan and mix it in well. Bring the mixture to a boil, stirring occasionally. The cooking liquid will thicken lightly as it comes to a boil. Cool to room temperature, then cover and refrigerate the prunes and liquid together.

Divide the prunes and juice among 6 bowls. If desired, serve with slices of pound cake or cookies.

Per serving: 217 calories, 0.4 g. fat (2% of calories), 0 g. saturated fat, 0 mg. cholesterol, 6 mg. sodium.

Raspberry Soufflés in Raspberry Sauce

Raspberry Soufflés in Raspberry Sauce

Yield: 6 servings

his showy dessert is for special parties. Containing egg whites with a little sugar and a puree of fresh berries, it has a wonderful color and concentrated berry taste. Although I make individual soufflés here, you can make one large dessert by baking the mixture in a 1-quart mold for 25 to 30 minutes.

10 ounces fresh raspberries or 1 package (10–12 ounces) frozen unsweetened berries, thawed

⅓ cup seedless raspberry jam

1 teaspoon peanut or corn oil

4 large egg whites

⅓ cup sugar

½ cup fresh raspberries

Place the 10 to 12 ounces of raspberries in the bowl of a food processor or blender. Add the jam and process the mixture until it is pureed. Strain the puree. (You should have about 2 cups.)

Preheat the oven to 400°. Brush 6 molds (½- to 1-cup capacity) with the oil.

Place the egg whites in a large copper or stainless steel mixing bowl. Beat by hand with a large balloon whisk or with an electric mixer (fitted with a whisk attachment) at medium to high speed. When the whites hold a firm peak, gradually beat in the sugar, then continue beating the mixture for 10 seconds. The whites should be stiff and shiny.

Crush the ½ cup of raspberries coarsely and fold them into the egg white mixture. Divide the soufflé mixture among the oiled molds. (It should extend in soft peaks above the tops of the molds.)

Arrange the filled molds on a baking tray and bake for 12 to 15 minutes, until the tops are browned and the soufflés are well inflated and firm.

To serve, spoon 2 tablespoons of the sauce on each of 6 dessert plates. Run a sharp knife around the edge of the soufflés, unmold them and arrange a soufflé, browned side up, in the center of each dessert plate. Drizzle the top of each soufflé with an additional tablespoon of sauce and serve immediately.

Per serving: 135 calories, 1.1 g. fat (7% of calories), 0.1 g. saturated fat, 0 mg. cholesterol, 39 mg. sodium.

Cold Sweet Strawberry Soup

In the style of nouvelle cuisine, this dessert is called a soup because it is served in a flat soup plate and eaten with a soup spoon. It consists of a flavorful mixture containing ripe strawberries that's cooked gently, cooled to room temperature and served with a garnish of nonfat yogurt.

- 2 pints ripe strawberries (about 2 pounds), washed and hulled
- ½ cup strawberry jam
- ½ cup sweet wine (muscatel, sauternes or port)
- 1 lemon
- ½ cup plain nonfat yogurt
- Fresh mint leaves, for garnish

Place the strawberries, jam and wine in a large saucepan.

Remove 10 to 12 strips of rind from the lemon with a vegetable peeler. Then stack the strips, 3 or 4 together at a time, and cut them lengthwise into thin julienne pieces. (You should have about ¼ cup.) Squeeze the lemon to extract the juice (about 3 tablespoons).

Add the lemon rind and lemon juice to the saucepan. Bring the mixture to a strong boil, cover, reduce the heat and boil gently over medium to low heat for 4 minutes.

Remove the pan from the heat and cool the mixture to room temperature. Then transfer it to large bowl, cover and refrigerate until cold.

To serve the dessert, divide it among 6 soup plates (about ½ cup per person). Spoon a rounded tablespoon of yogurt into the center of each serving and garnish with a few mint leaves. Serve with soup spoons.

Per serving: 148 calories, 0.6 g. fat (3% of calories), 0 g. saturated fat, 0 mg. cholesterol, 20 mg. sodium.

Cold Sweet Strawberry Soup

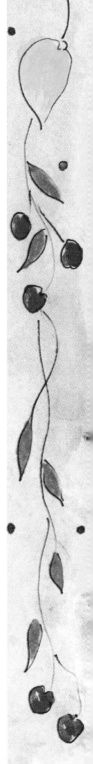

Strawberries in Creamy Orange Sauce

Yield: 6 servings

I imitate the flavor and consistency of a conventional dessert sauce (made with milk, cream, eggs and sugar) by combining nonfat yogurt with frozen orange juice concentrate. The resulting sauce—creamy, rich-tasting and rich-looking—enhances the flavor of ripe strawberries and blueberries in this recipe. Pistachios are an appealingly crunchy final touch.

- 3 cups plain nonfat yogurt
- ⅔ cup frozen orange juice concentrate, thawed
- 2 tablespoons Grand Marnier liqueur (orange brandy) (optional)
- 36 medium to large strawberries (about 1½ pounds), washed and hulled
- 1 cup fresh blueberries, washed, drained and patted dry
- 12 unsalted pistachio nuts, shelled and broken into small pieces

Place the yogurt, orange juice concentrate and liqueur, if using, in the bowl of a food processor. Process until emulsified.

Place ½ cup of the sauce on each of 6 dessert plates. Divide the strawberries among the plates, standing 6 of them upright in a circle in the center of each plate. Fill the center of the circle with blueberries and sprinkle the remaining blueberries elsewhere around the plates. Drizzle the remaining sauce over the strawberries and sprinkle the pistachios on top.

Per serving: 198 calories, 3.3 g. fat (15% of calories), 0.5 g. saturated fat, 2 mg. cholesterol, 91 mg. sodium.

Strawberries in Strawberry Sauce

Yield: 6 servings

The nicest strawberries are served whole—or if they are very large, halved—in a sauce made from the less ripe or slightly damaged berries in the batch. The flavor of this dessert is enhanced greatly if the berries are allowed to marinate in the sauce for an hour or so before serving. The berries and sauce are particularly good served over thin slices of Yogurt Cake (page 287).

- 3 cups ripe strawberries, washed and hulled
- 3 tablespoons strawberry jam
- 2 teaspoons dark rum (optional)
- 24 seedless grapes, halved, for garnish
- Mint leaves, for garnish

Cut up enough of the slightly unripe, overripe or bruised berries to make about ¾ cup. Place the berry pieces in the bowl of a food processor with the jam and rum, if using. Process until smooth.

If the remaining berries are very large, halve them; otherwise, leave them whole. Place in a serving bowl and pour the strawberry sauce over them. Cover and refrigerate for at least 1 hour before serving.

To serve, divide the berries and sauce among 6 dessert dishes and garnish with the grapes and mint leaves.

Per serving: 53 calories, 0.3 g. fat (4% of calories), 0 g. saturated fat, 0 mg. cholesterol, 2 mg. sodium.

Strawberry Granola Parfaits

Strawberry Granola Parfaits

Yield: 6 servings

his is a quick, easy recipe. I make it by layering an intensely flavored strawberry puree with yogurt cheese and granola in fluted glasses. Healthful and delicious, the finished parfaits are beautiful topped with whole strawberries.

    2   pints ripe strawberries (about 1 pound), washed
        and hulled
    ⅓   cup strawberry jam
    2   tablespoons crème de cassis (black currant liqueur)
        (optional)
    1½ cups low-fat granola (4 ounces)
    1½ cups yogurt cheese (see page 263)

Reserve 6 nice berries to use as a decoration. Place the remainder of the berries in the bowl of a food processor with the jam and cassis, if using. Process the mixture until it is pureed.

Using 6 fluted glasses, layer the ingredients in the following order until the glasses are filled: about 2 tablespoons of yogurt cheese, 2 tablespoons strawberry puree and 2 tablespoons granola. Top each serving with a reserved strawberry.

Per serving: 212 calories, 3.6 g. fat (15% of calories), 2.2 g. saturated fat, 1 mg. cholesterol, 92 mg. sodium.

Crêpes

Yield: 12 crêpes

For me, crêpes are best when eaten as suggested here—hot from the pan with a light coating of good homemade jam. They also form the base for Crêpe Purses with Mushroom Duxelles (page 86) and Crêpes with Caramelized Apples and Pecans (page 294). Make them ahead and refrigerate or freeze them for those dishes. Notice that these crêpes, made in an 8" nonstick skillet, are larger than conventional crêpes.

½ cup all-purpose flour

2 egg whites

¾ cup skim milk

1 tablespoon canola or peanut oil

1½ teaspoons sugar

½ teaspoon vanilla extract or 1 tablespoon dark rum

Assorted jams, such as raspberry, plum, apricot or quince (optional)

Place the flour in a medium mixing bowl. Whisk in the egg whites and ¼ cup of the milk, beating the mixture with a whisk until it is smooth. Then whisk in the oil, sugar, vanilla or rum and the remaining ½ cup milk.

Lightly coat an 8" nonstick skillet with vegetable cooking spray and set it over high heat until hot. Place 2 tablespoons of the crêpe batter in the bottom of the skillet and immediately tilt and shake the skillet until its entire bottom is covered lightly with the batter. (The faster the batter is spread, the thinner the crêpe will be.)

Allow the crêpe to cook over medium to high heat for 35 to 45 seconds, until it is browned on the bottom. Then, using a fork, loosen it around the edges. Grab hold of the crêpe along one side with both hands, carefully turn it over in the skillet and cook it for 30 seconds on the other side. Transfer the crêpe to a platter and continue making crêpes in the skillet (no additional spray is needed) until the batter is gone. (You should have about 12 crêpes.)

If desired, spread each crêpe with about 1 teaspoon of jam and serve immediately, 2 per person. Or securely wrap and refrigerate or freeze the crêpes.

Per plain crêpe: 47 calories, 1.8 g. fat (35% of calories), 0.1 g. saturated fat, 0 mg. cholesterol, 17 mg. sodium.

Meringue Shells

Yield: 15 shells

hese shells are always good to have on hand; they can be made weeks ahead and will remain crisp and flavorful if stored in a moisture-proof container. They are especially appealing when served with Fruit Sorbets (page 308), Melon with Lime Sauce (page 313) or Strawberries in Strawberry Sauce (page 335). As an alternative to using a pastry bag to form the shells, you can simply spoon the meringue mixture onto the cookie sheet.

> 6 **large egg whites**
> **A few drops of lemon juice**
> 1½ **cups sugar**

Place the egg whites in a large copper or stainless steel mixing bowl and add the lemon juice. Beat the mixture by hand with a large balloon whisk or with an electric mixer (fitted with a whisk attachment) at medium to high speed. When the whites hold a firm peak, gradually beat in the sugar, then continue beating the mixture for 10 seconds. The whites should be stiff and shiny.

Preheat the oven to 180° to 190°. Spray a cookie sheet lightly with vegetable cooking spray.

Fit a pastry bag with a fluted tip and fill the bag with the meringue mixture. Squeeze out 3″-diameter spirals of meringue to form the base of individual shells, then pipe a border around the exterior of each base to create a nest effect.

Bake the shells for 2 to 3 hours, or until they are dry and pale beige in color. Cool completely and place in an airtight plastic container until ready to serve.

Per shell: 79 calories, 0 g. fat (0% of calories), 0 g. saturated fat, 0 mg. cholesterol, 22 mg. sodium.

Chocolate Sauce

Yield: 6 servings

*B*ecause this concentrated chocolate sauce is made with unsweetened cocoa powder instead of chocolate, which is high in fat, it is suitable for people on low-fat diets. The sauce goes particularly well with Angel Cake (page 284) but is also good with most other plain cakes.

½ cup water
½ cup sugar
½ cup unsweetened cocoa powder

Combine the water and sugar in a medium saucepan and bring the mixture to a boil. Boil for 1 minute, then add the cocoa and whisk the mixture until it is well blended.

Strain the sauce into a jar and set it aside; it will thicken as it cools. When it is cool, cover the jar with a tight-fitting lid and store in the refrigerator. Rewarm the sauce or serve it cold over cake or frozen yogurt.

Per serving: 74 calories, 0.7 g. fat (7% of calories), 0 g. saturated fat, 0 mg. cholesterol, 5 mg. sodium.

Don't confuse unsweetened cocoa powder with the sweetened ground chocolate used to make instant drinks. Be aware also that different types of cocoa powder have different flavors. Dutch cocoa is one excellent choice for this chocolate sauce. Mexican cocoa is also good and has a subtly different taste. Experiment with different types to see which you like best.

Apricot Sauce with Dried Fruits

This sauce can be made weeks ahead and refrigerated in a jar with a tight-fitting lid. It makes an excellent substitute for blueberries as a topping for Yogurt Cake (page 287) and is good with cookies and soufflés or on top of ice milk or frozen yogurt.

- 3 strips lemon rind removed with a vegetable peeler
- 3 strips lime rind removed with a vegetable peeler
- ⅓ cup honey
- ⅓ cup lemon juice
- ¼ cup strained apricot preserves
- 2 tablespoons cognac (optional)
- ⅓ cup dried apricot halves, cut into thin strips
- ¼ cup raisins
- 8 prunes, pitted and cut into ½″ pieces
- 2 dried peach halves, cut into thin strips

Stack the pieces of lemon rind and lime rind; cut them lengthwise into thin julienne strips.

Mix the honey and lemon juice together in a mixing bowl and stir in the lemon rind and lime rind. Add the preserves and, if desired, the cognac; mix well.

Stir in the apricots, raisins, prunes and peaches. Cover and let stand for at least an hour. To store, tightly cover and refrigerate.

Per serving: 174 calories, 0.2 g. fat (1% of calories), 0 g. saturated fat, 0 mg. cholesterol, 5 mg. sodium.

Index

Note: **Boldface** references indicate photographs.

Special Thanks:
Cassis; Christofle Silver, Inc.; Deruta of Italy
Corporation; Bill Goldsmith for Goldsmith/
Corot, Inc.; LS Collection; Palais Royal;
Quimper Faïence, Inc.; Solanee New York;
Vietri